Red Robert

Red Robert

A Life of

ROBERT BIRLEY

by

ARTHUR HEARNDEN

HAMISH HAMILTON

LONDON

First published in Great Britain 1984
by Hamish Hamilton Ltd
Garden House 57–59 Long Acre London WC2E 9JZ

Copyright © 1984 by Arthur Hearnden

Indexed by P. S. H. Lawrence

British Library Cataloguing in Publication Data

Hearnden, Arthur
  Red Robert.
  1. Birley, Robert   2. Educators—Great
  Britain—Biography
  I. Title
  370′.92′4   LB775.B/
  ISBN 0–241–11158–7

Typeset by The Spartan Press Ltd, Lymington, Hampshire
Printed in Great Britain by
St Edmundsbury Press Ltd, Bury St Edmunds, Suffolk

To Josephine

Contents

Acknowledgements

It is a pleasure to acknowledge the generous help I have received in the writing of this biography from so many relations and friends of Sir Robert Birley. Above all I wish to thank his widow Lady Birley for her trust in putting her late husband's private papers and the Birley photograph albums at my disposal. I am grateful to have had her encouragement, and that of her daughter Rachael Hetherington and her sons-in-law Brian Rees and Paul Hetherington. Other members of the family who helped me were Robert's sister, the late Marion Birley, and his cousins Joy Jourdain, Arthur Markham, Margaret Markham and Sister Veronica Markham.

I have, too, greatly valued the co-operation that was spontaneously forthcoming from the three schools with which so much of the book is concerned. James Woodhouse, formerly Headmaster of Rugby and now of Lancing, Brian Rees, formerly Headmaster of Charterhouse and now of Rugby, Peter Attenborough, the present Headmaster of Charterhouse, Lord Charteris of Amisfield, Provost of Eton, and Michael McCrum and Eric Anderson, successive Head Masters of Eton, all gave their support by putting library facilities at my disposal and giving me leave to quote from the various official school sources.

For the opening chapter Brian Summers of Kirkham Grammar School helped by putting me in touch with the Kirkham and District Local History Society, and one of its members, F. J. Singleton, provided information about the Birley family history. This was supplemented by Bryan Matthews, Librarian and Archivist of Uppingham School, who supplied information about the Birleys at Uppingham. For the account of life at Rugby I was greatly helped by the School Librarian, Jennifer Macrory; Edward Bradby was kind enough to read the chapter in question and made valuable suggestions.

For the help I needed over details of Robert's travels in

Europe after leaving school I was able to turn to a number of German and Austrian friends, Dieter Tscherning, Franz Eschbach, Peter Marzolff, Emil Siess and Gerhard Mayr. Among his contemporaries at Oxford I met or corresponded with Lord Brooke of Cumnor, Sir John Hicks, Sir Roger Mynors, Godfrey Samuel, Sir Walter Oakeshott and George Rink. Among those who knew him as an Assistant Master at Eton, whether as friends, colleagues or pupils, I would like to mention with appreciation Nigel Nicolson, Lord Gore-Booth, Lord Donaldson, Sir Victor Fitzgeorge-Balfour, Wyndham Milligan, George Pike and especially Grizel Hartley and David Astor.

For the two chapters on Charterhouse I had extensive and generous help from a great many people connected with the school in various ways – Sir Edward and Lady Tuckwell, Mrs Hope Sellar, R. L. Arrowsmith, John Waterfield, Sir Ronald McIntosh, Sir Geoffrey Johnson Smith, John Ehrman, Michael Hoban, Robert Neild, Dick Taverne, Sir William Rees-Mogg, Conrad Dehn, Simon Raven, Gerald Priestland, David Raeburn, Otto Fisher, Peter May, Frederic Raphael, and James Prior who also accepted very readily the invitation to write a Foreword. Brian Souter of the present staff went to great trouble to find the illustrations I wanted.

The quotations in the chapter on Germany are taken from *The British in Germany* which I edited and which was published by Hamish Hamilton in 1978. I was able to speak to a great many of those who saw Robert Birley's work as Educational Adviser at close hand, in particular his interpreter Berta Humphrey and Dame Lilo Milchsack, founder of the *Deutsch-Englische Gesellschaft* and the Königswinter Conferences. Among the former members of Education Branch I should mention Tom Creighton, Geoffrey and Joan Bird, Edith Davies, Kathleen Davis, Harry Beckhough, Ray and Barbara Perraudin, George Murray, Ken Walsh, Trevor Davies, Muriel Lambert, Caroline Cunningham, Geoffrey and Veronica Carter and Valerie Dundas-Grant. I have talked to or corresponded with all of them at one time or another about Robert Birley, as well as Margaret McNeill and Bertha Bracey who worked with the Friends' Service Council in Germany. I am also grateful to Gerda Hanko for observations about post-war Berlin and to Gerald Mortimer of the *Derby Evening Telegraph* for information about Derby County Football Club.

For the later chapters on Eton I appreciated greatly the time which so many present and former members of staff were prepared to spare in order to recall Robert Birley's time as their Head Master. They included David Macindoe, the present Vice-Provost, Oliver Van Oss, Kenneth Rose, Peter Lawrence, Giles St Aubyn, John Wells, Norman Addison, Roger Thompson, Michael Neal, David Guilford, James McConnell who kindly gave me permission to quote from his book *Eton Repointed*, and Paul Quarrie who found useful material in the College Library for me. A number of Old Etonians contributed too. Lord Snowdon kindly allowed me to reproduce Robert Birley's letter to him. Jasper Ungoed-Thomas read through all the Eton chapters and made perceptive suggestions for their improvement. Others who responded equally helpfully were William Waldegrave, Paul Channon, Lord Gowrie, David Howell, Lord Camoys, Winston S. Churchill and Sir George Young. In addition Lady Donaldson permitted me to quote from her recent biography of P. G. Wodehouse, and Charles Hastings of Radley College drew my attention to some other published references to Robert Birley.

Where South Africa was concerned I would have been completely at a loss without the help I received from various sources. Professor Edmund King put me in touch with Professor Napier Boyce of Johannesburg College of Education and Professor F. R. N. Nabarro at the University of the Witwatersrand, and Joan Biddles sent me much helpful material from the Wits archives. In Oxford I benefited greatly from being able to talk to Lord and Lady Redcliffe-Maud, Professor Richard Cobb, Colin Wood, Ann Yates, Copper and Penelope Le May, Professor Kenneth Kirkwood and Francis Wilson while he was on sabbatical leave from Cape Town. I also had valuable talks with Mary Benson, Randolph Vigne, Philip and Myrtle Radley and, especially, Michael O'Dowd of the Anglo-American Corporation of South Africa.

Many others helped at various stages of the work, including Sir James Tait, formerly Vice-Chancellor of the City University and David Jenkins and Brian Enright who were colleagues of Robert's during his time there. Former headmasters I was able to consult in addition to those already mentioned were Sir Desmond Lee, Walter Hamilton, Rhodes Boyson, Sir James Cobban, Robson Fisher and Frank Fisher. R. M. Knight provided information about the Eton Fives Association, Professor W. S. Watt about Balliol College, and the Revd Paul Rowntree Clifford, Frank Bell, Doris Krug, Michael Schweitzer and Alec Dickson also helped with contributions about the later years.

The book was not commissioned but once it was completed, publication was made possible with help from the Robert Birley Fund, to which the three schools contributed, as did the Mercers' Company, the Radley Trust, the Bell Educational Trust and the German Academic Exchange Service. Frank Bell, John Waterfield, F. P. Lykiardopulo and Otto Fisher contributed as individuals and the Fund was administered by R. H. Symes-Thompson, Bursar of Eton. This collective generosity is a mark of the esteem in which Robert Birley was held in so many different circles. Had more extensive support been needed, I am quite sure it would have been readily forthcoming.

In conclusion I have three special debts of gratitude to record: to Peter Lawrence who helped me to assemble the illustrations, a number of which are also reproduced in his book *An Eton Camera 1920–1959*, and who also undertook the indexing; to Walter Hamilton who read so much of the text and taught me so much; and to John Waterfield whose warm friendship and encouragement carried me through the most difficult times. With all this help I am sure the book ought to be better than it is.

Arthur Hearnden

Foreword

It is a privilege to be educated at one of our great public schools. Robert Birley was enthusiastic in his recognition and acceptance of that fact, and it was one of the reasons why he wished the opportunity to be more widely shared. He was very much a 'leveller up' rather than the reverse and was irritated by those who thought that this was socialism. Some of his pupils and a number of reactionary old boys regarded his views with great suspicion: to them he was almost the Trojan Horse. This nonsense irritated him but did not deter him. False labels were frequently pinned to people and if this was the price which had to be paid for implementing progress, so be it.

Robert was a gangling mass of intellectual energy, of boundless and impish enthusiasm. He used the opportunities presented by being headmaster of Eton and Charterhouse to put forward ideas and propound principles in the best tradition of those who recognise their fortunate position and use it to advantage. He would bend the ear mercilessly of visiting politicians, service chiefs, bishops and industrialists. The bombardment might begin at lunch with the boys present, but it would be continued for ever after if the recipient showed understanding and interest, and it would be an extraordinarily wooden person who was not captivated by his enthusiasm and argument. By letter or conversation, encouragement and approval to a course of action would be given. Some new initiative might be suggested and all argument would be accompanied by personal anecdote so that the recipient would have some special reason to remember, this in itself showing the quality of a really great teacher.

Many anecdotes one remembers but I wish to recall one. It related to the unemployed of Slough amongst whom Robert worked when a young master at Eton. They were paid benefit in new notes which quite often stuck together, but the honesty and fair play of the recipient always resulted in over-payment being returned. It was illustrative, Robert said, of the basic honesty and decency of people who, through no fault of their own, had fallen on hard times. The lesson was that these were good people who should be helped, trusted and respected. Without doubt it was a different message to the one conveyed by many parents to many boys, but re-told in wartime it fitted the theme of national unity.

In later years national unity extended to European unity and embraced strong views on racial equality in South Africa and elsewhere. Idealistic yes, but Robert knew the pitfalls and cynicism awaiting the idealist, and knew also that young men need inspiration. He was one of the few in his generation who was able to give it. Is it surprising that some of us were caught up in his enthusiasms, fired by his idealism, and found our views fashioned in his image?

We were taught to believe that there were responsibilities as well as rights and that we lucky ones had duties to others which we were bound to honour. If one didn't remember the VE-Day sermon, the message was relayed to us throughout his life. We are haunted by that simple homily, 'never let this country become a house with empty rooms'. Many have much for which to thank him as he stirred the conscience and by his enthusiasm and the vigour of his intellect encouraged us when the going was rough and hard. If his views on social policy were fashioned in the pre-war years of poverty and high unemployment, they came to acceptance and fulfilment in the successes of the thirty post-war years. There are those who now decry those years and those who guided us through them. Only time will be able to tell us who was right, but Robert Birley argued his case from a deep understanding of our nation's history, and he more than most would be content to be judged by it.

The Rt Hon James Prior, MP
July 1983

CHAPTER ONE

A Lancashire Ancestry,
A Bournemouth Childhood

'Spiritually we are a thirsty and dry land. The water is there all right, but it is strictly restrained. Now I can hope to see fountains playing before I go.' So wrote an elderly colleague on the threshold of retirement at the end of Robert Birley's first term as Head Master of Eton. At that time no one could have been better fitted by background and temperament to be the source of fresh inspiration for the most famous of English public schools, to preside over its peculiar alchemy in which stereotypes dissolve. Oxford scholar, brilliant teacher of history, outstanding Headmaster of Charterhouse, distinguished public servant, Birley had done just the right things to enable him to achieve his principal ambition. But his way of doing them was incomparably his own, and at every point somehow right for one whose descent had its tap root in defiant northern soil.

Birley is a Lancastrian name with the agreeably bucolic derivation of byre lee – cowshed by a field. The first bearer of it to make a mark in Lancashire history would make a fitting ancestor for a distinguished teacher. A manuscript quoted in *The Victoria History of the County of Lancaster* tells how

'Isabell Birley, wife of Thomas Birley, born in Kirkham, daughter of John Coulbron, an ale house keeper all her life and through that imployment attayned to a good personall estait, being moved with a naturall compassion to pore children . . . in the yeare 1621, having gotten a good stock of money into her hands,' repaired to the church where 'the thirty men of the parish being assembled with £30 in her aporon, telling them that she had brought that money to give it towards the erecting of a free schole for pore children, to be taught gratis . . . wishing them to take it and consider of it, (as) they were . . . the most like persons to move their several townshipps to contribute everyone something' towards the accomplishment of so charitable a work 'and not doubting but their good examples in their contributions would be a strong motive to excite others. This was thankfully accepted. . . .'

Thanks to Isabel Birley's persistence a total of £170.40s. was collected for the 'free schole', but this was by no means the end of the story. Having raised the money to pay the piper, Isabel was determined to call the tune. Her interest in the school and her influence with the governing body were such that she was able to have her own personal candidate elected to the mastership. However, most of those who had contributed the money were Romanists and since her protégé was a Protestant of whom they disapproved, they were provoked into retaliation. They used their power to unseat the governing body, all but one of whom were forced to resign. Thereupon Isabel appealed to the Bishop and a new constitution was devised whereby

the whole parish or so many as shall appear at some day prefixed . . . shall elect six or nine lawful and honest men feofees . . . whereof a third part to be chosen by the towne of Kirkham and the other two parts by the parishioners generally, of which feofees Isabell Wilding's husband [Isabel Birley had married a second time] and her heirs, because she gave 30*l* to the schole maister, shall be one.

How long this hereditary right to a seat on the governing body of Kirkham Grammar School was exercised is not known, but from a distance the Birley family has taken an affectionate interest in the affairs of the school ever since.

Robert Birley liked to think he was descended from Isabel, although no connection has ever been proved. *Burke's Landed Gentry* traces the ancestry back to John Birley of Kirkham, a West India merchant born in 1710, son of John Birley of Skippool, Poulton-le-Fylde. According to family tradition this latter John Birley had come over from Ireland with his mother before 1700. It is therefore a matter of speculation whether some relative of Isabel had gone to

Dublin – where there were many English merchants at that time – and whether John Birley was a descendant who returned to the Fylde where he had family connections. At all events he appears to have been a prominent citizen of Poulton until his trade declined in the 1760s, whereupon he moved to Kirkham to join his brother-in-law in the firm of Langton Shepherd, flax merchants and sail cloth manufacturers. The firm, which in due course became Langton, Birley and Shepherd, traded with the Baltic countries, importing flax from which to make sail cloth and ropes.

John Birley's son Richard married Alice Hornby, the daughter of another Kirkham flax merchant, and went to Blackburn where he joined his brother-in-law John Hornby in cotton manufacture. Richard's three sons moved on to Manchester where they, too, prospered in cotton manufacture, in partnership with Charles Mackintosh the inventor of the waterproof process. All three were Deputy Lieutenants of the County. Indeed so prominent were they that when in 1819 the 60,000 workers marched, bands playing and banners fluttering, to St Peter's Field for a parliamentary reform meeting, at which the popular orator Henry Hunt was to speak, it was one of them – Robert Birley's great-great-uncle Hugh – who led the charge of the Yeomanry. With eleven killed and more than 400 injured (one of whom, Thomas Redford, brought an action against Hugh Birley), it was this most rancorous episode in the class war which more than anything cradled the liberalism to which the family subsequently adhered.

In the next generation the Birleys were at their most prolific. Joseph, the youngest of the three brothers, had seventeen children; Robert Birley's grandfather Arthur was the youngest boy in this family. A prospering business made it possible for Joseph's sons to be educated at Winchester and three of them went on to Oxford, two to Balliol and one to Pembroke. Two were Deputy Lieutenants and three were Justices of the Peace. One was Liberal MP for a Manchester constituency for fifteen years and another was an Honorary Canon of Manchester Cathedral. The strong commitment to public service in this prominent generation exemplified the social conscience with which the Lancashire middle class sought to put the Peterloo Massacre behind them. Schooling was in the forefront of their charitable activities and Manchester still has a Birley High School by which to remember them.

Arthur Birley went into the family business and reinforced this burgeoning progressive tradition by marrying Julia Peel, a cousin of Sir Robert Peel. They had met during the 'cotton famine' when both were doing voluntary teaching in classes for the unemployed. Less dynastically inclined than the previous generation, they had only six children of whom the youngest boy, Leonard, was Robert Birley's father. In education, Winchester was forsaken for Uppingham which was at that time approaching the culmination of Edward Thring's thirty-four years of reforming headmastership. Leonard entered the school as a Scholar in September 1888 and in his first term came top in Classics, French and Maths. There was something of the archetypal public schoolboy about him, for this academic potential was matched by comparable promise in sport.

It was a time of heated controversy over how football should be played. Was Uppingham to abandon its own rules for the game in favour of those of Rugby, thereby making it possible to play matches against the growing number of other schools which were adopting the Rugby code? The idea had been roundly denounced as capitulation to the spirit of professionalism. A Cambridge undergraduate signing himself 'Old Blue' wrote to *The Uppinghamian*:

> The football season never seemed so oppressively dull when I was at Uppingham, and rather would I see not a single foreign match than that Uppingham football players should have that 'Pro'-ish spirit that is so painful to see in some school men. (It is especially noticeable in men from a certain school, whose name shall not here be mentioned, on whose match list I have seen twenty-five fixtures for one season.)

Leonard Birley's elder brother Maurice, later a well-known social worker and Warden of Toynbee Hall, was at this time at the top of the school and a leader of the pro-Rugby faction. It fell to him as Captain of Games in his last term to put up the historic notice: 'In future Uppingham will play football according to the Rugby code. Signed, M. Birley.'

Leonard followed in Maurice's footsteps as one of Upping-ham's leading sportsmen and played a prominent part in the increasing number of 'foreign' matches. Among the thumb-nail sketches of 'characters of the Fifteen' he was described as 'a variable forward who is very good on his day' and as one whose height made him a great asset in the line-out. He made still more of a mark as a cricketer, scoring fifties for the Eleven in victories over MCC and S. Christopherson's XI. His academic development kept pace with his sporting achieve-ments. In the sixth form he was frequently instructed to show his work to the Headmaster. These 'good copies' were in Classics and English, the two subjects in which he consistently distinguished himself. His all-round ability and strength of character earned him the captaincy of his House and, as crown to his successful school career, he won an Open Scholarship to New College in 1893.

At Oxford Leonard Birley flourished. He read Classics, taking a First in the preliminary examination ('Mods') and a Second in his Finals ('Greats'); he also had a trial for the Cricket XI. Then, in 1897, he joined the Indian Civil Service and was sent to Bengal. It was a fascinating place to begin a career; Calcutta, still at that time the capital of India, was a powerful commercial centre of great importance to the Empire, and Bengal was among the most advanced provinces. Leonard Birley grew to like the local people and developed a keen interest in the Hindu-Moslem rivalry which permeated their politics. At the age of twenty-seven, he married Grace, the nineteen-year-old daughter of Maxwell Smyth, an indigo planter who had gone out to Bihar from Moffat in Dumfries-shire. A year later, on 14 July 1903, their son Robert was born at Midnapore.

The early twentieth century was a critical time in the affairs of Bengal. A succession of proposals which were being advanced were to culminate two years later in the ill-fated partition. The prosperous, mainly Hindu West Bengal was created a separate province; the more backward and pre-dominantly Moslem East Bengal was tacked on to Assam. Whatever the administrative logic of the arrangement, it stirred the latent nationalism of the Bengali people and fuelled anti-British sentiment.

In this troubled year of partition the Birleys had a second child, Marion.

In one respect Leonard's marriage to Grace might have enabled their two children to claim a genealogical record. For Maxwell Smyth's parents – like Arthur Birley's – had had seventeen children. In later life Robert and Marion enjoyed being able to say that each of their two grandfathers was one of a family of seventeen.

Looking back in the critical light of modern attitudes, the upbringing of the children of the members of the Indian Civil Service seems severely deprived. Normal home life ended once they were old enough to return to England to prep school, and the time and expense involved in a passage to India meant that in general it was only when the parents came back on leave every three years or so that families were reunited. School holidays compounded the bewilderment when, as was too often the case, the children were moved from pillar to post, either boarded out or using up their parents' credit with a succession of relatives. This discontinuity was probably more true of the Birley children than most, for their home life was disrupted even earlier than was normal, and in a tragic way. After four years of marriage Grace died. Robert was three, Marion one. The only sensible course open to Leonard was to bring the two of them home to England and leave them in the care of his parents who had retired to a large house in Cavendish Road, Bournemouth. He was then free to return to the administration of West Bengal.

The Deceased Wife's Sister Act had come at a fortunate moment in that it made possible Leonard's second marriage, to Maxwell Smyth's other daughter. Grace had become a wife and mother too young to allow time for her to train for any career. Her sister Jessie, on the other hand, who was somewhat older, had qualified as a nurse at Calcutta Hospital and worked in a nursing home before marrying. A warm-hearted and outgoing personality equipped her well for the task of dispelling the sadness of Grace's death and rebuilding Leonard's domestic life. He was shy and somewhat awkward, and could all too easily have retreated into misanthropy. Jessie understood how to steer him away from this introspective path, and his career prospered. He was made Companion of the Indian Empire in

1914 and, on his retirement in 1926 as Chief Secretary to the Government of Bengal, Companion of the Order of the Star of India. He had retired at the earliest possible moment – twenty-five years was the minimum period of service – because of his reluctance to accept official policy. To his colleagues he had seemed destined for still higher office. But he was determined to leave, and he and Jessie returned to England. They too settled in Cavendish Road, at Number 8, far enough along from the grandparents' old house to be able to overlook the Hampshire County Cricket Ground.

The turns that Leonard's life had taken suggested that by the rules of psychology Robert and Marion would be insecure and unhappy children. They were handed over to their grandparents at the age of three and one respectively. They acquired a stepmother whom they did not meet until five years later. But if these were circumstances which might have led an observer to predict a difficult upbringing, nothing could have been wider of the mark. In the first place the grandparents provided complete continuity, and Cavendish Road was the children's home until they left to take up their respective careers in teaching and nursing. In the second place, if Jessie Birley was a devoted wife, she became an even more resounding success in the more difficult role of step-mother. From the time they first met her, Robert and Marion hardly felt they were not her own son and daughter. And though it was not until their school days were over that she was regularly at hand, she inspired an affection and had an influence on their lives out of all proportion to the time that they were able to spend together.

The successful home life created out of adversity was matched by a successful early education. This too was against the odds, for a childhood spent with grandparents in a sedate residential district of Bournemouth was not the most obvious environment for early intellectual stimulation. The regime was the standard one of meals in the nursery in the charge of a nanny, and half an hour in their best clothes in the drawing room in the evening. Yet the upbringing which Robert – Bobbie, as he was called in the family – and Marion received was by the standards of the time strikingly liberal. Their nanny, Ada Hayter, discharging her duties with the firmness expected

of her profession, nevertheless contrived to reconcile traditional discipline with encouragement of imaginative and educa-
tive pastimes. Not many nannies would have tolerated the
accumulation of coins, shells, fossils and assorted litter which
small children delight in hoarding, and which Ada's two
charges assembled as a museum. For Bobbie the nursery
afforded splendid opportunities to experiment in leadership. At
hand was a compliant younger sister to act as innocent
accomplice in outbursts of minor vandalism such as the hurling
of all the toys out of the bedroom window. (Grandmother's
punishment for this offence was to permit only one toy to be
retrieved each day, leaving the others to rust tantalizingly on
the grass.)

The fertility of the earlier generation of Birleys had paid its
dividend in the form of innumerable cousins, and the scope of
nursery life was widened when various among them came to
stay from time to time. On these occasions Bobbie was usually
in the grip of some craze or other. And so they painted pictures,
tamed lions, conducted bands, got up magazines, wrote and
performed plays, in short did many of the things that would
most excite modern theorists of progressive primary education.
The theatrical activity centred largely on Shakespeare, with
parts being rehearsed on nursery walks. *Julius Caesar* was the
favourite play, performed, with sheets as costumes, for a
captive audience that comprised Grannie, Ada and the maids.
One of the cousins, Veronica Markham, wrote a romance called
Claudio and Lucia, set in Venice. A play by Bobbie about a
Praetor was considered by the others to be very dull. The
performances were taken so seriously that another cousin, Joy
Roberts, was only once allowed to have a part – a non-speaking
one.

When they grew older and went away to school, these nursery
pursuits gave way to more sophisticated holiday activities.
There was the 'Kenilworth Debating Society' (named after the
grandparents' house), for which records were scrupulously
kept:

Summer Holidays

Aug. 4th

The Debate was opened by Mr R. Birley in his position as President of the Kenilworth Debating Society for the holidays before. He was returned to that post.

———

The following points were then discussed –

(i) *The Magazine.* There were several heated discussions between R. B. and I. M-S. but at length the following points were decided:–

   (i)   That the magazine should be a special Illustrated Number.
   (ii) That it should also be a summer number.
   (iii) That the number of contributions should be increased very much as far as possible, and that the public also might contribute if desired.
   (iv) That 'criticism pages' should be abolished.
   (v)   That there should be more variety.
   (vi) That the date of publication should be fixed at least 1 week before Sept. 24th.

   The following were elected to the posts:–

   Editor   R. Birley
   Secretary & Printer   I. Maxwell-Smyth
   Illustrating Editor   M. G. Birley
   Treasurer   S. C. Monckton

(ii) *The Play.* It was unanimously agreed that it should take place *after* Sept. 1st, when S. C. M. should have returned.
   On the point as to where it should take place there was much discussion, and it was left open. It was however agreed that it must be in the garden.

(iii) *Fines.* Fines, the money gained by them going to a fund for providing books for the library, the play (if necessary) etc., are to be imposed on:–

(i)	The use of slang between 5.30 & 6	½d a time.
(ii)	Negligence of duties (given below)	1d a day.
(iii)	Late for meals	½d a meal
(iv)	Neglect to pay fines 1 day after announcement	1d a day
(v)	Play fines as last holidays.	
(vi)	Magazine fines if necessary.	

N. B. It was pointed out that this did not in any way rob the Red Cross fund, but it aided it by adding books to be read.

(iv)   *Books* The following list of books was voted to be obtained by the money obtained:–

List 1

'No Man's Land' (Sapper)
'The Lost World' (Conan Doyle)
'The Money Moon' (Jeffery Farnol)
'Captains All' (W. W. Jacobs)
'Ayesha' (H. Rider Haggard)

List 11 *(Supplementary)*

'Rupert of Hentzau' (New Edition)
'The First Hundred Thousand' (Ian Hay)
'The Long Trick' (Bartimeus)
'Pearl Maiden' (H. Rider Haggard)
'A Gentleman of France' (New Edition)

———

(v)   *The Library.* Everyone taking a book from the library must enter his name in a book provided for that purpose putting name, name of book, author, date taken out, date returned, if paid for. For neglect of any one of these things the fine is ½d.

R. Birley was elected as Librarian, & S. C. Monckton as Treasurer.

(vi)   *Duties.*

To keep the room supplied with flowers ..... M. G. Birley
To arrange expeditions .... R. Birley
To arrange Tournaments in tennis etc. ..... I. M-Smyth

> *To record the same* .... I. M-Smyth
> *To see to the fines* .... R. Birley

N. B. The debate, which lasted 1½ hours, was the most successful yet held by the Kenilworth Debating Society.)

R. Birley
(President of Kenilworth
Debating Society.)

The Society met again the following day, the main business being to appoint a Deputy Treasurer to stand in for Sybille Monckton who was going to be away for a few weeks. No further records have survived.

Through all this activity Ada Hayter worked especially hard to ensure that Marion was not too much overshadowed by her elder brother's effervescence, constantly reassuring her that her work was just as good as his, 'even if you are not quite so clever'. The most important thing in Ada's life was to see the two of them through these early years. She had become engaged when quite young, but refused to get married until the family no longer needed her. Sidney, her fiancé, simply had to wait.

It was grandmother who provided the more formal side of Bobbie and Marion's early education, for Arthur Birley was something of an invalid. Indeed it was for the sake of his health that they had moved south, their doctor in Manchester having suggested either Bournemouth or the Canary Islands. Although he endeared himself to his grandchildren by keeping a box of rose lozenges on the mantelpiece, Arthur was not in a position to make a great impact. He died in 1912. His wife on the other hand was formidably dynamic, with a lively imagination. Although she had never been there, she wrote two novels set in India, based on Leonard's account of his experiences. Published by Mowbrays under the pen name of Alice Clifton, they remained in print for many years: *The Unwilling Wife* was about an arranged marriage at the time of the Mutiny, and *Lord Branca's Promise* was a story about a lost heir. Both books were praised for their authenticity of background.

For someone who had had no formal education herself, Julia

Birley had a remarkable store of knowledge, and, what was more, a flair for imparting it. In Bobbie she found a precocious pupil with whom she could discuss political and religious questions as though he were an adult. By virtue of her Peel connections she was steeped in progressive traditions and considered the Liberal Party to be more true to these than the Conservatives. When the Tories won Bournemouth in the General Election of January 1910 Bobbie shared the consternation in the household, but Grannie reassured him by declaring that despite this setback the Liberals would still win in the country as a whole. She taught him to know the catechism by heart, but paved the way for metaphorical interpretation of the scriptures by telling him from the start that the story of Adam and Eve was not true. She encouraged him to follow the Balkan War of 1912 with such thoroughness that for the rest of his life he continued to be stirred at any mention of Kirk-Kilisse, Bunar Hisse-Lule-Burgas or Çatalca. By the time he was eleven she was discussing with him the question of Papal infallibility in a carriage going along the seafront at Paignton. This remarkable lady died shortly after the outbreak of the Great War. But there was no question of breaking the continuity of Cavendish Road life. A widowed aunt, Katie Dixon, came to take over the household.

Leonard and Jessie Birley had come home on leave in the long hot summer of 1911, part of which they spent at Weymouth. This was also the year in which it was arranged that Bobbie should go to a day prep school called Wychwood. It was an old-fashioned place of which he remarked years later that it must have been the last of the Dame schools. This new phase of his education opened with the excruciating mortification of being packed off by Grannie on the first day wearing a sailor suit. Further embarrassment was to follow when on wet days she made him take an umbrella. He had the initiative to hide this in the hedge, and needed all his presence of mind to explain away the occasions when he arrived home wringing wet. Wychwood was a pretty average school, by no means a magnet for ambitious parents with their eye on scholarships to leading public schools. Bobbie had had such a good grounding in the fundamentals from his grandmother that he was well ahead of his age group. When he came home for lunch at 1.20 each day he was far from exhausted by his morning's labours.

Old-fashioned and run of the mill or not, Wychwood did provide some memorable experiences. When Bobbie was about twelve a retired West Indian planter joined the staff and proceeded to teach mathematics brilliantly. More impressive still was his teaching of geography. His hobby was meteorology and he instructed the boys in its complexities to a level that in retrospect seemed amazing. In one end of term examination they were issued with duplicated maps of South America marked with isotherms, isobars, wind currents and so on. There was only one question: 'What is the normal climate of Bolivia in June?' To Bobbie it seemed a good question, difficult but not unfairly so. The excitement of these lessons was something which he could remember clearly years afterwards as his introduction to scientific thinking.

We can only speculate whether this inspired teaching was the most efficient preparation for Common Entrance. It did not have to be put to the test in Bobbie's case, for he got chicken pox a few days before he was due to take the examination, and was accepted into his public school on the the strength of his headmistress's recommendation alone.

CHAPTER TWO

Schooldays at Rugby

Although he had himself done very well at Uppingham Leonard Birley was not one of those who necessarily wanted his son to follow him to the same school. He was convinced that what mattered most in a boarding school was the personality of the housemaster, and enquiries among his friends produced a short list for him to visit during one of his periods of leave. His final choice fell on G. F. Bradby at Rugby.

Bradby was a man supremely well connected to the schoolmastering ascendancy of the turn of the century through the network of influence bequeathed by Thomas Arnold. When C. J. Vaughan, a former pupil of Arnold's at Rugby, followed in the steps of the master by reforming the monitorial system at Harrow, one of the men he appointed to his staff was an Old Rugbeian, E. H. Bradby. He too was an ex-pupil of Arnold's and from being the first to preside over what is still today Bradby's House at Harrow he went on to be one of the most remarkable Headmasters of Haileybury. Patriarchal figure and radical churchman, he edited several books of the Bible in the light of the latest scholarly criticism and published sermons and addresses on such subjects as thrift and church reform. Naturally enough, Bradby sent his own sons to Rugby and two of them returned to teach there and become housemasters.

They were a remarkable pair. Both were keen games players, especially the younger one, H. C. ('Kit'), who as Sir Frank Fletcher recalled in *After Many Days* 'could outrun the fastest of the school football players at an age when most men take to golf for their only exercise [and] whose cricketing eye lasted up to the day when he reached the age for retirement'. Both had a gift for humorous versifying, and Kit was an occasional contributor to *Punch*. G. F., who unlike his brother remained a bachelor and liked to pose as a woman-hater, had been in his younger days something of a leader in a Rugby common room which included a dozen or so future distinguished headmasters.

Not only was he by this token an influential figure in public school circles but a historian, poet and novelist into the bargain.

It was a perceptive choice of mentors. For a future history specialist it was stimulating to have as housemaster the author of *The great days of Versailles, studies of court life in the later years of Louis XIV*. For someone who was himself to become a house-master it was valuable to absorb the insight of a man who, in a poem called 'The Tutor's Nightmare' published in 1902, wrote:

> I told him he was just a boy
> Whose life was still at dawn,
> That tears *must* mingle with his joy
> Like dewdrops with a lawn
> But when I wanted to explain
> The mystery and use of pain
> He stopped me with a yawn.

And for someone who was to play a major part in the politics of the public schools it was salutary to be made aware from Bradby's novels of the penumbra of pretentiousness that threatened to obscure their virtues.

Published in 1913, his *The Lanchester Tradition* fairly romps through the absurdities of public school life. A new young headmaster has been appointed to Chiltern School, an institution built up from respectably obscure origins by the great Dr Lanchester in the nineteenth century. The school has colours of 'a happy combination of cerise, orange and green' which are a familiar sight in all parts of the Empire; classrooms which though dark, have an indefinable charm which 'together with the sense of continuity with a remote past are generally regarded as a substitute for ventilation'; a school song which 'without ever lapsing into poetry maintains throughout a fair rhythm and a high level of imbecility'; a house captain and captain-designate of the Eleven who 'had with difficulty fought his way into the senior fifth'; and a senior master who personifies 'that narrow but confident prejudice which blocks progress and strangles reform'. Hugely successful, the book was devoured in the public schools where the vignette of the senior master set innumerable bells ringing. There is a story, a shade improbable, that on reading it two Eton housemasters, each convinced that this ineffable character was modelled on the other, hurried to each other's houses one evening and met half-way. Each was clutching a copy of the book, mischievously intended as a gift for his colleague.

Another novel *The Chronicles of Dawnhope,* published in 1921 – near the end of Birley's time at school – was also about a new headmaster. For this fresh quiverful of satirical arrows the target of blind adherence to tradition had been replaced by that of ill-considered obsession with democratic change. But whereas *Lanchester* had not been based explicitly on Rugby, *Dawnhope* was much nearer the bone, for it was an obvious and cutting lampoon of A. A. David the Headmaster. David's offence, unforgivable in the eyes of Bradby and other masters of older persuasions, had been to interest himself in Homer Lane's pioneer work on the application of Freud's theories of psychoanalysis to education. In fact this crusty disapproval was by no means representative of opinion in the school. By and large the boys thought the world of their Headmaster. In his review of the book in *The Rugbeian,* Edward Ashcroft, a future distinguished journalist whose younger sister was to become Dame Peggy, roundly declared that Dr David was 'not the pompous, foolish egoist whom Mr Bradby knows'. *Dawnhope* was a parting shot published shortly after its author had retired, and about the time when David left Rugby to become Bishop of Liverpool. It was meant to leave a scar. But it was an admonition which was also wickedly funny and which did much to bring a sense of proportion to the problems of moving with the times.

It is interesting that it should have been these two very different personalities, the traditionally-minded housemaster and the progressive headmaster, who left the most distinctive impression on Robert Birley. It is something of a truism that for public school headmasters the course between tradition and change can be a particularly awkward one to steer. Bradby, down to earth and disingenuous, and David, kindly and a shade naïve, might be said to have put down valuable early markers, and each was nearer to the golden mean of common sense than the other was likely to admit. Both were convinced Christians and in their different ways both had the gift of treating boys as individuals and not simply as one of six hundred or so pupils.

However, neither of these indelible influences was immediately brought to bear. When Birley arrived at Rugby in September 1917 he was placed in a 'waiting house' for the first term, there being no immediate vacancy in Bradby's. His immediate reaction was pure delight. His first letter to his parents began: 'Rugby is a *ripping* place. I like it awfully, and am settling down quite all right.' The account continued in this vein, illustrated by detailed diagrams of the dormitory, and the study which he shared with four other boys. His favourite companion was William Plomer, the future author and wit, who was in the queue for School House. Cosmopolitan and intellectually precocious, Plomer had first been to a school in Johannesburg which he had found infinitely preferable to the dreary English prep school to which he was sent at the age of ten.

The early excitement of life in Troy House under Mr Cole was not altogether matched in lessons, for the quality of teaching had suffered as a result of the war. The question of whether or not schoolmasters should be called up was a delicate one and War Office policy had been to take only those who could be spared without impairing the work of the schools. But though the intention was to avoid devitalizing the teaching force, it was inevitable that some of the best people should be among those who went, leaving things often in the hands of 'dotards or weaklings', as Plomer put it in his autobiography. The contemporary worm's eye view in Birley's letter was less scathing. French with Mr Brigstocke he described as 'some sweat' and went on: 'It is awfully difficult to hear him, and he's always pouncing on you for not listening, and you have to listen *most* intently. He's quite a nice old chap, but the work's jolly hard and the French dictation awful.' The geography master was 'an awfully jolly old chap, and you can rag like fun'. As for maths, despite coming top in the set, he declared that he did not much care for the man teaching it. After Christmas Birley and Plomer moved on to their respective houses and from the following September the atmosphere was revitalized by the return of the younger masters.

Bradby's had its share of the harshness characteristic of public school life at that time. Birley did not relish his introduction to the regime and indeed before long was among the leaders of a successful protest against the conduct of one obnoxiously dictatorial senior boy. But having taken the indispensable step of demonstrating that he could stand up for himself, he was able to pursue his naturally individualistic course, relatively untroubled by the need to belong to any particular group. His housemaster played a part in all sorts of ways. On one occasion when Birley had come top of Bradby's class in history, he awaited his end of term report with pleasurable anticipation. The report read: 'First out of 25; bad, but the others were worse.' Years later it was a useful anecdote for the numerous occasions when the victim of this comment was called upon to give away prizes at school speech days.

One of the most important initial decisions at Rugby was whether a boy was placed on the classical or on the modern side. Plomer was one of those who chose the modern, Birley wanted to do classics. But on the strength of the recommendation from Wychwood he did not begin at the bottom of the school and a place could only be found in the 'non-Greek' form. Special arrangements were made for him to have Greek with the parallel form, with a view to moving across later on. However, for someone whose Greek was already weak, the effort was too much and the idea was soon abandoned. Birley's father was not consulted and was furious. He had kept up his own classical interests through the clever device of whiling away Church services by translating the psalms into Greek verse. However, communications with India being even more long-drawn-out than usual owing to the war, by the time he found out what had happened it was too late to do anything about it.

So it was to some extent by default that Birley found himself on the intellectually rather less fashionable modern side. Yet what was at the time a disappointment was in fact also something of a landmark, for he was later to be one of the first public school headmasters vigorously to question the common assumption that classical languages were the best test of academic potential. Already at prep school his own best subject had been history and the path he had taken led naturally to his becoming a history specialist when he entered the sixth form. A Balliol scholarship later proved the point. He left another, unwitting, legacy to the cause of history specialism at Rugby. The future High Master of St Paul's, T. E. B. Howarth, who

Bobbie Birley, aged two, at Midnapore

onard Birley with Bobbie and
arion in Bournemouth

Grannie, his first teacher

Bobbie and Marion with nan
Ada Hay

At prep school in Bournemouth

entered the same house a decade later and who was also on the
modern side, recalled being offered help with some difficult
history essays by his house captain. It came in the form of
model answers which had been handed down from year to year;
they had been written, he was told, by 'some fellow called
Birley'.

Promotion to the Lower Bench, as the Rugby first year sixth
was called, had not followed an orthodox path. Failure in Latin
had brought failure in School Certificate, for which passes in a
certain combination of subjects were required. But Bradby
nobly told the Headmaster that it was not Birley but the
examination system that was at fault and that he should be
moved up anyway. He was, Bradby said, so obviously cut out
for the sixth form. There were special arrangements whereby
the two or three most promising historians were excused certain
lessons to allow them to prepare a weekly essay for the senior
history master, C. P. ('Tiger') Hastings. The sooner opportunities of this kind came Birley's way the better, and in due
course he derived enormous benefit from the tutorial style of
teaching practised by Hastings. It was exactly the kind of thing
which he was so much to enjoy doing himself years later,
though he was more adventurous than his mentor who was
reputed to regard anything after the reign of Queen Anne as too
dangerous to teach.

There was one especially significant preliminary to this
valuable propædeutic. In the middle of the summer term of his
first year in the sixth, when he was just seventeen, Birley's form
master fell ill and was replaced by a temporary master. Long
afterwards, in an address entitled *Freedom in Education,* Birley
recalled what happened, summing it up in three words: 'We did
nothing.' By that he did not mean that they were lazy or ill-
disciplined. He meant simply that in the formal sense they did
nothing. No work was set, no text books were brought into
school, no questions were asked them. Fortunately the boys
were a somewhat highbrow bunch. On one occasion, to their
astonishment, the temporary master suddenly asked one of
them what he was reading. He answered, quite truthfully,
Browning's *The Ring and the Book.* The master never tried
again. A deep peace brooded over the room. For two halcyon
months in glorious summer weather, except for occasional

periods when he had to take some subjects not taught by the master, Birley did no formal work at all. It was a vivid illustration of the adage that the taste for reading is caught, not taught.

It was a lucky coincidence that had made this possible. The school was in its last term of David's kindly and easy-going stewardship. Nothing of the kind could have happened under W. W. Vaughan who became Headmaster the following September. At any rate, for Birley the release from classroom discipline had come at exactly the right moment. He read as he was never able to read again. The whole world of literature, as he later recalled, seemed to have simply unlocked its gates for him, and he had time to enjoy the right of entry. He read every novel of Joseph Conrad in the complete edition in the school library, and most if not all of Shakespeare's plays. He read the whole of Macaulay's *History of England* and Motley's *The Rise of the Dutch Republic*. 'Revelling in my idleness, like some Pasha of the East, I read in a deck chair in the evenings, while my companions in other forms struggled at Latin proses or mathematical exercises.' As he was expecting to spend a further year at school he was not yet required to take the Higher School Certificate. The fact that some of his companions in the house were having to spend much of their time in furious revising for this examination only heightened the enjoyment of his own sublime freedom.

The Lower Bench also provided him with a memorable introduction to the natural sciences, for as a new venture in the school all arts specialists were to study them for two periods a week. 'A natural clumsiness and a lack of patience, along with a sad weakness at mathematics,' as Birley later recalled, had ensured that he was not much use at science. He had taken physics and chemistry in the School Certificate and, to his own astonishment, passed in both. But that in his view was quite enough. Like so many arts specialists in sixth forms ever since, he had made up his mind to have nothing more to do with science. The form as a whole shared this lack of interest and they were incensed at the imposition of the two weekly periods. The Daniel who entered this lion's den of indignation was E. R. Thomas, a remarkable teacher who went on to be Headmaster of Newcastle Royal Grammar School for more than a quarter of a century. At the start of his first lesson he looked at them and said, '"what is Truth, said jesting Pilate, and would not stay for an answer." Now who wrote that?' Some of them recognised the quotation, but none could remember where it came from. 'Well,' he said, 'it is from Bacon's essay on Truth. Now I suggest that we begin by discussing what a scientist means by truth and then comparing it with what other people mean, like a philosopher, for instance.' This was not at all what they expected and before long they were entranced.

After the shock tactics of this opening gambit Thomas went on to devise what he called 'communal experiments' for the form, in which they had to compare their results. But it was by no means plain sailing. Birley remembered his writing the instructions for one of these experiments on the blackboard and adding at the foot: 'For the purpose of obtaining an average of these results, Birley's experiment should be ignored.' Obviously the conventional approach to the subject would not entirely do. In the end Thomas allowed his way-ward pupil to make a study of Paracelsus and the early chem-ists on condition that he eventually gave a lecture on the subject to the form. The supreme moment was the occasion when, as the rest of the boys were reaching for their bottles of hydrochloric acid and their litmus paper, the student of Paracelsus came proudly into the laboratory with the materials for an experiment which he intended to conduct – a bottle of wine and an egg.

It was of course significant that in their exposure to physics and chemistry in the lower school the form had all learnt something of the grammar, as it were, of these subjects. But when it came to biology which they had not previously studied, this foundation was lacking and things became more difficult. Dr Thomas got round the problem by concentrating almost entirely on the study of one man, Louis Pasteur. He went on to suggest that it would be an excellent idea if they acted Sacha Guitry's play *Pasteur* before the rest of the school. And they did, in French.

Most memorable of all was the lesson in which Thomas talked to them about the work of Ernest Rutherford and what in those days was known as splitting the atom. He said that this would eventually give men far greater power than they had ever possessed before. He told them that all power brought with it responsibility and that they ought to be aware of how immense the new responsibilities would be. At the end of the lesson he said that he did not think they had discussed it as extensively as they might and added that any who were interested could come to tea with him on the following Sunday to resume doing so. Birley was one of those who accepted the invitation. That experience was the first thing that came into his mind when, twenty-four years later, he heard on the wireless the news of the bomb dropped on Hiroshima.

Memories of the inventive teaching of E. R. Thomas later prompted many thoughts about the problems of specialisation in the sixth form, problems which became particularly acute during Birley's time as Head Master of Eton. He had no doubt that it was due to his own experiences at this stage that he himself – a common or garden teacher of history, as he put it – taught a course in the history of science to the history specialists. Although, as he characteristically added in recalling this, 'some might say that it shows what dreadful results may flow from rash educational experiments.'

The most important feature of the non-specialist science taught by Dr Thomas had been that there was no question of the form being examined on their work, and this was a small instance of Birley's own general good fortune in evading formal examinations. It was not just that he had missed out Common Entrance by contracting chicken pox and been admitted to Rugby on the strength of the recommendation from his prep school. Nor that he had failed School Certificate and, thanks to his housemaster, been promoted to the Lower Bench without having to take it again. His luck held still longer, for he left school the term before he was due to take the Higher School Certificate. Even the examinations for admission to Oxford did not pass off in totally straightforward fashion. All this made him in later life profoundly suspicious of the ever more time-plundering national system of public examinations. It was largely due to their dominance that time spent on unexamined work had come to be seen as wasted. But it was only by escaping from examinations that he himself had been able to savour what he referred to as 'that most stimulating educational experience, complete irrelevance', something which he never ceased to value after the unforgettable summer term of unbridled reading in the Rugby Lower Bench.

These classroom tales seem a far cry from the conventional image of a regimented public school existence founded on the trinity of chapel, games and the Officers Training Corps. It was partly that in David's time the atmosphere was less severe than it would have been under most other headmasters. One of his innovations was to make Sunday evening chapel voluntary. But what by modern standards must seem a remarkably harmless change was in fact one of the controversial ideas which aroused strong opposition in the common room. For the older staff it was of a piece with David's 'trust the boy' philosophy of which they profoundly disapproved. It is difficult to believe that they need have worried. The school routine was by any standards a busy one. There was a highly demanding timetable of lessons which in the summer term included school before breakfast. Games were compulsory, with only a few like William Plomer managing to escape them, and even then only by way of organised alternatives. And on top of chapel and the OTC there was a wealth of corporate activity. The music was especially good. The City of Birmingham Orchestra came regularly to the school and before their concerts the Director of Music, A. H. Peppin, gave splendid illustrated talks on the structure of the musical compositions which were in prospect.

Birley joined in most of these activities with enthusiasm. He took to rugger with a will and in due time his lanky figure made its appearance in the succession of team photographs that lined the gloomy corridors of the house. He was less enthusiastic about cricket – to the disappointment of his father – and having served the statutory two-year apprenticeship, gave it up in favour of tennis and swimming. The varied nature of his activities put him strongly in the running to be Head of House but in the event this went to another boy who unexpectedly stayed on for an extra year. It proved a beneficial disappointment in so far as it contributed to his desire to leave school earlier than intended and spend the summer term on a tour of Europe. In any case he was getting on for nineteen by this time and had amply savoured the all-round enjoyment of school life which could so easily generate the inclination to take up school teaching as a career.

The picture of life at Rugby as Birley experienced it differs in a quite fundamental way from the public school stereotype which inflamed a section of radical opinion in the years following the First World War. One of the most prominent features of the identikit image that was put about at that time was the subordination of intellectual values to the various orthodoxies conveyed by the idea of 'good form'. Over the years Rugby has probably been, by virtue of its famous name and history, more vulnerable than most to this over-simplification. Thomas Arnold's reputation has scarcely been freed of the implications of the remark made in an address to his præpostors and quoted in the Stanley biography: 'What we must look for here is, first, religious and moral principle; secondly, gentlemanly conduct; thirdly, intellectual ability.' Ever since this was seized on by Lytton Strachey in *Eminent Victorians* it has invited the sardonic inference that for Arnold intellectual ability came a poor third behind morality and principled conduct, and indeed that he held intellectual development to be somehow incompatible with moral principle. In fact, an undervaluing of the intellect is the very last charge that could be laid at Arnold's door. His lasting contribution to the development of the public schools lay precisely in his insistence that intellectual merit should be the criterion according to which boys were selected for positions of power and privilege.

In Birley's own time at Rugby it was, to be sure, the best part of a century since Arnold's headmastership but the importance of the intellectual criterion had endured. Of course the games cult had developed in the meantime and since most schoolboys will always find something fascinating and of value in sporting prowess, it is hardly surprising if it is assumed to go hand in hand with qualities of leadership, given that senior boys are called upon to do most of the day to day running of a public school. But at Rugby it was neither a necessary nor a sufficient condition for the exercise of authority. If a boy was moved up into the sixth form he was automatically given the powers of supervision and discipline which in most schools are confined to selected prefects. Occasionally there would be a boy of strong character and sporting ability whose work was not up to standard for promotion to the sixth. The housemaster could use his discretion in conferring disciplinary powers on such a boy but G. F. Bradby was reluctant to do so. Birley remembered one contemporary of his, subsequently a Cambridge Blue, who was allowed no greater authority than, in Bradby's quaint phrase, 'sixth-form power in the bedroom'.

So even if much was made of the gladiatorial virtues of the playing field it was certainly not at the expense of a vigorous intellectual life. In Birley's recollection the hero of the time was Rupert Brooke and there were obvious reasons for idolising him. As he was the son of one of the masters, Rugby had been his home for the first twenty-three years of his life, and the fame that followed his death in 1915 reflected on the school through his fulsome tributes. Soon after leaving he had declared himself to have been happier at Rugby than he could find words to say. This was the nostalgia of the successful all-rounder who had played cricket and rugger for the school and won prizes for his poems, who had been Head of House and who was now tasting freshman unsureness at King's. Once settled at Cambridge he had scaled the enticing heights of radical undergraduate ambition, becoming the point of inter-section of the most modish charmed circles. A founder of the Marlowe Society, he had sparkled in the eclat of the produc-tion of *Comus* commissioned by Christ's for the Milton Tercentenary. Having been at Rugby a somewhat mischievous champion of the Labour Party, he had at Cambridge become President of the University Fabian Society. Prizes for scholar-ship, a Fellowship at King's, national renown as a poet and poignant valediction in *The Times* over the initials of Winston Churchill – these were natural ingredients of a recipe for hero worship.

Sir Edward Marsh's memoir which brought so much of the story to light was published in Birley's second year at Rugby and in the years that followed the myth gathered strength. It helped to consolidate the public school values, endorsed by a heroic figure who had attended the literary teas of the young G. F. Bradby and who was, in Churchill's phrase 'all that one would wish England's noblest sons to be'. Perhaps the legend did something to lighten the earnestness of the mark that Arnold left on the school by linking it with the fashionable and vivacious elite of Cambridge, as described by Marsh. Perhaps too it helped to nurture the questioning strand in a tradition which embraced, among other radically minded Old Rugbeians, the towering figure of R. H. Tawney.

Certainly when it came to Birley's turn to test the water it was not considered at all odd that he should read a paper to the School's Literary Society on the subject of the anarchist Kropotkin. He was himself far from having any really anarchistic attitudes: 'embryonic liberal reformer of prized institutions' would be nearer the mark. It was entirely in character that in a mock Parliament in 1922 he should, as Minister of Education in a Labour Government, introduce a bill for the democratisation of forms and sets, maintaining that his new measures 'would encourage the slothful to take an intelligent interest in their work'. As it happened, his reputation for intellectual insurrection would not be denied and, as *The Rugbeian* records, his Tory opponent was able to persuade the House to reject the bill on the grounds that it would lead to anarchy.

Debates of this kind reflected a post-war climate in the country at large which was receptive to any talk of reform. In education in particular, the upheaval had set in motion one of those periodic waves of agonising over the interminably vexed question of 'what to do about the public schools'. At the most radical end of the scale the argument about their being a bastion of an irrelevant established order which needed to be swept away was enjoying a certain vogue. In fact they were not under any serious threat, but the general climate was salutary in prompting a wave of wholesome self-criticism.

With this in the air it is hardly surprising to find Birley cutting his teeth in *The Rugbeian* with a mild polemic entitled 'What is wrong with Rugby?' For this and other contributions to the magazine he used the pen-name Saraswati. Dayananda Saraswati was the nineteenth-century Hindu nationalist leader whose revolutionary teaching claimed that there was no Vedic authority for customs such as rigidity of caste, untouchability and child marriage. Birley's critique does not perhaps have quite the passion of Hindu nationalism. He begins by chiding with elegant detachment: 'You may say that there is nothing wrong with Rugby. If so, I am afraid we must agree to differ. . . . If you think Rugby perfect I advise you to turn to the next article, for you are unlikely to be in the frame of mind

for this one'. The theme then emerges of the self-conscious
and priggish public school all-rounder who takes himself too
seriously. Of course it was perfectly all right to be an all-
rounder – Rupert Brooke, he recalled, was described as being
'always with a ball in his hand and a book in his pocket'. But
Rupert Brooke would change from the one to the other
without any conscious effort and though the memoir alluded
to his assertion of decadence at Rugby he did not, in this case
at any rate, take himself seriously. It was artificial striving for
effect that Birley was tilting at. 'By all means let us act plays,
and read books and write papers on them and play football,
but let us stop thinking of ourselves in doing so. Let us have a
House Dramatic Society because we want to act, or, if you like
it, because we want to give people something to do, but not by
a conscious effort because (this is, after all, the reason) it is
comme il faut.'

The illustration of house drama was one that was close to
the heart. At the time the article was written Mr Odgers's
House Dramatic Society ('Hearty Odgers' had taken over from
Bradby as housemaster) was about to present two plays 'for
the first time on any stage', *The Eternal Feud* by J. T. G.
Macleod the House Captain, and *Ulf Builds a Church* by R.
Birley. The reviewer in *The Rugbeian* later described Birley's
performance in the first of them in the part of 'Rory Macleod,
age eighteen, philosopher' as 'very brilliant'. Birley's own play
went on record as 'altogether a very jolly affair' about a Danish
merchant who had made his pile by 850 AD and was
determined to keep up with the younger generation. With
floods of rhetoric he emancipated his slaves and declared his
intention of reviving the Saxon tongue of which he considered
himself a champion. He had built a church, and proposed to
dedicate it with an inscription in Saxon. When he proceeded
to read this, however, his daughter tactlessly pointed out that
he had committed a grammatical error. This precipitated the
dénouement, with Ulf flying into a towering rage at the
realisation that his attempt to keep up with the younger
generation was doomed to failure.

Elsewhere in *The Rugbeian* Birley kept popping up as the
author of various off-beat and humorous pieces. One of these,
a disquisition on the delights of roast turkey, begins with the

observation that a dictionary has a sense of humour and goes on
to explain that, on the question of turkey, it is at its greatest.

> Listen to what it says. 'Large (esp. domestic) gallinaceous
> bird, native of America; related to pheasant, esteemed as
> food, and associated with Christmas festivities.' Observe the
> order. First you are told that it is 'a gallinaceous bird'. (Page
> 337. 'Gallinaceous = Of the order gallinea, including
> domestic poultry, pheasants, partridges, etc.') Then you are
> told that it came from America. This has an importance
> which I will explain later. Then that it is related to pheasant.
> Redundant, you say. Not a bit of it; you know quite well you
> would not have looked up page 337. Now, having whetted
> your excitement, and led you off on one false trail, it comes to
> the point. 'Esteemed as food and associated with Christmas
> festivities.'

He then remarks on how differently the ordinary person would
have written this:

> We would have left out the little domestic touch, and begun:
> 'A bird chiefly associated with Christmas festivities, and
> much esteemed as food, native of America, and of the
> gallinaceous order.' How inferior it is! Who, after reading
> the first clause, would go further? How else could the bird be
> associated with Christmas, if not as food? How vulgarly
> emotional is the inclusion of the 'much'. No, I prefer the
> dictionary.

The piece then develops into an apologia for the turkey and
proceeds, through the case for incorporating it in the Royal
Standard, to its irresistible climax:

> Everything is against it, and yet, once before you, with
> sausages and stuffing, potatoes and bread sauce, it lifts you
> away to that region where America is no farther than Surrey,
> and where the fogs and mists of London are as strange and
> foreign as the blazing sun of the pampas.

Another of his contributions to *The Rugbeian* prefigures a
later penchant for roaming on the Continent. He had been on a
walking tour in Normandy with his cousin Ian Maxwell-Smyth
and was impressed by the cathedrals in the conventional way.

The conventionality of his essay, however, lasts no longer than the opening paragraph. The rest turns out to be more characteristically unorthodox, concerning itself with those which he did not visit, 'the queer erections which pass for cathedrals in the South of France'. He had read about them in a book and they had usurped the place of the orthodox Gothic ones in his affections by virtue of their weird incongruity. In the illustrations to the book La Rochelle was like a bank, Perpignan like a prison, Marseilles, in the midst of wharves, 'like an ornate warehouse, built perhaps for rich Eastern goods, but terribly ugly, and Nice, with a carriage drawn up in front, like a General Post Office'. A photograph of Albi made it seem like 'some Moorish castle, narrow windows, turreted roof castellated like the entrance to a white fortress'. The keynote of these dazzling effects is, he points out, the Southern sunlight and, aware that his readership by now probably requires a more homely point of reference, he concludes, 'New Big School may look the very epitome of ugliness in the midst of Rugby, but set it in Provence and you will see the difference.'

Le style c'était le jeune homme. It is these juvenilia with their mental agility and malice-free humour that best convey the personality that was beginning to flower towards the end of the days at Rugby. The natural next step was Oxford or Cambridge.

As his father had been at New College, this was Birley's first choice for the scholarship. In the meantime he had in the matriculation examination managed to demonstrate an adequate competence in Latin. The attempt ended in disappointment. The story went that his papers were marked by an Old Rugbeian don from another college, who was sufficiently incensed by Birley's somewhat radical, and no doubt tiresome, essay to declare that Oxford must not have this man at any price. More probably the failure could be attributed to the classical bias at New College. At all events the dismay that followed the rebuff soon gave way to elation. The tutors of Balliol were more impressed and awarded him the Brackenbury Scholarship for History. In so doing they made Higher School Certificate as irrelevant as Common Entrance and School Certificate had been. He was now in a position to go up to Oxford without having passed any of the national examinations.

CHAPTER THREE

Your Affectionate Son, R. Birley

The jubilation and relief at the Brackenbury success released a surge of wanderlust. A final term at Rugby was a tame prospect compared with the possibilities elsewhere, and Birley set about persuading his father to allow him to leave school at Easter in order to spend the time wandering about the Continent. What has now become commonplace as a way of putting in time between school and university was then rather enterprising and just a shade eccentric. But his father agreed, provided that it was not going to cost him any more than the term's fees at Rugby. The money was to last well, for it was 1922, the year when the great inflation was just beginning, and in several of the countries he visited the stability of sterling gave it an increasing real value.

Altogether Birley was able to roam for four fascinating months, consolidating at first hand the sense of European history which he had been acquiring from books. He went first to Florence where he set about his sightseeing quite ready to be bowled over by the art and architecture, but at the same time retaining enough of his wit and critical disposition to resist slipping into undifferentiated admiration. His letters home, generally signed 'Your affectionate son, R. Birley', demonstrated an emerging touch with anecdote which was to be one of the qualities that later endeared him to so many audiences. At the Monastery of St Mark, where Savonarola had lived, he was shown round by a guide who ended all his sentences with a kind of refrain: 'This is the original ceiling, Fra Angelico Savonarola. This is a picture by Fra Bartolomeo, Fra Angelico Savonarola. This is a *very* old pen, Fra Angelico Savonarola. . . .' At the Palazzo Vecchio there was only one room that he found really interesting, in which there were cupboards all round the walls, and on each one a painted map dating from the mid-sixteenth century. The one he especially liked was of Abyssinia 'looking rather as if there was a sunset over it, and standing in the middle one solitary, very dejected elephant!'

A visit to the opera helped him to get the feel of Italian life. At a performance of *Tristan and Isolde* many of the audience had been caught out by the fact that it started only seven minutes late, half an hour being more usual. The result was that people were coming in through the whole of the first act. Punctuality, he learnt, was not an Italian virtue. This, and the over-acting, and the fact that the performance did not finish till five past one in the morning, all helped to take him outside his English sense of order and moderation.

He soon began, too, to learn the essential skills of student travel, dodging the tour parties over which Cook's appeared to have something of a monopoly, and surviving the unfamiliar intense heat. The latter was the lesson of a day trip to Pisa. A little air blew in to his carriage while the train was moving, but while it was stopped at stations – no inconsiderable portion of the time – he was denied even that relief. Indeed, even on the journeys between the stations his Italian fellow-travellers would draw the curtains, ostensibly to keep out the sun, but more probably – it seemed to him at the time – to ensure maximum stuffiness and discomfort. Another skill to be acquired was that of eating spaghetti, which in those days had not made any inroads into English culinary culture. He thought he did better than the Pisans in the restaurant where he had lunch. His abiding memory of Pisa was one of eeriness, whether induced by the sensation that came from leaning over at the top of the Tower and seeing the walls receding beneath him; or by the magnificent frescoes in the Campo Santo which were mostly of Hell; or by the old man in the Baptistry who for a few pence would sing falsetto, making a sound exactly like an organ.

In Florence Birley was involved in a somewhat un-Florentine episode when a shop assistant tried the confidence trick of adding 12 per cent for a bogus tax on the purchase of some handkerchiefs. He was saved from paying this by two American ladies who happened to be in the shop at the time. 'Tax', one of them declared. 'We never had any tax before. There is no tax. This gentleman likes the handkerchiefs. He will buy them. If there is a tax, we will give you our names and you can send them to the authorities.' Birley handed over the money, minus the 12 per cent, the girl gave him the handkerchiefs meekly and the three of them swept out.

The best day trip of all from Florence was to San Gimignano, the magnificent fourteenth-century 'city of the towers'. After taking a train to the nearest station at Poggibonsi Birley discovered that the bus which did the remainder of the journey was entirely enclosed. Since the main point of visiting San Gimignano is the view from the outside, this did not seem satisfactory and so he resolved to be bold and ask the ticket collector if he could get a carriage privately. The collector beckoned to a nearby group of peasants, one of whom offered to take him for 35 lire. 'Following out the excellent instructions of Baedeker to bargain with people in remote parts, I stuck my chin out, looked firm and said "25 lire"'. He was then treated to a variety of tactics – not understanding, misunderstanding, shrugging of shoulders in indifference, and so on. Just as his Dutch courage was beginning to falter, one of the group agreed on the 25 lire for the journey.

Five minutes later Birley was asked by a very old man to follow him and they wound their way by queer and tortuous streets up through the village until they reached a stable by an inn. He was glad to note that the objective was not to entice him to have a meal but to take him to a horse that was being harnessed to a rickety cart. The horse was 'rather weak in the flesh but extremely willing in the spirit' and they got all the way up the formidable hill to San Gimignano without the driver having to beat it once. Although Birley had expressly stipulated that he wanted to go up only, on the way he agreed to a return ride for 25 lire, and 10 lire for food for the man and his horse while he looked round the town. This deal having been concluded, the man then stopped his horse and climbed up a bank into a field from which he stole a large bundle of hay.

The cathedral and the other buildings lived up to expectations, and the seal was set on the day by a return journey on which, with the aid of his dictionary, Birley got into friendly conversation with the driver. In the midst of the usual exchange of information about home and family the man suddenly asked him if he had any babies. During the pause, while Birley looked up the words with which to phrase his startled answer, the driver went on: 'I suppose you have a wife?' The episode developed into a comparison of English and Italian views of matrimony; any self-respecting Italian villager married at twenty, Birley learnt. After a further stop to steal an even larger bundle of hay they got back to Poggibonsi in comfortable time for the nineteen-year-old bachelor to catch the train back.

In Florence itself, incident followed incident. At the serene end of the scale was a visit to the Russian Church to hear a concert of Russian sacred music. The choir was the best that Birley had ever heard and the music, apart from four familiar items by Tchaikowsky, compellingly strange. At the turbulent end was the pandemonium when a row broke out between a group of students drinking beer in a terrace cafe and a family party having a photograph taken. The students had been larking about, trying to put the slow and deliberate photographer off his stroke. A young man from the family group then suddenly went over to them, knocked over their table, smashing the glasses, and was with difficulty restrained from fisticuffs. Old ladies fled and waiters withdrew quivering into the background, but before long everything settled down again. The climax to Birley's stay in Florence had a whiff of danger as well as of excitement; he found himself having to crouch in a doorway while insurgents fired from one end of the street and the police fired from the other. He had stumbled on one of the preliminaries to the Fascist march on Rome.

Next came Ravenna, hot and dusty but memorable in a positive way too. On the evening of his arrival Birley met an American, a graduate of Oxford, who showed him that it was possible to peer into the tomb of Dante after dark; inside a lamp was kept burning night and day on behalf of the people of Florence, as a kind of penance for having exiled Dante from their city. The Mausoleum of Galla Placidia was quite overwhelming, with the mosaics looking like a kind of soft braid in the half-light of the alabaster windows. Later the American friend showed him the best way to see the Baptistry mosaics, which was to lie down at full length on the edge of the vast font. With a letter, written to his mother, aunt and sister, Birley enclosed a picture of the Baptistry, the floor of which he had marked in two places. This was the pitch of his game of cricket with the custodian's grandson who was about three years old and 'of such an imperious disposition that his commands were

quite obvious without the aid of words'. The letter, sent on to
his father in Bengal, was signed

> Your affectionate
> son
> brother   R. Birley
> nephew

Going on from Ravenna to Venice Birley found the churches
disappointing by comparison – 'ripping' from the outside, he
thought, but close up, almost all hideous. Inside he found them
full of horrible statues, ornaments, and tombs 'of the most
terrible taste'. Nor did he care much for Venetian painting,
except for one or two early artists like Carpaccio, Giorgione and
Bellini. Most of the more famous artists, like Titian, Veronese
and Tintoretto, failed to excite him. The one glorious exception
to the mediocrity of the churches was St Mark's. The mosaics
which covered the roof of the narthex were especially engaging
representations of Old Testament stories. There was God
breathing a soul into Adam, the soul portrayed as a minute little
man with wings, looking like a dragonfly; God giving clothes to
Adam and Eve, with Eve looking doubtful and Adam surveying
the shirt allocated to him with an expression of extreme disgust.
There was Adam naming the animals – it was the lion's turn
and his tongue was hanging out as though, panting with
excitement, he was wondering what his name was going to be.
And there was Noah, bundling animals into and out of the Ark
by the scruff of the neck. These were a prelude to a feast of
mosaics in the main body of the basilica.

Behind the high altar was an immense gold altarpiece about
seven feet square and raised four feet above the floor, a mass of
jewels and panels with Byzantine enamel miniatures. It was
difficult to see them, partly because of the dark and partly
because of the height. Most visitors satisfied themselves with a
view of the bottom two or three rows of panels, but Birley
managed to obtain a candle from the custodian, which enabled
him to spend a couple of hours examining the rest. This made
him extremely popular and he was repeatedly asked to illumin-
ate the top row but one, which was the highest he could reach
with his candle. One of the beneficiaries, an American lady, was
a professional worker in enamel and repaid him with an account

of how this kind of work was done. The following day Birley returned to St Mark's with a walking stick. By tying a candle to this he was able to reveal the former secrets of the top row of panels, which was in fact the oldest and the finest of all. His equipment proved such an attraction that the place was crowded out in no time.

While in Venice, he once again saw political disturbance at close quarters. His hotel bedroom had been built over a passage very near the Piazza San Marco where, in the course of a confrontation, a Fascist was shot by a policeman. The next day there was a funeral and all the hotel flags were at half-mast. The manager of Birley's hotel was an anti-Fascist and was prevailed upon to follow suit only after much excited argument. In the evening some troops arrived to march round the city in a display of authority. However, as there is not much of Venice that lends itself to marching, their scope was restricted, and much to Birley's amusement they tramped under his bedroom again and again throughout the night. So ended, with a flavour of comic opera, his first-hand experience of the rise of Fascism.

The three blissful weeks in Italy were followed by a rude shock. At Basel Birley discovered that the box with all his belongings, which had been sent separately, had not come through. At this point he was, as he put it in a letter to his father, 'much helped spiritually and materially' by a little interpreter who was 'cheerful and imperturbable of countenance' and who assured him firstly that his situation was not unique and, secondly, that Basel was a beautiful city. The obvious course was to forget the worries by exploring it, which he did, greatly enjoying the contrast with Italy. On his return to the station he learnt that the worst had happened. At Domodossola the Italians had refused to allow the box through customs. He had to send the key, and this meant staying at least two nights in Basel. 'Weak in spirit, I trailed across to the hotel opposite the station, asked for a room and got one.'

However, the days in Basel were far from uneventful. The letter to his father describing his experiences gathered momentum:

The next morning I paid another visit to the Cathedral and walked about, paying every now and then quite useless and hopeless visits to the station. That afternoon I meant to go to Arlesheim, a village near Basel, in the tram, but I never got there. I started off by doing something simply terrible, one of those quite simple, but nevertheless awful things that you might dream about.

I saw a tram coming marked for Arlesheim. The Basel trams do not have marked up where they are going to, but simply two names, X – Arlesheim, or perhaps Arlesheim – X, it does not matter which. At any rate I jumped into it, and the conductor came towards me. Suddenly I realised the awful fact that I had got a tram going the wrong way. I passed by a shop that I knew and it gave me my sense of direction. Now in Bournemouth this would not have mattered. I should have asked for the next stopping place and got out. But not only did I not know *any* stopping-place along the route, but I also did not know the terminus, not having noticed it, and what is more, I did not know sufficient German to explain my position. In English or even in French I might have brazened it out and pretended to be eccentric and said, 'Oh, any old place. I don't mind. I want a ride.' But my German would not go as far as this. The position was *terrible*.

Meanwhile, as all this was flashing through my brain, the conductor was getting nearer; he was just standing over me when I had what I really think must be counted as one of *the* achievements of my career. I suddenly remembered that the Rhine went through Basel from north-west to south-east. As Arlesheim and I were on the left bank of the Rhine, the odds were that the unknown terminus was on the right. Steadying myself for a moment I said, *'Die Rheinbrücke'* [the Rhine bridge]. There was a moment of awful suspense and then, *'Jawohl. Das ist fünfundzwanzig.'* With a trembling hand I gave the money and sank back with relief.

This achievement, dramatised with revealing innocence, had been based on somewhat obscure reasoning since the Rhine in fact flows through Basel from south-east to north-west. A later episode lent itself more naturally to dramatisation:

Having got out at the *'Rheinbrücke'*, I was waiting for a tram to Arlesheim, when it suddenly struck me that it might be worth while finding out the address of the German Consul in Strasbourg for visa purposes. I found that there was no German Consul in Basel, but a '*Bureau de Passeports*' which would do as well. It was at the Bavarian Railway Station. I am glad I went, among other things, because I saw the cubist fountain outside the station, the first cubist work, I believe, ordered by a town. It was of distinct decorative merit, but seemed to be entirely without real importance. There are two animals, a bull and a horse, facing one another, representing the Rhine and the Weser. They are sitting down and in front of each is a naked woman, also facing each other, kneeling. The whole thing is of course very roughly cut.

I had a hard time at the passport office, but it was worthwhile. I found that there was no German Consul at Strasbourg, so I decided to get a visa there. Out of four officials I had to deal with, only one could speak French. It was *terrible*! I also had a long wait. The official who could speak French spoke it even worse than I do, if that were possible, and so we didn't get along very fast. He said that my passport was good for as many voyages into Germany before June 30th as I liked. As a matter of fact I found at Strasbourg that it was only good for one. I must make good use of it! However, I can get across the Rhine into Germany at Kehl in French Occupied Territory without a visa.

At five o'clock I paid another visit to the station and this time I found to my *intense* surprise that the box had arrived. The Italians apparently had relented. The only train I could take for Strasbourg left at 5.20. I found this out by 5.05. I had a quarter of an hour. It was an intensely dramatic one! I gave the porter the registration ticket and fled to the hotel. Bursting in, breathless, I explained the situation to the hall porter. The whole hotel became fired with excitement. The lift-boy helped me to pack my bag. My bill was made out hurriedly. As if by magic, servants appeared from the depths, waiting to be financed, and I distributed largesse as I went. I very nearly tipped the hotel proprietor by mistake! He was immensely excited and said I hadn't a chance. The lift-boy however (at this moment democracy ruled even in the hotel) thought otherwise. Spurred only by this hope I rushed across the Zentralbahnplatz, the lift-boy with baggage at my heels and an excited audience. Flying to the Customs Office I told the man that I had not the key, that the Italians had it, that it depended solely on him whether I could reach my destination, and that I threw myself on his mercy and his behaviour as a gentleman. He passed me with a wave of his hand. My passport was soon stamped and I fled to the platform. I had three minutes to spare. The lift-boy got 3/-.

To continue the history of my box, the key has not yet arrived. It was on Tuesday evening that I reached Strasbourg, on Saturday evening I called in the doctor and he operated. The proceedings were ignominious. Chloroform was unnecessary. The doctor merely took an aged meat-skewer from his bag, plunged it into the lock and opened it. I could see that he was not a little surprised at this easy victory, but with wonderful restraint he merely looked up and said, '*Et voilà*,' as if he had done it by some wonderful skill or by means of magic. He charged me 1 franc 50 and, admiring his self-control, I gave him two.

This explains the delay of this letter. Owing to my immense correspondence about my box and to Mother, assuring her that I am well, I have borrowed practically all the paper Madame Motsch has, and I simply couldn't ask for 15 more! But now all is well. *Et voilà*.

The idea of going to Strasbourg was to spend a month with the rather improbable purpose of learning French and German in that time. If that was less than successful there were compensating pleasures. Birley soon became friendly with the family of a conductor ('music not trams!') called Schlochow; he was to meet Naomi, one of the daughters, again twenty-six years later when she was the wife of Hubert Ripka, a member of the Czech Government and one of the leaders of the resistance to the Russian-backed *coup d'état*.

There was good company in the *pension* too, and in particular an Irish lady called Miss Piggott whom he took to, and an interesting Belgian called Hosti who was Secretary of the International Commission which was looking into the *Titanic* disaster. There was also an American lady whom he found very trying at first since 'she seemed imbued with the idea that something clever was expected of her, and her remarks consequent on that sentiment consisted chiefly of ridiculous comparisons of everything in Europe with similar or dissimilar things in America, the latter naturally coming out on top'. With this group Birley went walking in the Black Forest, with the object of reaching the summit of the Feldberg. In the course of the expedition the American lady abandoned her compulsive comparing and 'became more her ordinary self, which was so naïve, and *so* killingly funny (unintentionally, of course) that we had the most terrible time not bursting out laughing and Miss Piggott, who found it more difficult than the rest of us, quite gave way once or twice'. As they had not calculated their time correctly, they had to be content with climbing the Herzogenhorn instead of the Feldberg, but with the compensation of a splendid meal at an inn somewhere between the two, and superb views on the way down to Titisee.

Strasbourg was also a good base from which to explore the Vosges, where Birley spent the most energetic day of his entire tour. Having climbed the Grand Ballon, the highest mountain in the Vosges, he had intended to go on to the Hartmannwiller-kopf, the scene of some fierce fighting in the war. He did in fact see some of the trenches, dug-outs, barbed wire and torn-up trees. However, it was evident that if he climbed the Hart-mannwillerkopf, he would not get back to Strasbourg that evening. It was quite enough to walk the sixteen or so kilometres to Bollwiller station. He had had a good lunch, but this had used up nearly all the money he had with him. When he arrived at Bollwiller, hot, dusty, and thirsty, and had bought his ticket, he had 55 centimes over. A cup of coffee was 60 centimes:

This was terrible. I began asking the Mademoiselle in my best French, with a profusion of *s'il vous plaîts, voudriez-vous biens, est-ce que je pourrais, je regrette beaucoups, je suis desolés* etc, etc, to give me a 55 centimes-worth cup of coffee, when she cut me short by saying 'It doesn't matter' and handed a very obviously tired warrior an excessively large and full cup. This was very nice of her indeed! The coffee was very easily the best I have ever tasted, *very* easily. Perhaps, however, I was biased!

Towards the end of the time in Strasbourg he was joined by a cousin, Willie Robson-Scott, with whom he had shared a study at Rugby and who was now an undergraduate at University College, Oxford. Together they went on to Southern Germany.

Birley's whereabouts were now going to be less predictable, and so he wrote home promising to send a postcard once a day. He went to still further lengths to put his stepmother's mind at rest by impressing on her that she must not fret:

> DO NOT GET WORRIED if no postcard arrives. The chances of my being dead or hurt in that case are so small as to be negligible. Here are a few reasons why a postcard might not come.
>
> 1. I might forget.
> 2. I might be too tired.
> 3. I might have no stamps.
> 4. I might have no postcard.
> 5. I might miss the post.
> 6. I might be staying at a place where there would be only one post a day and so be late.
> 7. It might be delayed anywhere.
> 8. In particular it might be delayed at Bournemouth.
>
> You see therefore that there is no cause for alarm!

The first place that Birley and Robson-Scott made for was Freiburg and, after another abortive attempt to climb the Feldberg, they continued via Konstanz to Ulm.

At their Konstanz hotel there was a memorable interlude when Robson rushed into the bedroom saying that he could not stop his bath tap running. Frantically they turned on and off every tap in the room, one result of which was that Robson drenched himself under a cold shower. At the same time Birley kept up a continuous ring on the bell. The chambermaid arrived just as the water was within an inch of the top of the bath. She rushed off immediately, shouting, '*Abstellung! Abstellung!*' and eventually they concluded that she must have turned the water off at the main.

They did not stay long in Konstanz which Birley considered an ugly town with the most hideous cathedral he had ever seen. Ulm too was disappointing, and to begin with they were unimpressed by the cathedral spire, highest in the world though it was. They did not intend to climb it, but on entering the cathedral they bought tickets to do so by mistake. They were then bullied into going up by the custodian but got over their annoyance when they realised what a splendid view it gave them.

Their next stop, Oberammergau, was more enjoyable, exciting and impressive. The American ladies whom Birley had met in Florence had given him the name of someone to stay with, a certain Herr Zwinck. Although there turned out to be eleven Herr Zwincks in Oberammergau, they ran the right one to earth fairly quickly and were quite overwhelmed by his hospitality. It had been important not to miss going to Oberammergau since it was the year of the Passion Play, and it turned out that one of the Zwinck family was Judas. The performance lasted from 8.00 to 11.30 a.m. and from 2.00 to 6.00 p.m. The weather was unkind, with showers of rain throughout, and there were only hard wooden seats to sit on, but it was so good that they never felt in the least bored or tired – 'I have often been much more tired after one hour's lecture in the Speech Room at Rugby!'

From Oberammergau they headed on for Vienna with brief stops at Munich and Salzburg, where, appropriately enough, they visited a salt mine. It was a very bad time for Austria. Before the war there had been about 20 Kronen to the shilling. When Birley and Robson-Scott arrived in Vienna there were 90,000. When they left, the rate was 130,000. 'This does not mean, of course that things are 6,000 times as dear but it shows that things are *very* bad and getting worse', Birley wrote. His account of the situation finished with the sadly prophetic remark, 'The Austrians long for a dictator as the only way out!' The happier side of the story in Vienna was the beauty of the buildings and the impression of the Austrian character – 'inefficient, entirely happy-go-lucky and haphazard, gay, imaginative, romantic and with real taste.'

By comparison there was a pervading oppressiveness about their next stop, Budapest, where the counter-revolutionary forces of Admiral Horthy had seized power from Bela Kun, chief of the Hungarian Soviets. But there were light-hearted moments too:

There was one ripping café we went to in Buda, where there was a Hungarian orchestra which played with the most terrific 'go' you can imagine. All Hungarian cafés and restaurants have one peculiarity. You don't have your bread given to you on the table and then pay for it, but there is a special young lady called *das Brotmädchen* (bread girl) who brings it round to you, and you select your amount at the beginning of the meal. The *Brotmädchen* is always selected on the same principle as the chorus-girl, and is really the great advertisement of the restaurant. She carries a huge tray of bread high above her head, and her business is to be young and charming. This particular café had a very beauteous *Brotmädchen*, who knew no German but only Magyar. This made us friends at once. I have noticed for some time that if you know nothing of the language of the other person, it creates a great bond, as the only thing you can do is to laugh in common. Also if they know English it is a bond, as the other people don't know what you are saying and you both have a sense of superiority. But for me to speak German or French to a man is no bond at all, unless I speak it badly enough to cause laughter, as with my Italian.

The three main points about the rest of our stay in Buda-Pest were:

    (a)   the bath;
    (b)   the picture-gallery;
    (c)   the zoo.

The bath incident was terrible and something like that in Konstanz. To begin with, as happened so often in this country, all the notices on the taps were in Magyar. It was moreover a *very* complicated tap system, all coming out in one large spurt. When I got to the bath I found that it had been filled much too hot, so after various attempts I got the cold to run in. A few minutes later I was feeling the water to see how it was getting on, and bending over the bath (luckily undressed) when there was a sudden 'Phew' noise above my head and a solid sheet of water descended without warning from a cold shower, hitting me fairly and squarely in the middle of the back! Luckily this sudden influx made the bath cold enough, otherwise I think I should have had to wait!

The picture-gallery was an immense surprise. It had some really excellent things, in particular one by Goya, the man who painted the lady with the mantle on my dressing table; the one here was almost as good as that one.

The Buda-Pest Zoo is not a good one, but it has two great show points. One of these is a wonderful armadillo. It is very difficult to explain why it was wonderful but perhaps you will understand. The other thing was the elephant. If you gave it a one or two Kronen note, it took hold of it in its trunk and gave it to the keeper, who exchanged it for a hunk of bread. You can imagine the crowd! Willie had some small change and managed to get to the front and give it a note with the desired effect. (He was obviously very frightened, as I had told him that an elephant could break a man's finger with the tip of his trunk!). I had nothing smaller than a 10 Kronen note and I didn't dare to give that or I might have been lynched by the crowd as a profiteer!

We left Buda-Pest on Sunday night. The journey to Vienna was pretty uncomfortable, though not as bad as that from Hofgastein. We got to Vienna at 7 in the morning and there I left Willie. He went to Nürnberg and then to England. I had enjoyed being with him immensely and wish he could have stayed longer.

So for what was to be the climax of the tour, his visit to Czechoslovakia, Birley was on his own again.

After Hungary the sense of democratic freedom in Czechoslovakia was a final elixir of delight. He was utterly enraptured by Prague and the Czech people, and it was the beginning of a lifelong interest in the country and admiration for Tomas Masaryk, its first President. Many years later, writing in one of the Oxford pamphlets on World Affairs, Birley recalled the calm assurance with which Czechoslovakia was administered, something that was amazing in a new state. 'When the financial systems of Central Europe collapsed in the period between 1920 and 1924, it remained an island of financial security. But what is most remarkable was the lack of any hysteria, any panic in face of the new and troublous world. In Czechoslovakia the Truth remained free.' This seemed to Birley to convey a kind of adult national assurance which he summed up by quoting a remark made by Masaryk: 'What's the use of talking? A normal individual does not go about trumpeting abroad the fact that he loves his parents, his wife, his children; that is taken for granted . . . I was always held back by a kind of shame from saying the words "my country", "my nation".' The seeds of this sympathetic understanding of Czechoslovakia were sown in the days of Birley's pre-Oxford tour.

By the time he had reached Prague his trip was nearly over. On his way home he stopped again at Munich and rounded things off by going to see the entire *Ring* cycle – and *Peer Gynt* for good measure. The whole enterprise had been an ideal way of purging himself of the extreme Englishness of schooldays at Rugby and holidays at Bournemouth. The contrast to life in England was overwhelming and exhilarating, and in later life he always felt that it had transformed his outlook. Above all, it engendered a sense of being European which pervaded his history teaching and culminated in his Reith Lectures on European unity.

CHAPTER FOUR

Undergraduate Days at Balliol

Leaving Rugby had prompted thoughts about the future and how Oxford would help in the business of finding a career. Birley was in two minds. The natural course was to follow his father into the Indian Civil Service. But he was also attracted by an academic life, either as a don or as a schoolmaster. Having given it a good deal of thought he seemed to be leaning towards the Civil Service. And certainly a letter to his father on the subject, written in his first term at Balliol, displayed an analytical turn of mind that would have put him very much at home in the world of administration. 'The points,' he wrote, 'seem to me as follows:

(1)   The work in the I.C.S. ought to be more 'unusual' than in a school. This is not merely a desire for originality! Nor is it a question of routine work. I know there is plenty in both. What I mean is that the kind of work you do as a schoolmaster is so much written about and talked about, while that in the I.C.S. you have to pick up and think about yourself more.

(2)   In either case I am likely to come up against the possibility of my superiors telling me to do something of which I disapprove on principle. This, I should imagine, would be more disagreeable in the I.C.S. than as a schoolmaster; the consequences of doing what you firmly believe is wrong must be greater and so you must be more annoyed about it.

(3)   In either case the great annoyance of being held up by the apathy of those above you must be a fairly common experience. This obviously is worse in the I.C.S., as in a school there is much more chance of seeing people about things instead of writing. In fact there must be a much closer touch.

(4)   The scope of the I.C.S. seems to me to be much greater. There are of course heaps of opportunities of trying original ideas etc. as a master, but there cannot be the same sequence of different events, not matters of 'original ideas', but of the right way to treat ordinary events. This to a certain extent is gained at a school by the different kinds of boys etc. but this cannot come up to the variety of the I.C.S. (except perhaps when you get a House, but that is a long business).

(5)   There is of course the great question, would I do better dealing with men or boys? That I, of course, cannot say. It seems to me of some importance, but I suppose cannot be answered until I try one or the other.

You will see that 1 and 4 are in favour of the I.C.S., 2 and 3 of the schoolmastering. At the moment I think I still lean towards the I.C.S. But you will notice that 1 and 4 are general, 2 and 3 particular. I cannot say as yet how much I am likely to feel the disagreeableness mentioned in 2 and 3.

There were other considerations beyond those of the nature of the work. With his parents abroad, family affairs would be much more easily handled if he stayed in England. He thought too that he might want to do some writing, which would be easier as a schoolmaster, and the possibilities of continental travel in the school holidays were a further enticement. It boiled down to the proposition that, as the letter continued, 'the I.C.S. would be some very good ointment with a rather large number of biggish flies (family, 2 and 3 etc.) and the schoolmastering would be not such good ointment but with fewer and smaller flies.'

The implications for his years at Oxford were quite clear. The matter would have to be settled by the end of his second term. 'In March 1923 I will take History Previous, and, on paper, I ought to pass. I then have to decide what to do. If I am going in for the I.C.S. I will have to take my degree at the first chance and so I will work all out for History. If I am going in for the All Souls Fellowship or to be a schoolmaster I will probably try for a double first. You stand a better chance all round and, I believe, as a schoolmaster your pay is higher. To do this I will try for two schools, History and Greats.'

His father's advice settled it. Leonard Birley was far-sighted enough to guess that the Indian Civil Service would not last for another generation and he did not recommend it. So History and Greats it was, a combination which was not as odd as it might nowadays sound. The new school of 'Greats without Greek', a proposal that had lapsed owing to the war and was revived largely at the instigation of A. D. Lindsay and George Adams, was to be started in 1923. The idea that modern society could be studied in the way that classical civilisation had been, was enormously appealing to someone of Birley's temperament. He had picked up the gossip, via one of the masters at Rugby, that it was going to be 'quite the thing' to read Modern Greats after History. As he wrote to his father, 'It would mean that I would have to arrange my work for the History School so as to concentrate on those subjects useful for Greats. I would, of course, first of all, consult the History people, to see whether I would run any risk of foozling my chances of a 1st in History, as that is the really important thing'. It was therefore with no small measure of ambition that Birley went up to Oxford in October 1922.

If Rugby had been a happy choice, Balliol now turned out to be ever more so. Not that New College would have been a bad idea in view of its stimulating Junior Common Room. But Balliol could offer the more lively history teaching and was also attracting more than its share of the most able young men. The other Brackenbury scholar of 1922 was Cyril Connolly whose nimble wit betokened such prodigious promise among many budding *littérateurs*.

Birley did not give anything like this obvious impression of great things to come. He was by no means someone to be ignored, being noticeably tall and very talkative, and he had plenty of friends on the arty, as opposed to the hearty, side of the College. But he did not in any sense set out to cut a figure in the University. He was interested in political questions, especially foreign policy, and joined the University Labour Club. But he was no fledgling parliamentarian and did not play any active part in student politics. He attended Union debates but never spoke at one. Like the great majority of undergraduates at any time his education followed for the most part the unobtrusive course of reading, essay writing and endless discussion. This was the path of faithfulness to the intentions which he had vouchsafed to his father.

One of Balliol's great virtues was the way in which new undergraduates were initiated into the peculiar intimacy of the intellectual life of the College. Each week they had to write an essay on a topic unconnected with their normal work and read it to a don who taught a subject other than their own. It was through this arrangement that Birley struck up a lasting rapport with the Mods Tutor Cyril Bailey. Later on, Bailey took his pupil in hand when he had to sit an examination in Greek history and literature-in-translation before he could take his Final Schools. Together they read through the first four books of Plato's *Republic*, and imperceptibly a daunting chore was transformed into an unforgettable pleasure.

The other obstacle that had to be got out of the way before Final Schools was the rather quaint Divinity Examination. This was on its way to becoming an unlamented relic since exemption was granted to those – by now the majority – who had passed School Certificate with Scripture as one of their subjects. It was now that the emerging national examination system, to which Birley and G. F. Bradby had between them shown such indifference at Rugby, could get its own back. 'Divvers' had to be passed. Though it was a simple examination largely concerned with the Gospels and the Acts of the Apostles, the more simple minds had not always found it so. Their saviour had been the omni-inventive Ronald Knox. During his time as Chaplain and Mods Tutor at Trinity he had made up, on the model of Snakes and Ladders, a board game in which the players followed the missionary routes of St Paul; where the Apostles were well received you shot up a ladder and where the reception was hostile you slid down a snake. Knox being originally a Balliol man it was natural to claim 'St Paul to Rome' as a College game. It enabled Birley to get some fun out of belonging to the assorted group who had come up technically unversed in the teachings of the New Testament. And of course it did the trick. After a few rounds they were comfortably able to clear the faintly ridiculous hurdle.

Greek literature-in-translation and Divvers were however only mild distractions from the study of history which Birley pursued with single-minded industry. His teachers ranged from the celebrated to the unsung. At one end of the scale was Humphrey Sumner whose sublime presence made it seem that he was somehow not made of quite the same stuff as other men; lent to the planet, as it were, from some other galaxy. At the other was a tutor who was superb in a quite different way. This was C. G. Stone, one of those extraordinarily improbable people whose pupils speak of their teaching with hushed admiration. He was deaf and had a severe stammer, disabilities which made communication difficult and accentuated a naturally retiring disposition. His modesty was such that he gave up being a Fellow in 1924 because he did not consider himself good enough. He did scarcely any research or writing himself, but he had an extraordinary gift for inspiring others, as he did in, for example, the case of George Jennison, the superintendent of the Zoo in Manchester, who under his guidance wrote a distinguished book entitled *Animals for show and pleasure in ancient Rome*.

Stone was universally known as 'Topes', a nickname thought to be derived from the Greek *topos* which was Rugbeian slang for lavatory. Perhaps the fact that they had both been to the same school had something to do with the affinity between him and his new pupil. At any rate it was Stone who really taught Birley how to tackle historical questions. He was a Roman historian himself but also greatly interested in the medieval period and able to nurture his pupil's fascination for the reign of Pope Gregory VII – to the extent that Birley had for the rest of his life a sneaking ambition to write a history of the Papacy. Stone was in fact guiding his pupil in the footsteps of a long line of Balliol historians which included three successive Regius Professors at Oxford and one at Cambridge, not to mention professors at other universities and distinguished schoolmasters like Henry Marten at Eton.

Scholarship was of course only a part of the wider tradition of public service. It was well known that Balliol men were rather expected to excel, whatever the walk of life in which they found themselves. A few would, very properly, pursue erudition for its own sake and as a career in itself, but for the others scholarship was viewed as the precondition for success in national affairs. In giving teaching a higher priority than research the tutors were consciously promoting this Balliol colonisation of national life. H. W. C. Davis, another of Birley's teachers, pointed out in his history of the College that Jowett's comment about 'inoculating the world with Balliol' was not entirely meant as a joke. In the 1920s, however, profound changes were in the making in Oxford, and the idea of Balliol – or New College or any other College for that matter – as *the* education for Church, State and especially Empire was becoming out of date. What had been a matter of pride in Leonard Birley's time, when some fifteen per cent or more of the public servants of India were reputed to be Balliol men, was no longer relevant for his son, whose penchant for academic life in preference to the Indian Civil Service was gradually being vindicated.

Balliol, however, had found a new way in which to take a lead in public service under yet another in its great line of history tutors, A. L. Smith, who was Master of the College when Birley went up in 1922. Smith's radical outlook was rooted in the idea of studying history as a means of understanding the problems of modern society. He was preoccupied with the thought of the whirlwind that might one day be reaped if progress were not made in educating the industrial proletariat. And so with his active involvement in the adult education movement he had taken the College beyond the naturally conservative boundaries of Oxford on a new path also trodden by such characteristic Balliol men as Arnold Toynbee, R. H. Tawney, G. D. H. Cole and William Temple. All of them were convinced of the urgent need to go outside the privileged precincts of the Universities and put their tradition of education within reach of a wider public.

For Birley's generation of undergraduates, therefore, the genius of the College was still at least as worldly as it was scholarly but the focus had become the social and political crusades of the time. Sadly, A. L. Smith had by this time become ill and was seen less and less about the College. Birley was one of the few who were fortunate enough to get to know him, and his stunningly handsome wife, in the last couple of years of his Mastership. This was partly because such time as 'A. L.' had for undergraduates he devoted to the historians. And partly because Birley belonged to a small group of favoured undergraduates to whom Mrs Smith gave a key to the private door of the Master's Lodgings so that they would not have to climb over the wall if they arrived back late.

The Balliol scholar visiting a salt mine at Salzburg in 1922

Birley (*third from left*) practising Morris dancing at Oxford, with some embarrassment

Robert Birley outside Chambers
in the autumn of 1932

With other masters on the
occasion of the retirement of
Alington, 1933

Mr E. L. Churchill calling Absence for the Staff on Alington's
retirement. Birley's head is just visible on the left above those of his
colleagues

The array of historians with whom Birley came into contact in his first year was so stimulating that in his second he was emboldened to enter for the Gladstone Memorial Prize Essay. The subject – the English Jacobins from 1789 to 1802 – was far removed from his medieval preoccupations, but this did not deter him. For most of the year he poured his energies into the extensive research that was necessary, visiting the British Museum in the vacations for the purpose. When the pressure was at its peak A. L. Smith stopped him one day in the quad to say that he was sure he was overdoing things, and benevolently ordered him to take the afternoons off. In the end the essay was an undergraduate *tour de force* and carried off the Prize. The examiner, the Regius Professor, had himself written a paper on the subject and was impressed at the new information that Birley had unearthed.

What was the most impressive however was the remarkably topical use he made of the information. He presented the struggle of the Reformers as the beginning of the class war, at a time when Oxford was preoccupied with negotiating an armistice to end it. He was fascinated by the English mistrust of political doctrine and he attributed the ineffectiveness of the Reformers in these years to their neglect of immediate economic facts. 'The English Jacobins were ideologues and England is fortunate that she is not given to gaining victories with her head in the clouds'. It was a theme which recalled some of the foundations of Balliol's nineteenth-century tradition as described by 'Fluffy' Davis. 'First lesson, men are greater than theories, practice is the end of life, practice grounded in the faith which is innate in the human mind. Second lesson, this faith is not bound up with the dogma of any sect and in no way depends on the truth of so-called historic facts. Third lesson, within the limits prescribed by faith, reason is the only trustworthy guide.'

It turned out that his performance in the Gladstone anchored Birley in a tradition that was to be maintained in Balliol throughout the inter-war period. For when A. L. Smith died in 1924, the election of A. D. Lindsay to succeed him confirmed the radical trend and confounded the more conservative temperaments in the College and the University at large. Lindsay was as committed to the values of a community of scholars as any of his predecessors had been. But at the same time he was convinced of the need to be outward-rather than inward-looking. The sermon which he preached in the College chapel at the memorial service for his predecessor interpreted the Balliol tradition for Birley's generation. The text, as Drusilla Scott records in her biography of her father, was from Hebrews: 'Let us therefore go forth unto him without the camp, bearing his reproach. For here we have no abiding city, but we seek one to come.' The point was that the camp represented the historic tradition of the Jewish people, loved for its safety and stability, but also enriched by those who were ready to go beyond it. 'All the permanent camps were of use because they helped to keep alive what had been won by the men who had gone out before. Each of these men when he went seemed to himself to be leaving all that was stable and certain and secure – all the elements of the continuing city – and going out after something very unsubstantial and visionary. Yet the camps had got nobler just because the men who loved them had been willing to go beyond them.' It was this spirit that A. L. Smith had embodied and that Lindsay declared his intention of keeping alive in what was the year of the first British Labour Government.

Lindsay became a still more important figure in Birley's life than A. L. Smith had been, though no doubt it was largely in more informal ways that through a Chapel sermon that the young men of Balliol imbibed the spirit of his teaching, and that the seeds were sown of a social conscience which later expressed itself in various kinds of voluntary work from the time of the General Strike through to the recession of the early 1930s. Lindsay encouraged them to teach W.E.A. (Workers' Educational Association) classes and to help with the Maes yr Haf Educational Settlement in the Rhondda Valley. Walter Oakeshott and John Hicks, who had both come up with Birley in 1922, edited the broadsheet *British Independent* as part of the Master's conciliation movement at the time of the General Strike. Henry Brooke, another of the 1922 vintage, was one of the first to work at Maes yr Haf. And when unemployment was at its worst, Balliol men were prominent in such initiatives as the Pilgrim Trust Unemployment Enquiry which resulted in the report *Men Without Work* in 1933. It is not surprising that

Birley, himself teaching at Eton in these years, was from time to time impelled to leave this most secure of all 'camps' and interest himself in the affairs of Slough.

In the meantime there was undergraduate life to be enjoyed. Apart from the excesses provoked by the legendary antagonism to neighbouring Trinity, Balliol was not a particularly boisterous College. There was no need to become embroiled in the raffish revelries of the *beau monde* rowdies. The exaggerated picture presented in Evelyn Waugh's *Diaries* is hardly one that Birley and his friends would have remembered. There was of course scope for self-indulgence. Gourmet meals could be sent up to one's rooms from the Buttery without immediate payment. Inevitably there was some questioning of whether this was an altogether proper atmosphere in which to educate future leaders of society. But if the undergraduates were aware of their good fortune they had no great reason to be inhibited by it. It was a time to be enjoyed.

Apart from a little hockey and some folk dancing in a club which a friend talked him into joining, and from which he made his escape as soon as he could, Birley's own pleasures were predominantly intellectual. Few things capture the spirit of his Balliol days as well as a game which he and a group of his contemporaries invented. This consisted in choosing a topic of broad general interest for discussion and taking the part of historical characters in order to argue it out. Though the game did not survive for long, it began as a huge success. The subject of the first debate was Poverty and there were two star performers. One was Denis Brogan, whose name, along with that of C. E. M. Joad, was to become a household word as a member of the BBC Brains Trust. His choice was Brother Elias, the financial founder of the Franciscan Order, which enabled him to propound a peculiarly literal interpretation of the theme. The other was Birley, who chose to be Hildebrand, giving himself the opportunity to teach his companions just how difficult it is to argue with the Roman Catholic church.

Although acting parts had appealed to him ever since his school days at Rugby, Birley did not pursue this inclination in any of the drama societies of the University at large. Nor did he join the Balliol Players, a group which existed for the purpose of touring with productions in the summer vacations.

But when, in his second year, a production of one of the Coventry mystery plays was being got up for special Christmas performance in the College Hall, he took part with great enthusiasm in what was for then a rather unusual venture. One of the most vivid memories of some of the Balliol men of the time was the figure of Death making a sudden apearance at Herod's feast. This was Birley, totally encased in a skin-tight black outfit on which the skeleton was painted in white, and holding a great spear in his hand. His friend Roger Mynors recalled him looking at least eight feet high.

Outside the College Birley's most active involvement was with the Stubbs Society, one of the university historical societies. Perhaps it was characteristic that it should be another friend, John Hicks, who became President of the Society after Birley had introduced him to it. He himself was much more at home in the informal intellectual life of Oxford which the Balliol dons made a particular effort to foster. The Science Tutor, Harold Hartley, kept more or less open house in his rooms and Birley was one of those undergraduates who appreciated the opportunity to go there at any time. Quite often they had the pleasant surprise of finding themselves in conversation with some distinguished visiting scientist. This was what has come to be romanticised as the ideal of College life, suplemented of course by the celebrated reading parties in the vacations. Here the dominant figure was F. F. Urquhart, widely known as 'Sligger'. Indeed so much has been made of the select groups who went to Sligger's chalet on the slopes of Mont Blanc that it is perhaps a distinction on Birley's part to be a Balliol man who rose to prominence without having been part of this particular College élite. Furthermore, some of the élite actually learnt to lean on him; more than one of Cyril Connolly's essays was written by Birley.

His own vacations were happiest when he was going off with one or two friends on expeditions which turned out to be memorable in the jovial way that undergraduate expeditions generally do. On one occasion he went to Ireland with Godfrey Samuel, younger son of Herbert Samuel. Having started by looking round Dublin they decided to cycle to Cork and hired two bicycles for the purpose. Before very long both machines collapsed and had to be abandoned. So they proceeded by train and for their first stop got as far as Thurles in Co. Tipperary, where a jaunting car was needed to get them from the station to the town. Seated back to back on the jaunting car they failed to notice that the luggage fell off on the way. Fortunately this was efficiently picked up by some Gardai and delivered to the hotel. Thurles was the place where in 1884 a small group of men had founded the Gaelic Athletic Association, in the conviction that the widespread adoption of English games had been a significant part of the wider betrayal of the Irish national heritage. Birley and Samuel were oblivious of the town's particular tradition of fervent nationalism but they were aware that memories of the Black and Tans were still fresh. So, being so very obviously English, they did not feel much at home. The solution was the agreeable one of ensconcing themselves for the evening in a quiet corner of the bar from where Birley claimed he heard the landlord's wife describing them to one of the local habitués as 'a couple of hated Saxons'.

Another jaunt with Godfrey Samuel was to Italy which provided an apt setting for their respective interests to crystal-lise. In Venice as they gazed at the Palazzo Vecchio, the much beloved model for Victorian factory buildings, Samuel (who was beginning to be absorbed by architecture) remarked on the hideousness of the façade. Birley's reply was, 'Ah, but the important thing is that Savonarola was burnt in front of that building.'

Apart from travel the vacations provided precious time for reading, relieved in the summer by periodic visits to the County Cricket Ground only a couple of steps away from Cavendish Road. As for term time, the extraordinary industry which brought success in the Gladstone Prize was constantly apparent in the recondite knowledge which Birley delighted in acquiring. The earnestness was lightened by a mischievous humour which he shared with his sister Marion. On one occasion he had sent her news of one of their friends who had, somewhat improb-ably, become engaged to be married. Her telegrammed reply which greatly amused him read simply, 'Incredible, if true.' His sense of humour was tickled, too, by the unlikely things that had a way of happening to him. Once at a tutorial he was reading a long essay to Humphrey Sumner who, having fallen asleep, awoke with a start and said with great conviction '*maurische Baukunst*'. Nothing in the essay had been remotely to do with Moorish architecture.

The test of Birley's original ambitions came with Final Schools and turned out to be a continuation of his series of unorthodox encounters with the world of examining. Given a *viva* after his written papers, he was greeted urbanely by the examiners with the observation that they had read all his answers very carefully and had decided that the only grade they felt able to award was alpha/delta. The reason for the oscillation between triumph and disaster in his papers was his obsession with the Middle Ages. He had skimped the work on everything else. However, having realised in the meantime what it was that had prejudiced his chances of doing well and precipitated the *viva*, he had mugged up his modern history before being orally examined. One of the examiners was the same don who had been so scathing about his essay in the entrance scholarship for New College. But all went well and he was awarded his First.

It was the soundest of foundations for an academic career. He had already gained a little experience of teaching by spending a few weeks filling in for someone at Bradfield and it was beginning to be evident that he would prefer the life of a schoolmaster to that of a don. Indeed he had begun to say quite readily to his friends that he could envisage a career as a headmaster – not, they noted with amusement, as a schoolmaster. But there was for the moment no obvious post available and the attraction of going on to try Modern Greats was very strong. He returned to Oxford in the October of 1925, the same term in which his sister Marion came up to Somerville. PPE in one year, whatever the gossip which had suggested it was 'quite the thing', was however a tall order. Before long it was so very obviously a mistake that the ever solicitous Cyril Bailey, who had advised against the short cut to Modern Greats in the first place, stepped in. A temporary vacancy had arisen at Eton and Bailey steered Birley towards it, knowing that it was urgent for him to cut his losses and get away. It would have been a pity if three happy and successful years had been soured by a disappointing fourth.

By comparison with some of the more obviously promising careers that began their flowering at Balliol, Birley's had been an unobtrusive seedtime. It was not all that obvious, even to his close contemporaries, just how fertile the ground was in which the seeds were germinating. But then most of his associates were men of great ability and promise themselves, as their subsequent achievements demonstrated: Henry Brooke, Home Secretary in the Macmillan government; John Hicks, Professor of Political Economy at Oxford and Nobel Prizewinner for Economics; Roger Mynors, Professor of Latin successively at Cambridge and Oxford; Walter Oakeshott, Headmaster of Winchester, Rector of Lincoln and Vice-Chancellor of Oxford; Godfrey Samuel, Secretary of the Fine Art Commission. It was not company in which it was easy to stand out.

CHAPTER FIVE

Teaching at Eton

The appointment to Eton was a temporary one and it was intended that Birley should teach various groups of ruffians in the lower school. However, he was one of four new men who joined the staff in January 1926 and the flexibility which this created worked to his advantage. The man he had to thank for the opportunity that came his way was Henry Marten, who had also been a Brackenbury scholar of Balliol and had been one of the first schoolmasters to foster history as a fully-fledged specialism to rival classics in the sixth form. When Marten discovered in conversation that Birley was a Balliol historian, he at once said, 'Then you had much better teach history specialists than those lag boys in C', and moved him over. As Oliver Van Oss recalled many years later, 'the wretched counterpart man who was thus consigned to the rabble was mobbed off his head and left soon afterwards.' For Birley, on the other hand, it was a flying start. From his very first term he had the astonishing good fortune to find himself teaching history to some of the cleverest boys at the top of the school.

It was a time when a university diploma in education was rarely taken seriously. Public school masters were the gentlemen farmers, so to speak, of the teaching world and their view of professionalism is summed up in a letter from George Lyttelton's correspondence with Rupert Hart-Davis. This legendary character, who had a House at Eton throughout Birley's time as an Assistant Master there, remarked: 'I see that some important ass has been saying that three years' training is essential for every teacher – when nobody knows what education should be aiming at.' No one at Eton would have dreamt of trying to tell Birley what he should be aiming at, but Henry Marten did give him two pieces of advice. The first was this: 'Before you have a lesson to teach, look up something on the period you are dealing with and think about it on your way across.' The second was: 'Before you take a lesson, make sure

you find time to prepare some notes – but, for Heaven's
sake, don't keep to them!' Birley's professional training began
and ended with this brief conversation. For him it was
enough. He had the two really important qualities that go to
make a teacher, he was fascinated by his subject, and he was
enormously interested in young people. A gift for imparting
knowledge was a natural consequence. As for the opportunities to develop this talent, they were superb, if not
unique. Eton's tutorial system made it the nearest thing to a
'university for boys' and as such provided the perfect solution
to Birley's dilemma as to whether he would be more at home
teaching in a school or a university.

By the end of his first half (the Eton word for term) he had
made such an impression that Marten was keen to keep him.
This was welcome news and it was followed by an offer of a
post by the Head Master, Dr Alington. Officially there was a
two- year probationary period during which either side could
terminate the contract without breach of faith, but for all
practical purposes it was a permanent appointment. Alington
was clearly concerned to make the offer financially attractive,
as Birley explained in a letter to his father:

> The one difficulty is that as I shall not be able to take
> pupils in the ordinary way a classical master does, after
> five years on the present system my salary would stop
> short at about £800 or £900. Alington said, however, that
> both he and Marten are prepared to put my case before the
> School Fund to get the normal amount later of about
> £1000, without taking the full number of pupils. (A
> Histor-
> ian, pure and simple, cannot very well take more than
> about 20 or 25. The maximum is 45). He said he was
> prepared to give me a written promise whenever I wanted
> it and to put my case before his successor, if necessary. He
> said that if I liked he would bring the matter before the
> School Fund Committee now, but he advised waiting for
> three or four years until I was more of a 'fait accompli'.
> This seemed to me to be sound.

It was still more encouraging to learn from Alington that he
would certainly be on the list of prospective housemasters if
he stayed:

The difficulty here is that being youngish for the job, I should get a house young (which he approves of) but that I should probably have to give it up when I was about fifty, as there is a fifteen-year limit. However, that does not seem to me, (and he agreed with me) a very bad thing. I could go on teaching here without a house, of course. Being a house-master here is such a paying job that it ought not to land me in financial difficulty, unless I very much play the fool with my money. There is, I suppose, (and I think you'd agree!) something to be said for being able to retire soon after fifty. (Alington prophesied that I'd be offered a professorship in History at fifty!)

In the end I accepted, and I am now an accredited permanent master at Eton.

At this time Birley's parents were making preparations to come home from Bengal for good, and he finished the letter by enjoining his father to keep him informed of his decline into pedagogery 'and I will strive to retard it as far as possible!'

For a newly appointed master the work was hard and the responsibilities at first slightly intimidating. 'Today I had my first parental interview, with the father of my pupil, a jolly old man with a red face and an eye-glass. He was very nice and the meeting passed off very well, though I had quaked with fear beforehand. I implored him to force his son to work three hours a day during the holidays up to the Balliol Entrance and to make him read the paper daily.' Entrance to Oxford and Cambridge was the real test of Birley's work and at the end of his second half one of his pupils was awarded a scholarship to Trinity College, Oxford. The others did reasonably well too, and a boy who was not his pupil in the Eton tutorial sense, but whom he taught twice a week, won the only Brackenbury scholarship to be awarded that year. Very rapidly the number of Birley's pupils increased, with some of the most able boys in the school among them. Jack Donaldson, Paul Gore-Booth, Con O'Neill and Victor Fitzgeorge-Balfour were just a few of those he taught. When, some years later, Alington was asked to write a reference for Birley he declared in it that 'there is no teacher of history who is more sought after as a tutor and I considered myself very fortunate in getting him to take my son as a pupil. I cannot be too grateful for his influence on him, both in pupil room and out of it.'

Alington's initial prophecy was very soon shown to be not all that wide of the mark, for in the summer half Birley was invited to go and teach history at Christ Church. It was flattering that Oxford should want to reclaim him so soon after he had gone down, and the offer was tempting. But it was already too late. He was enjoying himself so greatly at Eton that there was really little question of giving it up. Those who have turned down a post at Christ Church in their mid-twenties must be a select group indeed. There could scarcely be a more eloquent proof of the exhilaration of the job than that it was a victorious rival attraction to the life of a don at one of Oxford's best known colleges.

The exhilaration of Eton came from the all-absorbing nature of the life. In many ways it was not so very different from what Birley would have encountered at Christ Church. There was more teaching of course, but a good deal of it was in conditions every bit as conducive to intellectual excitement as those of university life. Birley threw himself into it with prodigious energy. What it meant to some of his pupils is described by Paul Gore-Booth in his autobiography *With Great Truth and Respect*. Here was a boy who had been taught elementary history superbly well at his prep school and who now needed someone to appear who could put flesh on its bones and breathe life into it:

The occasion produced the man. Robert Birley became my history tutor as soon as I had passed the School Certificate in 1925 and the period chosen was the Middle Ages. In company with Robert I attended the coming of Charlemagne at Aix, I walked to Canossa with the Emperor Henry IV, I marched with the early Crusaders in formation out of Antioch, I thundered imperially into Italy with Frederick Barbarossa, listened in on the Papal thunder of Innocent III and cheered at the glamorous ingenuities of Fredericus Secundus Stupor Mundi. And when in 1250 Conradin died and the curtain came down on it all, we just stopped. One cannot live all the time at this grand level. But without

Robert Birley I could never have thought of human events on this scale at all. It was my first essay in thinking big.

Gore-Booth's crowning achievement at school was an essay on Barbarossa which was so thoroughly researched that it was a subject on which he expected to shine when he went up to take the Balliol examination. But this was a worry to his tutor on the grounds that if he were to write about it once again, he would overdo things and become rather boring. So Birley sent a last-minute telegram to the young man while he was staying at Balliol for the examination, with the instruction that if a question on Frederick Barbarossa came up in the paper, on no account was he to answer it. The question did come up, the self-denying ordinance was fulfilled – and Gore-Booth was awarded his scholarship.

The contact with pupils was about much more than history teaching. As Gore-Booth put it, 'Birley also filled the odd hours, in which you studied what you liked or what your tutor suggested, with reading Jacobean dramas, notably *The White Devil* and *The Duchess of Malfi*. We explored Chekhov and indeed anything within the hours available that could stimulate the mind and spirit to something beyond just learning.' And there was music. Birley was not, in any active sense of the word, 'musical'. Three piano lessons given by an aunt during his childhood had been sufficient to make it plain that it was a waste of time to continue. However, A. H. Peppin's remarkable concern for the boys at Rugby who were not interested in music had revolutionised Birley's attitude. He had been stimulated to take advantage of the opportunity to attend Dan Godfrey's weekly symphony concert at Bournemouth and from a seat behind the orchestra he had followed each work from a pocket score.

On the basis of the technique acquired at Rugby and Bournemouth Birley conducted a weekly session of musical appreciation for all his pupils. Although the idea of such sessions was well established at Eton, no one should underestimate the difficulty of the undertaking, and many are the golden rules that could be advanced. The most common would be not to attempt it. Those who did were well advised not to expect too much, and to keep a sense of humour. Birley's instructions on issuing the pocket scores were exemplary: firstly, when the notes go up, the sound goes up; secondly, if a note is filled it is half as long as one that isn't; thirdly, *fagotti* means bassoons. He always began with Beethoven's Seventh and claimed never to have had a failure. Some took longer than others and the Duke of Roxburghe took the longest. On one occasion after the end of the summer term three of his pupils left for Oxford in a hired car in order to deposit various belongings at their Colleges. On their way they stopped at a garage for petrol where they heard a Haydn symphony being played in a back room. Nothing would do but that they should persuade the bewildered garage owner to allow them to go inside and solemnly hear the symphony through to the end before resuming their journey.

The intensity of the commitment at Eton was enhanced by the fact that the great majority of Birley's colleagues made the school virtally their entire life in term-time. In consequence the atmosphere was highly congenial. Small groups of masters lived together in 'colonies'. Birley shared with Jack Peterson, later Headmaster of Shrewsbury and Dick Routh, a fellow historian who had been President of the Oxford Union. In the evenings the younger men were generally invited to dinner in the Houses. Studious efforts were made to avoid talking shop and on one memorable occasion in his first year Birley, true to his Balliol convictions, was outspoken enough to express views sympathetic to the General Strike. The reaction was shocked silence, until an older master broke the ice by saying: 'Look here, the young man is quite right.' The company remained unconvinced. It was an episode which foreshadowed the suspicion with which the more staid elements at Eton were later to view this provocative young man.

After dinner on these occasions the House Master would attend House prayers and then, along with any colleagues or men visitors, spend an hour or so going round talking to the boys while the women were left to survey their host's book-shelves. This convention, adhered to very strictly, was a convenient way for the House Master to put his boys in touch with stimulating teachers. In Birley's case such invitations came most frequently from A. H. G. 'Cyrus' Kerry, a popular figure, noted for his gift for improvising comic operatic recitative at the piano. The two men came to like each other very much, and it was only natural that Birley should take a keen interest in the boys in Kerry's House who specialised in history. As one of them, Nigel Nicolson remembered clearly the feeling on meeting a master who was almost as shy as he was himself. 'He would bounce off my wall, backwards and forwards, his hands behind his back, and neither of us knew quite what to say, but I always welcomed his coming, because he seemed so under-standing of one's unexpressed problems.'

This empathy would then be reinforced in divisions, as classes at Eton are called. Nicolson's recollections echoed those of Gore-Booth:

> He taught the Headmaster's division classical history, and his classes were always those most looked forward to. He would say, 'Today we are going to talk about one of the most extraordinary events in history – the Sicilian campaign' and would then describe the ships, the armour, the politics, the battle, the danger, the glory, all with such emotion and sense of fun (he adored speaking of war oddly enough) that we felt we were actually in Sicily in 420 BC, rowing in the galleys, slaving in the mines, speaking in the Assembly. Robert's very shyness made us adore him. It was as if he was another boy, not a master. Discipline was something unknown and unnecessary with him. He treated us like undergraduates. For the first time we saw what fun it was to be adult, and how it was possible for a shy man to be a dominating man, and that intelligence was not arid. Then he founded the Essay Society of his chosen pupils. We would meet in his house, and each person had to read an essay on any subject of their choice. We would then discuss the essay, and have cocoa, I think it was (in any case I can't spell it), and there was a fire in the grate and easy chairs and a sense that time did not press.

Birley had not in fact founded the Essay Society. It just seemed so, for no one remembered its previous obscure existence.

The conviviality gave life an elan which made this total absorption in the school a scarcely diluted pleasure to those who were cut out for it. Added spice came from contact with prominent figures in public life, some of whom could display the same blind spots about their children as are common in less sophisticated circles. Randolph Churchill was one of Birley's pupils, and this led to his getting to know Winston. On one of the occasions when the Great Man came to see him he spotted an essay on the desk in his son's handwriting. As a father he could not resist picking it up and reading it. It was about unemployment. It was evident that the boy's tutor had not thought much of it for he had written on the final page: 'Until you can tell the difference between insurance and the dole, you will get nowhere in dealing with unemployment.' Churchill was incensed and proceeded to admonish Birley, declaring that it was a very good essay which did not deserve this criticism.

It was only natural that the variety and intensity of activity at Eton should give rise to close relationships between masters and boys which could later develop into lasting friendships. Mutual loyalty could be fierce, as in the case of David Astor whose mother had resolved to take him away from the school. The reason was that his housemaster had come to the end of his term and Nancy Astor did not approve of the new man who had been appointed. Not many young masters would have relished taking on the formidably combative first woman MP. But Birley was utterly convinced that it was nothing short of insane to contemplate taking her son away and went again and again to London to remonstrate with her. He fought on behalf of his pupil and his housemaster colleague with all the tenacity that he was later to show in fighting for black refugees from South Africa. In the end he wore her down, and David stayed to become one of his most distinguished pupils.

Another gifted history specialist and protégé was Guy Burgess. Birley had a strong intellectual rapport with this apparently conventional success figure and under his tutelage Burgess won the Rosebery and Gladstone history prizes and a scholarship to Trinity College, Cambridge. In *The Climate of Treason* Andrew Boyle has recounted the subsequent meetings between the two men. The first was when Birley visited Burgess while he was an undergraduate at Trinity and was dismayed to notice an 'extraordinary array of explicit and extremely unpleasant pornographic literature' alongside the Marxist textbooks on his shelves. Twenty years later, on the day before he decamped to Moscow, Burgess visited Birley who was now Head Master of Eton. He had apparently been invited by Lady Gwendolen Cecil to write the third and final volume of the hitherto uncompleted biography of the Third Marquess of

Salisbury. But as an agnostic he was, he said, uncertain as to whether he was the right person to write about a convinced Christian. This struck Birley as a rather improbable scruple, though it could not have occurred to him that behind the contrived excuse for the visit was most probably a curiously emotional resurgence of an old loyalty to a teacher who had once been one of the people he had most respected. As soon as the news of the defection broke, Birley got in touch with an Etonian ex-pupil who was in MI5 and on whose instruction he kept the story to himself until he was given leave to relate it many years later. It is perhaps above all characteristic that Birley should have known someone with whom it was appropriate to discuss the bizarre Burgess affair. He kept up with a quite remarkable number of his ex-pupils. He spent hours writing to them, and for many he was the only one of their teachers with whom they kept in touch in later life.

Despite the exhilaration of being part of a wide and influential network, however, life at Eton was in its own way confining and it was important to get right away in the holidays. For Birley these were opportunities to get to know Europe better and better, pursuing, whenever possible, his arcane historical interests. One summer holiday he was staying with another Eton master, Kenneth Wickham, and their sisters, at Aulla on the Western side of the Apennines, a charming site which boasts an ancient castle perched on a hill. One day when the five of them were out walking they stopped at a small chapel in which Birley spotted an unusual crucifix with a clothed figure. For some time he had been fascinated by the Syrian tradition of representing Christ wearing a long tunic. It turned out that this particular example was a copy of the Volto Santo, the famous Holy Face of Lucca. Reading about it afterwards Birley learnt of the legend of Saint Wilgeforte, a Portuguese princess who, having taken a vow of virginity, prayed to God to preserve her from a forced marriage to the King of Sicily. The divine response was a luxuriant beard; the King, not unnaturally, repudiated her, and her father in his anger had her crucified. Art historians had deduced that it was she who was represented on the crucifix. In Lucca however it was believed that it was a carving of Christ, begun in His lifetime by Nicodemus and completed by divine intervention, and that over seven hundred years later it had been placed for safety in a ship which sailed to the West coast of Italy. It had then been taken to Lucca. A few years after the holiday which Birley had spent at Aulla, he discovered that there was to be the 1150th anniversary celebration of the arrival of the relic on the shore. There was to be a procession through Lucca and all the accompanying ceremonial. Birley was determined to be there but it was just after the beginning of the autumn half. He went to Alington therefore to ask if he could be allowed to arrive back a couple of days late and explained why. 'That,' said Alington, 'is the most absurd reason I have ever heard for being late for the beginning of the half. . . . Of course you must go!'

In another holiday he went on a Hellenic cruise and this led to his engagement to be married. His friends who did not already know Elinor Frere received the news with mild alarm, imagining a proposal by Mediterranean moonlight, or in other circumstances similarly conducive to folly. The way in which the encounter actually took place was in fact something of a promise of compatibility. During a particularly tedious lecture at some archaelogical site or other Birley had suddenly had enough and sneaked away to look at the ruins on his own. One other person had had the same idea. But the whole thing was even more providential than this, for Elinor had only gone on the cruise as a last-minute replacement for someone who had had to withdraw because of illness.

It was the most timely of meetings. Birley was twenty-six and securely established in the career that most appealed to him. The one cloud on his horizon was that he had begun to suffer from mental strain and had been sent by his doctor to see a specialist in Harley Street. It seemed clear that the principal cause was overwork and that it would not be too difficult to put things right. But there was still the worry that the anxiety state which had developed would recur and eventually impair his prospects of fulfilling his ambition. 'It is not at all a bad case of what is quite a common thing,' he wrote to his father in July 1929. 'The Headmaster for instance told me that another master here, now left, whom I knew quite well, suffered from it the whole time he was here. I could stay here quite well, I think, and do nothing about it. I do not think that my teaching has fallen off as a result, though at the moment I am pretty exhausted as a result. But it will really affect my chances of being a headmaster, as Alington agrees.' And he went on to quote the case of a contemporary headmaster who was known to have suffered in this way. The situation was not improved by an unpromising love affair with a girl Birley had known at Oxford. For all the convivial activity of Eton life he was at times acutely lonely.

His parents acted swiftly and arranged for him to accompany them on the cruise. From the moment of their meeting Elinor was just the right companion. One of Skipper Lynam's girls at the Dragon School in Oxford, she had gone on to St Leonard's and then read Greek at Lady Margaret Hall. They had much in common. On his return from the cruise Birley went straight to the London flat of George Rink, an Oxford friend who was now a barrister in Lincoln's Inn. His first words were: 'I now know that my infatuation for Joan is over.' His emotional life was transformed. The following year he and Elinor were married, with Willie Robson-Scott as a best man absent-minded enough to leave the ring behind in his overcoat pocket.

The absent-mindedness did not end there. In a burst of uncharacteristic extravagance Birley had bought a new suitcase for going away. It so happened that Dr Alington, who conducted the ceremony, also had a new suitcase. The result was that for the first night of the honeymoon, at Ford in the Windrush valley in Gloucestershire, the groom found himself with nothing to wear but the scarlet robes of a Doctor of Divinity. Fortunately there was time to rectify the mistake before they set off for Catalonia. There Elinor enthusiastically photographed the churches and sculptures in which the two of them shared a consuming interest. Photography was a hobby she had picked up from her father. He too had been greatly interested in churches, in the days when it was forbidden to take photographs in them. Finding his architectural studies hampered in this way he had outwitted the authorities by constructing for himself a camera shaped like a prayer book.

Thus in September 1930 Elinor Birley arrived at Eton, a striking addition to the very slowly increasing number of masters' wives. It was still a strongly male-dominated society, the great majority of the housemasters being still unmarried and so well looked after as to be inoculated against wedlock. It was important for the women to join in the life of the school, and in this they were given a lead by the universally popular Mrs Alington. When she herself had come to Eton there were only three wives and, as she once confided to Grizel Hartley, wife of another legendary Eton master, 'two of them were very queer'. Now however she could point out to the rather larger number in this select sorority how lucky they were to have a dozen or more interesting women about the place. They did indeed range from the charming – Grizel Hartley herself – to the alarming – Henry Marten's twin sister Isabel.

The Provost himself, Montague Rhodes James, was an important figure for Birley in one respect above all others. As one of the country's leading medieval scholars, Monty James delighted in the treasures of the Eton College library to which he had been introduced as a boy at the school. The permission which he granted to Birley to study the manuscripts with the aid of the catalogue he had put together was a watershed in the younger man's life. Birley's interest in the library led to his being entrusted with the responsibility for organising, along with Kenneth Wickham, a medieval exhibition on the occasion of the visit to Eton of the King and Queen in 1932. Among the items on display was a reproduction of the Arms of the Duchy of Teck, made especially for the benefit of Queen Mary. Her sole unbending comment was: 'They've got it wrong.' The acquaintance with the College Library was the beginning of a lifelong bibliophilia which reached its climax in the years after Birley returned to Eton as Head Master when he was able to devote such a remarkable amount of his time to making fresh discoveries in the collection and enlarging Monty James's catalogue.

It was apt that the Birleys should make their home where Henry Marten had lived for many years. In his address at Birley's memorial service in Eton College Chapel, Oliver Van Oss recalled how 'that long room in the Briary, once again lined with books, as it had been in Henry Marten's time, but now also ankle deep in volumes from the London Library, long overdue to be returned . . . and boasting an alabaster statue by a promising young sculptor, Henry Moore, on the top of the shelves, became a centre where his pupils and the Essay Society and others could escape into an adult world, that world of grown-up values which all the young so desperately seek'. The statue, known to the boys as Henrietta, and purchased long before Henry Moore became famous, was for many years a symbol of Birley's artistic leanings until an Old Etonian art dealer persuaded him to sell it. It was at the Briary that Elinor had her first baby. Named after her redoubtable great-grandmother, Julia was born shortly after the end of the summer half of 1931.

While marriage was just the stabilising experience that Birley needed, it did nothing to dilute the intensity of his commitment to his work. Those who came to enjoy the cosiness of the Essay Society, for example, had the impression that there were no limits to the time he could spare for them. On one such occasion, during the Birleys' frenetic final half in 1935, they were totally unaware that Elinor was having her second baby, Rachael, upstairs at the time.

The major preoccupation outside Birley's teaching duties was with the affairs of Slough, the rather dismal neighbouring town, dignified somewhat by having the beautiful church of St Lawrence, Upton, within its boundaries. He was one of those who liked to believe that it had a more long-standing claim than that of Stoke Poges to be the church of Gray's *Elegy*. He enjoyed pointing out that Upton was older than Windsor and Upton Church older than Windsor Castle. Birley's contact with Slough had begun when he became a member of the Eton Urban District Council, Eton apparently having the distinction of being the smallest urban district in England. This led to his being one of the two members for Eton on the Slough Town Planning Committee. It was a nomination that had a flavour of power about it since the other representative, a retired police-man, was so assiduous in following his colleague's lead that Birley had effectively two votes. All that was required in order to use the second one was to look over and catch the policeman's eye.

On the one occasion when Birley was unable to mobilise this second vote he suffered a memorable defeat. The issue, as he recalled it, was Horlicks Malted Milk. The Horlicks company wanted to put up a new building on some land scheduled for housing development and put great pressure on the Planning Committee to give its consent. Birley belonged to a faction which was firmly opposed to this on principle. When it came to the vote, one of the officials began to talk to him and was in such a position that the ocular exchange could not take place. Birley had been outwitted. The policeman voted the other way. The result was a tie. The issue now hung on the casting vote of the chairman – which went in favour of the factory. It was duly built and those who travel on a train from the West Country to Paddington pass close by the monument to this lost battle.

The involvement with Slough became more earnest in the early 1930s when the effects of the slump began to be felt in the town. With his knowledge of what was being done by A. D. Lindsay and some of those who had been his own contemporaries at Balliol, it was natural that Birley should want to find some way of promoting practical relief work. Adapting Lindsay's Unemployment Club idea, he set out to persuade factory owners to allow unused premises to be converted into carpentry shops. As for equipment, he wrote to every boy at Eton on the last day of the summer half of that year with a request to bring back after the holidays one carpentry tool – other than a hammer or a chisel. There was an enormous response to this appeal. From 1932 on Elinor joined him in the voluntary work, becoming in due course chairman of the Eton group of the Relief and Visiting Committees of the Slough Social Service Council.

It was a formidable task to relieve the distress in the homes of the unemployed in Slough and the Social Service Council became a powerful presence in the town. A reporter for the *Slough, Eton and Windsor Observer* spent a day visiting the families which had been given help; as a guide he had the Council's twenty-page document, setting out the names, addresses and needs of hundreds of necessitous cases. A typical entry read: 'Boy of 12. Girls 10, 7, 4. Baby 6 months. Very sad case. Only bread and margarine for three days. Have done all they can. Very urgent. (Milk, clothes, groceries and coal sent).' The impact which Elinor and her fellow committee members made in Slough was in proportion to the task. As the *Observer* journalist wrote, 'I have never heard the word godsend so many times in my life before. It ought to be written in capital letters and heavily underlined, because that was how the people said it – as if they meant it a hundred times over.'

While Elinor worked in this kind of relief, her husband's energies went into helping to organise the Unemployment Centres. Here, in addition to carpentry, there were classes in other crafts such as leatherwork, and in physical training and boxing, while football matches were organised using equipment provided by Eton. Reports which Birley circulated conveyed the realities of the situation to his colleagues:

> The unemployment figures in Slough have risen very sharply during the last month and there are now about 1900 out of work. The position is nearly as bad as last year.
>
> The Occupational Centre has now been going for over three months and it is almost always quite full. It has been necessary recently to introduce a shift system to accommodate the numbers attending.
>
> Over 150 articles of furniture etc. have been made or repaired, and those made include such articles as deal tables, chairs, meat-safes, toys, step-ladders, a bird-cage, a hat-rail, a child's cot, a bricklayer's hod, and fourteen trestle tables for the Soup Kitchen. . . .

On one occasion Birley found himself in court, giving evidence in a case of theft and explaining the very difficult straits which had led the defendant to break into his gas meter. Not only was the magistrate an Old Etonian, but he had with him five boys from the school who had been asked along to observe how the courts of justice operated. When the hearing was over, Birley was invited to join both generations of Etonians in another room before the court reassembled for the verdict. The man was given a suspended sentence. These were not activities that greatly commended themselves to the majority of the Eton masters. But one day Birley was asked by the Provost what he was up to in Slough. When he had explained it all, Monty James said: 'That is just the sort of thing that needs to be done. Would this be any help to you?' 'This' was a substantial cheque for £50.

But whether or not it made him popular among his colleagues, the work in Slough contributed to their impression that Birley was a potential headmaster. A similar reputation began to spread outside Eton too, once Spencer Leeson, Headmaster of Winchester, had successfully put him up for election as a member of the 'UU'. This society, of which the title was generally thought to stand for United Ushers, had been founded in the 1870s and met two or three times a year for dinner, after which one of the company would read a paper. As well as providing intellectual stimulation it was an agreeable way to get to know masters from other schools. Though only assistant masters could join, those who subsequently became headmasters could remain in membership. As a result it included some of the most influential figures in the public school world and by this token was an important recruiting ground for future heads.

It was however inside Eton that the earliest recognition of Birley's growing reputation came. In 1933 Cyril Alington announced his intention of retiring, whereupon two senior masters, Charles Gladstone and Eric Powell, Old Etonian wetbobs both, went to see him to suggest Birley as a successor. The very idea that anyone could contemplate the internal appointment of someone of thirty, and a controversial and not uniformly popular figure at that, is some indication of the impression he had made. Nor was his candidature dismissed out of hand. Alington was delighted at the idea, but the powers wisely considered him too young.

When in the event the mantle fell on Claude Elliott, his was no easy start. In the holidays before his arrival four masters were killed in an Alpine accident and had to be replaced at short notice. One of the new men was Walter Hamilton who found his first masters' meeting a miserable experience. He was not used to such occasions and it seemed to him that Elliott was being given a rough ride by his staff. The glumness must have shown on his face, for a note was passed to him on which Birley had written, 'Cheer up. It's not as bad as it looks.' Twenty years later, when Hamilton became Headmaster of Westminster, Birley wrote to congratulate him, and added, 'Do you remember when I sent you that note at your first masters' meeting at Eton? Now that you are Head of Westminster I would like to send you the same message – only it wouldn't be true!'

Being considered for the headmastership so young made Birley aware of the possibilities that lay before him. After an unsuccessful try for his father's old school, Uppingham, he was encouraged to put in for Charterhouse by Frank Fletcher who was due to retire in 1935. The appointment was made in March of that year, and all those directly concerned were delighted, except for Julia, now aged three, who declared that she had no intention of leaving Eton and that she would have to get another father.

The following summer brought to an end a period of eight and half years in which Birley had nobly carried on the tradition of history teaching begun by Henry Marten. It was this above all that the Editors of the *Eton College Chronicle* had in mind as they bade him farewell in verse attributable to T. F. Cattley:

R. B.

Sir, you have made Past Ages seem
Alive and real, and not a dream
And on your blackboard drawn strange trees
Polysyllabic pedigrees.
Right well we know, and we shall not forget
How deeply Charterhouse is in our debt.

CHAPTER SIX

A Very Young Headmaster

When a headmastership did come there was an element of the pre-ordained about it. Elinor Birley's father, Eustace Frere, was an architect who, having been a silver medallist at the Académie des Beaux Arts in Paris, had gone on to make something of a name for himself in the Edwardian period. He was one of those whose designs were later to attract the admiration of John Betjeman. In the latter part of his career he took on the job of looking after the London Charterhouse which he set about remodelling in various ways. It was a residential post and the Freres lived in what was called the 'Preacher's House'. For Elinor, therefore, the Charterhouse was home and it was only natural that Robert and she should be married in its Jacobean chapel. Although the school had moved out to Godalming in 1872 the links with the original hospice remained strong.

To be Headmaster of Charterhouse was a daunting preferment. At the age of thirty-two Birley was succeeding a man more than thirty years his senior. Frank Fletcher had become Headmaster before the First World War in succession to G. H. Rendall, a gentle donnish figure, remembered above all for having preferred persuasion to coercion and for trusting his boys implicitly. His civilised approach entailed some sacrifice of the outward signs of firm discipline and Fletcher was enticed away from Marlborough as the strong man who was needed to tighten things up. From the start he had taken firm charge and by the time he retired, nearly twenty-five years later, he was one of the most imposing and influential headmasters of his time. His academic distinction was acknowledged with an honorary Fellowship of Balliol and his services to the Headmasters' Conference were rewarded with a knighthood.

It was a case of one meteor making way for another. Not only had Fletcher been appointed Master of Marlborough at the early age of thirty-three, he had also been the first major public school headmaster not to be ordained. This new ground which he had helped to break was not long in being occupied, and by the time of Robert Birley's appointment a headmaster in orders was the exception rather than the rule. Very youthful heads, however, were still not common. Among the very few was John Wolfenden who was twenty-seven when he pipped Birley for Uppingham. At thirty-two his erstwhile rival was not far behind in precocity. But what was really new about Birley's case was something quite different. At that time headships went as a rule to classicists, exceptions being made only for the occasional Oxford or Cambridge history don. Having, as Ben Jonson said of Shakespeare, small Latin and less Greek, Birley seemed to be saddled with the wrong academic background. He had, however, one high card in a very strong suit. The tutorial system at Eton had enabled him to make quite a name for himself in academic circles. He got his full share of the credit for the successful passage into Oxford and Cambridge of the string of very bright boys who had been his pupils over the previous nine years. With this prestige as a counterweight to that of the classics he was in as good a position as any to break the spell of orthodoxy.

At Charterhouse he was entering the heartland of that orthodoxy. Fletcher had shared the teaching of the classical sixth with A. L. Irvine, a teacher of remarkable inspirational qualities who was generally known as 'The Uncle'. With their complementary talents these two had carried on a tradition handed down by a succession of eminent scholars on the staff. Foremost among these was Thomas Ethelbert Page, on whose classical texts generations of boys and girls are still brought up and who, as a notable Liberal, was paid the almost unique tribute of having his portrait hung in the Reform Club in his lifetime. T. E. Page had retired in 1910 but was still to be seen among the spectators at school cricket matches for many years thereafter. Indeed as his ageing and noble figure moved slowly in front of the sightscreen behind the bowler's arm on the way from one side of the ground to the other, the players would stand in reverent silence until he passed.

From the time of his arrival in 1911 Fletcher saw to it that distinction in the classics remained at the heart of the intellectual life of the school. The pervasiveness of his influence is illustrated by his teaching Divinity to the entire sixth form from New Testament Greek texts – presumably on Doctor Johnson's principle that 'Greek is like lace. Every man gets as much of it as he can.' The indelible impression which this left – for good or ill – on generations of Carthusians can well be imagined. But as his headmastership had worn on, so the dominance of the classics had begun to be undermined by what he referred to as 'the more superficially obvious "usefulness" of science and modern languages'. He had to admit that Greek and Latin needed, and in his view of course deserved, some artificial encouragement to help them to resist this challenge and maintain the balance.

The trouble had stemmed largely from the introduction in 1917 of the School Certificate which came to be taken by more and more boys at an earlier age than was necessarily intended. Those who did well enough were then able to go on to specialise, with an increasing variety of avenues open to them. What worried Fletcher was that these were opportunities to specialise in something other than classics. His misgivings on this count in fact amounted to one of the earliest of those warnings about over-specialisation of which C. P. Snow's Rede Lecture on the two cultures was a famous example. What Fletcher wrote in his autobiography would not sound out of place in modern debate:

> Even if we know a boy's bent we cannot always enable him to follow it. Vocational considerations cannot be completely ignored. A boy who wishes to be a doctor may have a real gift and taste for language and scholarship: but he cannot afford to follow a classical or literary course. The demands of the science examinations required for a medical degree, preparation for which is being forced more and more back on the schools by the universities, are too urgent to allow him to develop freely along the line which we should otherwise choose for him. What the medical profession has gained in scientific knowledge by these demands is balanced by a loss in general culture that may in the long run react upon their scientific and professional efficiency.

Whilst Birley would have endorsed Fletcher's analysis of the problem of over-specialisation, one in which he was to take a great interest in future years, he was less in agreement about his method of combating it. This lay in the use of all possible inducements to maintain the position of the classics. Almost all scholarships in Fletcher's time were awarded on a foundation of prowess in Latin and Greek. Charterhouse classicists rose to the highest standards of linguistic mastery under their succession of gifted mentors, whose tutelage bore fruit in a steady stream of scholarships and exhibitions to Oxford and Cambridge colleges.

The sporting tradition was if anything even stronger than the classical. Having been himself educated at the birthplace of rugby, Birley was taking over a school which had contributed to the origins of association football. Modern soccer grew out of the rules for fixtures such as the one between Charterhouse and Westminster, for which records go back to 1863. And with the Old Carthusians winning the FA Cup in 1881 and featuring prominently in this and various other competitions thereafter, a momentum had been built up which gave soccer uncontested dominance of the sporting life of the school. On the other hand, how cricket was regarded was memorably summed up by J. T. Morgan, an Old Carthusian who captained Cambridge in 1930: for him it was 'a device for keeping footballers in training during the summer'. Only towards the end of Fletcher's time was it taken seriously in hand by one of the masters, Wilfred Timms, who played for Northamptonshire in the school holidays. By the time Birley arrived as Headmaster, Timms had in three years made Charterhouse one of the strongest cricket schools. In one of the last matches before fixtures were disrupted by the war, Westminster were bowled out for 26 and the contest was over before lunch.

It was the intellectual rather than the sporting achievements to which Fletcher had been the more committed. He was himself something of an all-rounder, having played hockey for Oxford against Cambridge. But when he came to Charterhouse he was concerned at the aura of adulation in which he found the top games players basking. Things had come to a head towards the end of Rendall's time in the great moment of theatre, recounted by Robert Graves in *Goodbye to All That*, when three boys had the unbelievable effrontery to challenge the privileges of the members of the First XI, the so-called 'bloods'. This drama was played out before a dumbfounded congregation at a Sunday chapel in 1910. The three upstarts, posing as bloods, 'walked up the aisle magnificent in grey flannel trousers, slit coats, first-eleven collars and with pink carnations in their buttonholes. It is impossible to describe the astonishment and terror that this spectacle caused. Everyone looked at the captain of the first eleven; he had gone quite white.' The rebels got away with it and a corner had been turned. When Fletcher took over he set about speeding up the decline of the flamboyant conceits at which this outrageous snook had been cocked.

Indeed Fletcher seemed to bend over backwards to reduce the esteem in which games were held. He stubbornly refused to take sporting achievement into account in his appointments to the staff. By the twenties he felt he had managed to suppress the arrogance of an athletocracy without allowing the alternative arrogance of an intelligentsia to replace it. Looking back in his autobiography he liked to think that the Carthusian 'can be scholarly without being highbrow; he can admire and cultivate bodily skill and strength without making an idol of athleticism; he can care for literature and the arts without either effeminacy or intellectual arrogance'. But whatever the extent of his achievement it was at some cost in terms of relations with the Old Carthusians. For those among them with an intellectual turn of mind he would always be a delightful and immensely respected figure, but a good many others had little time for him. Birley too was an 'intellectual', and Eton had been a big enough school to be able to leave him entirely free of responsibility for games. But he did not have to fight the kind of battle that had preoccupied Fletcher. The fact of having no bee in his bonnet augured well for the task of reducing the tension over the role of games, and repairing the breach with the Old Carthusians. He took a good deal of trouble to get talented sportsmen on the staff for the very obvious reason that boys spend a great deal of their time at games and good coaching ought to be provided to enable them to excel in this as in any other aspect of school life. And when the school cricket professional Bob Relf left to take up another appointment, it was a stroke of luck to be able to replace him with the Leicestershire and England player George Geary whose warmth of personality made him into something of an institution at the school. All this reassured the Old Carthusians.

In the more general sense too there were great opportunities for the younger man. Fletcher's unbending discipline and scholarly integrity had kept Charterhouse pretty near the top of any of the imaginary pecking orders of conventional public schools. But by the thirties the realities of life beyond the school gates had begun to leave him behind. His overriding urge to mould an unassuming all-round competence had become ingrown, and detached from a society that was slowly becoming less authoritarian. If the ends remained admirable the means towards them were increasingly being challenged. Thoughtful parents were beginning to look for a rather less repressive atmosphere than the one that tough public school traditions had created. There were still plenty who put a high value on cold-bath harshness, but to cater exclusively for this persuasion meant losing ground in the longer run. It needed a new mind to perceive this clearly.

It was not only socially, but politically too, that Charterhouse was drifting out of touch. The other side of Fletcher's coin of stern and single-minded character-building was a certain cocoon-like lack of interest in contemporary affairs. The serenely picturesque school buildings in the lovely setting of the Surrey countryside made this detachment seem natural enough. A senior boy had once complained that it was quite unfair to be expected to field at third man with the view of Hindhead opening out in front of you. But all this was in sharp contrast to Birley's earlier teaching experience. Of course Eton had been insulated by its extensive playing fields from the industrial estates and suburbia of Slough. But it had at the same time been a place that was very much aware of the outside world, and for quite a number of the boys who had been Birley's pupils, politics was one of the obvious avenues of public life to follow. Birley had encouraged this through his own involvement in the problems of the unemployed in Slough. So coming from Eton of all schools, he very quickly became conscious of the less political atmosphere reigning at Charterhouse. If a new headmaster is expected to provide the inspiration to enable a school to strike out in a new direction it was quite evident in this case that the foremost priority was to foster a stimulating intellectual life which was rather more in touch with what was going on in the outside world. It was a task that in one respect was becoming easier. Not even in the idyllic isolation of Charterhouse was it possible to fail to become more politically aware in these years. Memories of the First World War were still vivid and painful enough to make what was happening in Germany cast a menacing shadow over the whole country.

On all these fronts Birley could see that change was overdue. But he was temperamentally not disposed to try to achieve it by a frontal assault on traditional practices. In any case control of the school's affairs was too widely dispersed for this to be even possible, let alone have a chance of succeeding. The housemasters really were masters of their houses and what happened in them was their business. Each of them had its own distinctive character and the Headmaster was in effect president of a federation, with his scope for action lying in the restricted realm where the school rather than the house was the corporate entity. This was of course true of the public school system as a whole. When it was working well there was a great deal to be said for it. The size of the unit was such that it could have something of a family atmosphere and every boy could 'get somewhere'. But equally, there were dangers in the potential lack of communication between houses. For a Headmaster setting out to modify conventions of this kind, the arrangement of the masters' common room at Charterhouse was particularly advantageous. Known as Brooke Hall, it had its own building, with a club atmosphere and dinner nights twice a week. It gave the Head much more opportunity than is accorded in most schools to discuss things with his staff in a leisurely and informal fashion. But even allowing for circumstances that were especially favourable for influencing opinion there was scope for only a limited number of overt changes in Birley's first few years.

The most obvious centre of school community life was the Chapel. Every day began with a very formal act of worship which reinforced the pervading sense of orderliness in the school routine. It would not have been very productive to tamper with this, but there was scope for fresh thinking in another direction. As at most public schools there were, in addition to early Communion, two major compulsory services every Sunday. They performed the convenient custodial function of ensuring that the entire school was under surveillance at two key points in the one day when, apart from an hour's divinity lesson, there was no organised work or sport to keep the boys occupied.. But it was a level of compulsory observance that was as likely to be a hindrance as a help in fostering Christian values and attitudes. Birley set out to persuade the housemasters to have Sunday morning chapel replaced by a voluntary service. He had got the idea from his own school days at Rugby, where David had done something similar. He succeeded, but not all that easily. For Charterhouse it was not an irresistible idea 'whose time had come'. Some of the older men like Uncle Irvine were shocked. So what must appear in retrospect as a minor decision hardly worth recording was in fact something of a breakthrough – above all in the eyes of small boys who lived in a pillar-to-post world where they seemed rarely to have a minute to themselves. So popular was the change that it ushered in a new informal kind of compulsory chapel. Certain houses saw to it that a respectable number of boys turned up each Sunday, just in case poor attendance should suggest that the experiment was a failure and cause it to be abandoned.

Another area of school life on which it was possible to gain some purchase was the curriculum. It was a straightforward and relatively uncontroversial matter to reappraise this and, being very much aware of the need to encourage science, Birley at once set about ensuring that all boys took physics and chemistry in the lower school. He was also anxious to have modern languages other than French more widely taught but, with Latin still a requirement for university matriculation, this was a slower business. Apart from his interest in the general trends, the attention which he paid to the detail of how the teaching was arranged was remarkable. In his autobiography *Promise Me You'll Sing Mud*, published in 1975, Ian Wallace recalls the unexpected and alarming experience of being summoned to the Headmaster's study on the first Monday of the first term after Fletcher's departure. The reason turned out to be that Birley had noticed that a small group of boys in a history set were, because of some inconvenient quirk in the timetable, going to waste their time by going over the same maths syllabus that they had covered in the previous term. This just would not do, and in accordance with his conviction that the Headmaster should do as much teaching as he could

ove left The new Headmaster,
ptember 1935

ove right and below General
avell inspecting the
arterhouse OTC

Bomb damage
Founder's Court
Charterhouse. T
school buildir
themselves remair
relatively unscath

Birley as Housemaster with Peter
May, House Captain of Saunderites
in 1947, and later England cricket
captain

For once, Birley in the unusual
position of the listener — with the
Chairman of the Governors, Michael
Ramsay, Archbishop of Canterbury

possibly manage, he resolved to give them some Carthaginian history himself instead. 'This shy mountain of a man took us across the Alps with Hannibal's elephants, and even in the half-light of early morning, rubbing the sleep from our eyes, it was impossible not to share his enthusiasm for this remarkable feat of arms.'

A third area where the Headmaster had obvious jurisdiction was school uniform. Between the wars Charterhouse boys were dressed as though their day was to be spent in an office in Threadneedle Street. It was not just the black jackets and striped trousers. Not even the smallest boy could go outside the school grounds without wearing a bowler hat. None of this ought to have surprised Birley, coming as he did from a school which could scarcely be surpassed in formality of dress. But the Charterhouse uniform seemed to suggest a more general rigidity which was not true of Eton. At any rate Birley's very first notice as Headmaster announced the banishment of the bowler. This certainly was a direct frontal assault on minor tradition. But there was little inclination among the staff to defend the conspicuously anachronistic headgear and the change caused no controversy in Brooke Hall. As for the boys, the announcement of the news was greeted with jubilation and legend has it that that evening in a number of houses ceremonial bowler hat bonfires were lit. After a decent interval came the further change when brown tweed and grey flannel replaced black and white, giving the school a sort of moulting look during the transitional period when the old coexisted with the new. One further liberalising gesture was Birley's decision, within his first week as Headmaster, to put the forbidden territory of the magnificent woods near the school in bounds. The staff were far less happy about this than about changes in uniform, predicting that the main benefit would be to the illicit smokers. Birley – a smoker himself – took a more realistic line in doubting whether restrictions on bounds were effective in deterring boys who were really set on smoking.

Such were a few of the more obvious outward ways in which it was possible to relax the rigidity of the Fletcher era. They epitomised a more general feeling of relief at the change, among masters and boys alike. They were tentative steps taken by a young man who knew what he wanted but who was without the imperious assurance of a predecessor whose inscrutable, faintly oriental features betokened inexhaustible experience. However, what his tall, fresh-faced and very scrutable successor lacked in confidence in those early years, he made up in warmth. Although towards the end of his time he had mellowed enormously, Fletcher still had an unnerving presence which made it more commonly an ordeal than a pleasure to engage in conversation with him. Birley was no easy conversationalist either, having little of that ready small talk which creates a relaxed atmosphere. But once the conversation hit upon something that really interested him he was a voluble talker who could sparkle with an adroit combination of wit and erudition. With the boys he had a gift for establishing relationships which encouraged discussion as between equals and yet at the same time he had a natural authority which never permitted over-familiarity.

This infusion of civilised values was epitomised in the Birleys' own home. In the twenties the school had acquired an adjoining estate, complete with a country house called Northbrook, and when Fletcher gave up being a housemaster this had become the Headmaster's residence. It was a quarter of a mile or so from the centre of the school, and under Fletcher distance lent awe rather than enchantment to the view of it across the playing fields. Within a very short time of their arrival, Elinor Birley's way with decoration had transformed the sombre interior. The succession of small boys invited to Sunday breakfast with the Headmaster's family found the grace of the surroundings in startling contrast with the dingy accommodation of the boys' side of their various Houses. These were mostly small boys in their first year. It was the Birleys' experience that the older ones were silent at breakfast time. The younger ones were, on the other hand, given to uninhibited chatter. For them it was another world, one of elegance, warmth and gentle humour.

But important as these glimpses of civilisation were for the boys, their real world was still one of hierarchical discipline. At Charterhouse, as at most public schools, social life was centred on the individual houses. Each was a miniature tribal society largely administered by the senior boys, and fraternisation with members of neighbouring tribes was actively discouraged.

Rank was denoted by the familiar array of esoteric symbols; it made all the difference in the world whether you were permitted to have one jacket button undone or two. This was the time-honoured way of making the system run smoothly by inculcating an unquestioning acceptance of authority. And with authority went the predictable scale of privileges, collectively known in Carthusian slang as *post tes*.

To maintain this elaborate structure, discipline had to be firm. In the more severe houses, when punishment was to be by beating, malefactors would be ceremoniously informed in the morning. The whole house would be aware of it. In the evening they would be summoned from their cubicles and brought down in pyjamas and dressing gown to the house hall past a row of glowering monitors. On entering the otherwise empty hall they would see at the far end the Head Monitor having a few practice swings at a cushion with an ash-plant specially cut that day by the School Sergeant. Scope for cruelty there certainly was, especially if the Head Monitor had a good eye and could strike the same place more than once. But the ash was not in fact a particularly efficient instrument, and it was as a safeguard against brutality that the regulations demanded the presence of the other monitors. In most cases the ceremony was probably more terrifying than the punishment was savage and in the long run it was the absurdity rather than the pain that was likely to be the most enduring memory. Other features of discipline like fagging have in retrospect a rather less distasteful touch of absurdity about them. House monitors could find themselves summoning fags who towered over them: Gerald Priestland, for example, was 6′ 1″ when he arrived as a new boy in a house where the senior boys of the time were unusually short of inches.

But not much of the absurdity was so evident at the time. There is a story of an Old Carthusian of the pre-war period who, on revisiting the school with the confidence of subsequent professional success, felt physically sick as he entered the grounds, so vivid were the memories of unhappiness. Some houses were of course more enlightened than others, and at least one abolished all beating within a few years of Birley's arrival. But by and large the regime added up to the familiar catalogue of conventions which, described in isolation, emphasise the philistine, conformist and barbaric side of public school life at that time. For a Headmaster setting out to bring Charterhouse up to date it was the more overt side of the challenge, and more bestrewn with hidden pitfalls than the straighforward business of widening the academic horizons and enriching the intellect- ual life of the place.

Whether it was the intellectual or the social life that was at issue, the Birley approach was the same characteristically oblique one. Awareness of the dangers of laying down the law led him to judge that in most things discretion was the better part. He was by no means the crusading reformer, dismantling at a stroke the network of privileges and punishments which made Charterhouse characteristic of the public schools more generally. In fact another generation was to elapse before serious cracks began to appear in that mould. Instead of fundamental change by edict, Birley set out to influence the atmosphere by as much informal contact with individuals as possible. This was in embryo the technique he was to employ as Educational Adviser in Germany after the war. So not only did little groups of boys make their way across the playing fields in the early morning for breakfast with the Birleys; other groups also gathered at Northbrook for various kinds of intellectual and aesthetic activity. For musical appreciation the Eton recipe of learning to understand a symphony by following a score was revived, and all sorts of school societies flourished.

One of the objectives dearest to Birley's heart was to get rid of the taboo of friendship between boys in different houses. Fletcher had been concerned about this but had been unable to break it. Birley found it easier to get on terms with boys about things of this kind. For one thing he spent a good deal of his time in his study, which was not in Northbrook but right in the centre of the school, with a good view of what was going on. (Though he was in favour of much freer association he still had the schoolmaster's instinct for spotting friendships that boded ill). The study was useful, too, as a convenient place to resume discussions left unfinished in class, rather in the way that he himself had experienced the informal extra tuition of Dr Thomas at Rugby. This was the most natural way to get to know boys and could be turned to good account if there was a particular social problem to discuss with them. Many such conversations contributed to the weakening of the non-fraternisation convention.

In none of these contacts did Birley set out to dominate people. His instinct was to discuss problems in the hope that sensible suggestions for solutions would come spontaneously from the boys themselves. If this did happen, he would snatch the opportunity to do things their way. On one occasion, when he was Head of the School, Michael Hoban, later Head Master of Harrow, jibbed at the idea of the school beatings which were conducted in the presence of some twenty to twenty-five school monitors. Birley seized on this chance to hasten the decline of the practice, which was already becoming rare.

The choice of Head of the School and the relationship with him were taken very seriously. Simon Raven's fictional account in *Fielding Gray* of senior boys spending part of the summer holidays with the Headmaster in 'Wiltshire' has a basis in fact. Soon after they came to Charterhouse the Birleys rented a farmhouse at Coate, near Martock in Somerset, and most summers small groups of boys of various ages were invited to stay there for one reason or another. The chief recreation was cycling round the neighbouring countryside exploring churches, with the Headmaster holding forth on an endless succession of historical vignettes associated with them. With adult friends of the Birleys, often old colleagues from Eton, also coming to stay now and again or visiting for meals, there was a very special atmosphere about Coate. Some boys took to it, others were recalcitrant, but all were being quietly educated whether they liked it or not.

These were unobtrusive contributions to a general intellectual atmosphere which in any school depends above all on the quality of the teaching and the receptiveness of those being taught. But receptiveness has to be worked for. In the traditional sense the teaching at Charterhouse was as good as anywhere, but the dash of inspiration and imagination which Birley brought to it made all the difference. He gave lectures to the school demonstrating his skill in making abstruse subjects interesting. Ian Wallace was only the first of many to be initiated into the strategies of Carthaginian campaigning. No one who was at Charterhouse in Birley's time is likely to forget the excitement with which he lectured on the role of the elephant as warrior.

It was however through his teaching of the history sixth that he had the most enduring influence. He got off to a splendid start. Within a year of his arrival he had the good fortune to be teaching one of the most distinguished groups of history specialists that Charterhouse had ever had. It was an academic subject which was already in good hands at the school, for John Morgan, the senior history master, was a first-rate teacher whose sound professionalism Birley was now able to complement with idiosyncratic flair. They were a formidable combination and five of the group they taught, including two subsequently eminent historians, John Ehrman and Lawrence Stone, won awards at Oxford or Cambridge in the examinations of 1937–38.

Part of the secret was, of course, that Birley simply adored teaching history to able boys. During the years at Eton he had amassed a repertoire of information of encyclopaedic proportions and it came bubbling out without any recourse to notes or textbooks being necessary. Sometimes it was ancient history and he would spend a whole term on, say, Alexander the Great. Sometimes it was modern, and Charterhouse boys found themselves studying American history, something which had not previously been in the syllabus. Indeed this soon led Birley to select and edit, for Oxford University Press, his *Speeches and Documents in American History*, prompting the *Times Literary Supplement* reviewer to pronounce that in British schools American history had 'at last got its colours'. But as ever it was the Middle Ages which fascinated Birley above all else. There was usually a moment of special excitement when he would tug furiously at his lapel and expound the central idea, the 'key' which, he declared, unlocked the mystery of the matter under consideration. He was, for example, fascinated by Thomas á Becket and above all the fact that he had become such an immensely popular saint so soon after his martyrdom, with churches dedicated to him from Sicily to Sweden. Birley's key to this was that in the conditions of the Middle Ages there was no such concept as individual liberty. The only liberty was that of a corporation, and so in defending the independence of the Church vis-à-vis the Crown, Becket was defending the liberty of individual people in their corporate rights. This was the kind of exposition which some of his pupils could remember in clear detail thirty-five years later. Above all Birley used his history to make them think. No sloppiness in their ideas or arguments was tolerated, and in consequence they discovered real enjoyment in intellectual endeavour. Some of them still recall the pleasurable anticipation with which they went to these classes. For this was sixth-form work of the very highest quality, sound on facts, full of ideas and with just that degree of over-simplification – 'one of the greatest, if not *the* greatest king/queen/prime minister/Pope of the century . . .' – necessary to make the story more vivid and convincing. Small wonder that those who went on to read history at University frequently found the teaching there an anti-climax.

This contribution helped to influence the quality of the teaching at Charterhouse right from the beginning. To influence the quality of those who would benefit from such teaching was a more mysterious process. Prominent public schools can rely on a reservoir of loyalty among Old Boys and other well-wishers which guarantees them a steady flow of applicants. But they can seldom afford to ignore the shifting clientele which seeks to be in the know about the fluctuations of academic reputations and is constantly on the look-out for the best buy. Within a few years of Birley's arrival at Charterhouse the messages on the grapevine were growing more and more favourable, above all among those for whom an enlightened atmosphere and intellectual distinction had a strong appeal. Enquiries about entry began to come in from new sources and the numbers of visits to view the school increased. Birley's shyness had never allowed him to become practised in the superficial arts of public relations. Being 'good with parents' was not one of his great strengths and it was not unknown for him to be spotted ducking into the Headmaster's garden to avoid them. Some of the more bluff, outgoing ones who came to size up the place were no doubt puzzled by the absence of conventional bonhomie. But for others the diffidence did not hide, and perhaps indeed added to, the impression of intellectual stature. They were meeting a Headmaster with a presence which conveyed something out of the ordinary, someone who was patently capable of making his school attractive to a wider than normal range of discriminating people.

Influencing the entry was nevertheless a slow business. In the first few years it was possible only to get the school into a position where it was attractive to thoughtful parents with outstandingly

able sons. But other schools too were in this position, and too
many factors are at work in this kind of choice to be conducive
to quick advance. Then as the peak years of Birley's headmastership were beginning, Charterhouse gained an unexpected advantage over some of its rivals. A number of schools in the
London area and the home counties were evacuated to safer
rural refuges. Westminster, for example, spent most of the war
at Bromyard in Herefordshire. From 1940 to 1945 Charterhouse was one of the reduced number of leading schools that
were still within easy reach of London. The upheaval brought
an infusion of new blood which in normal circumstances could
not have been achieved in such a short space of time. A number
of very able boys, originally down for other schools, found their
way to Charterhouse. And there were, too, talented sons of
Jewish refugees, some of whom had already arrived in the years
leading up to the war.

At the same time the culmination of competition for
outstanding talent continued to be the scholarship system. Like
any headmaster, Birley was determined to use this to the best
advantage but he brought an element of novelty into the way of
doing so. Fletcher had of course insisted on classics as the
foundation on which all awards were made and there was
nothing exceptional about this either in his own time or for a
good many years after he had retired. At Eton, for example, one
promising entrant for the scholarship in 1941 had written the
most brilliant history answers that any of the masters could
remember seeing from a boy of that age. But because his Latin
and Greek were relatively undistinguished and his maths poor,
Eton declined to give him an award. He then tried for
Charterhouse. Again his history answers were brilliant, again
his Latin and Greek undistinguished and his maths worse. It
would have been quite normal for the same thing to happen as at
Eton. But Birley was himself one of the panel which decided on
the scholarships and set more store on the interview part of the
proceedings than his colleagues. In this case he was convinced
that he had an outstanding candidate who should not be allowed
to slip through their fingers. He got his colleagues to agree that
because the maths result was so poor it would be a mistake to
make the judgment on the basis of the marks as a whole. This
created sufficient uncertainty to justify delay. Having thus

averted a decision which, if taken at once would have gone against him, he was able the following day to get his own way. The boy was the future Editor of *The Times*, William Rees-Mogg, who went on to vindicate his mentor's judgment by following in his footsteps as a Brackenbury scholar of Balliol. There had been something reminiscent of Birley's own progression to Rugby about this case of precocious interest in history and it became one of his cautionary tales of the dangers of orthodoxy. Years later at Eton, masters who marked the scholarship papers were sometimes taken on one side by the Head Master for a chat about what he called 'the matter of Rees-Mogg'.

The early wartime entry brought Charterhouse to the point to which new headmasters generally look forward, the point at which the school is made up entirely of boys who have come during their own time. With this generation it became Birley's school. The boys were his boys, and taking them through the war was what was to distinguish his headmastership above all else. It was an opportunity to grow to the stature of a national figure, and in what had gone before he had been well prepared. It was to be one of the more remarkable periods in Carthusian history.

CHAPTER SEVEN

A School in Wartime

Shortly after being appointed to Charterhouse Birley had written to Fletcher: 'You guided the school through the last war. I shall have to guide it through the next.' This conviction that Europe was heading for catastrophe had come at first hand from the experience of visiting Willie Robson-Scott who was now teaching at the University of Berlin. From the time that Hitler achieved his first electoral success in 1930 Birley was making his fear of how the situation would deteriorate more and more plain in the classroom. The impression that this left on some of his pupils was a powerful one. Some forty-five years later, while he was going round the *Neue Sachlichkeit* exhibition at the Hayward Gallery, an old gentleman came up and said: 'You won't remember me but you taught me history for two years at Eton. In 1933 and 1934 you used to tell us what dreadful people the Nazis were.' Birley replied: 'That was because I couldn't get older people to believe me – I took it out on you!' The Old Etonian was Lord Reading and the experience had led him and his friends to call themselves 'the group who knew'.

In the winter of 1933–34 Birley had given a series of lectures in Berlin on English education and this visit had reinforced his forebodings. It was, too, his last trip abroad before taking up his new post and it had ensured that he came to Charterhouse vividly aware of the turn that events were likely to take in Europe. Although the early years were naturally given over to learning the art of running a large school, he was nevertheless able to maintain the contacts with the world of affairs which he had established during his time at Eton. On the day in December 1936 when the Abdication was to be announced he had been taken to lunch by Harold Nicolson, along with Roland de Margerie, the First Secretary at the French Embassy. They had discussed German propaganda and the skilful way in which its appeal was directed towards adolescents in particular, and had then walked to the House of Commons in time for Nicolson to be in the Chamber to hear the Speaker's announcement and Baldwin's speech.

Birley's urge to be actively abreast of national and international affairs was heightened above all by his enduring attachment to Czechoslovakia. None of the other European countries he had visited in 1922 had made quite the same impression on him and he had gone back there periodically, acquiring a variety of contacts through the Czech wife of one of his Eton colleagues. The charm and grace of Prague and its inhabitants captivated him, and this emotional bond was reinforced by an intellectual one. In the difficult conditions of central Europe the Czech nation seemed to him to demonstrate in practice those principles of freedom and democracy which were guiding themes in his history teaching. In the summer of 1938 one of Birley's Czech acquaintances, a professor from Prague University, came to the school and talked to thirty or so of the senior boys about the Sudeten problem. The dangers were all too apparent. But even so, the Munich agreement between Chamberlain and Hitler in September came as a tremendous shock. In an Oxford pamphlet published the following year Birley denounced the deal concluded at the conference – without Czech representation – whereby the mountain defences were breached in a rearrangement of the frontier and the country was laid open to invasion.

On the day of the Munich crisis Birley simply could not put his mind to school affairs. He felt acutely ill at ease in the general atmosphere of relief at the settlement. There was nothing for it but to ask J. C. Thomson, who was soon to become Second Master, to take over his responsibilities until he himself felt ready to resume them. He and Elinor went up to London. It was a spontaneous act with no positive purpose behind it other than to get away and think. But in St James's Square they ran into Ronnie Cartland, an Old Carthusian MP whom they knew well. They talked for half an hour and found themselves in complete agreement over what was happening. Cartland was reassuring about the strength of the opposition to the Munich pact in the House of Commons, and the Birleys returned to Charterhouse in the belief that Great Britain would go no further along the road of appeasement. From being an ever-present threat, the idea of war was now as good as a reality.

From then on Birley's main concern was how to prepare Charterhouse for this new situation. Already during the summer all masters had taken a course of anti-gas training, and in the Oration Quarter – as the autumn term was called – first-aid lectures and fire drills followed. The Home Office instruction was that for a school situated like Charterhouse in open country and not near any obvious military objective, the best policy was to dig trenches well away from all buildings. Enough trenches to accommodate the entire school were dug in just over three days and, as Birley wrote in his end of term letter to the members of the Carthusian Society, 'in prospect, enemy aircraft seemed less alarming than pneumonia, following on a visit to a trench on a wet night (for which reason all boys were supplied with gumboots), or the expected arrival of about four thousand LCC schoolchildren in the immediate neighbourhood. The School would probably have enjoyed treating these refugees as their guests, but there was some apprehension as to the effect of this invasion on the food supplies of the neighbourhood. It is worth recording that only one parent took steps to remove his son from the school'. In due course the trenches were converted into complete underground shelters, covered with sheets of corrugated iron and piled up earth. Each held five boys and had a duckboard, a bench, a light and a curtained entrance protected above ground level by sandbags.

When the Germans marched into the Sudetenland in March the following year Birley addressed the school in Chapel. To bring home the significance of what had happened he turned once again to his musical appreciation technique. Smetana's symphonic poem *Ma Vlast* was chosen as the voluntary to be played by the organist after the service – the only sheet music available being one of the Headmaster's own collection of pocket scores. In his sermon Birley explained what it meant and invited the boys to listen to it after Chapel. Generally speaking only a handful used to stay to hear the voluntary; on this occasion only a handful did not.

The imminence of war brought to a head a feeling that Northbrook was too remote from the life of the school and that the proper thing was for the Birleys to take over a boarding house, which would enable them to be more at the centre of things. A number of factors contributed to this desire. To begin with, Birley had never been a housemaster and so lacked direct experience of one of the most influential appointments in boarding school life. Furthermore, if this life was to move with the times it was within the individual houses that it had to happen. But above all, to be a housemaster as well as Headmaster would put him in a better position to guide the school through the war.

As it happened, N. J. Chignell, the Housemaster of Saunderites, was due to retire at Christmas 1939. Saunderites had previously been the Headmaster's House, and it was from there that Sir Frank Fletcher had moved to Northbrook in 1924. At that time the Governors had foreseen the possibility that his successor might return to it. The Birleys moved in the January of 1940. It was a change that echoed the take-over from Fletcher. Chignell had been an old-fashioned housemaster, who left the running of things very much to the boys. His wife organised the domestic side of the house with firm discipline and made few concessions to graciousness in her surroundings. The very masculine atmosphere was reinforced by Mr Chignell's habit of taking groups of boys on caravanning holidays in which his wife took no part. Indeed she had little enough to do with the boys at any time, and the younger ones were not terribly sure whether she was his wife or his housekeeper. But it had not been all that odd for a married housemaster to be, as it were, a bachelor with a wife.

The arrival of the Birleys effected the same transformation to the private side of Saunderites as it had to Northbrook. Elinor's touch reappeared as the drawing room was redecorated to take advantage of the light that streamed in from windows to the south and west. White sofas with fluffy cushions, delicate water-colours, golden retrievers contributed to an atmosphere which contrasted with the former gloom, and perhaps was rather too civilised for some of the ruffians of the middle school to appreciate. For others it was a revelation. From the start it was quite evident that the Birleys were a team, both working equally hard to initiate their gauche charges into the proprieties of educated conversation.

For their first Head Monitor, John Waterfield, later British Ambassador to Mali, it was an awkward adjustment. Used to running the house his way, he now found subtle changes being suggested. When he resisted they were suggested again, and little by little the harsh masculinity was softened so that something of a family atmosphere could reign. Elinor came into house lunch – a startling innovation then, incredible as it may sound to modern ears. Other guests began to be invited. In its own small way the house was becoming less insular. But reform would be too big a word for what was happening. The rough justice of the boys' side continued as before with no great reduction in fagging, beating or other punishments. It was the Birleys' style to lead by civilised example rather than to drive by force of authority. They gave their lead with distinction, but they were rather too far ahead for some to be able to follow it.

In this respect Birley was an uncharacteristic figure in a profession with markedly autocratic tendencies. It was not his way to lay down the law. What he really wanted was for people to understand the moral force behind it. Consequently he was prepared to devote a phenomenal amount of energy to getting to know the boys individually and guiding their moral education. He wrote often to parents, confidential letters about their sons' personal and social development. They would always be in his own hand and extend generally to three or four pages. It was not part of the official reporting, of which as Headmaster and Housemaster he had more than his share, but he had observed it to be a standard practice for housemasters at Eton and it was well suited to his aim of creating, unobtrusively and as far as possible in collaboration with the family, an atmosphere that encouraged the growth of a stable code of values.

The unobtrusiveness was extremely important. Conrad Dehn recalled writing an essay castigating Gladstone for having 'preferred abstract morality to concrete success'. While at school Dehn had become a non-believer and this articulate piece demonstrated that he was happy to abandon morality as well as religion. Nevertheless he got a high mark and was sufficiently pleased with himself to show the essay to his father in the holidays. Appalled, and unknown to the boy, father Dehn got in touch with Birley. When the entire history sixth in the following quarter were asked to hand in their best essays for scrutiny by the Headmaster, young Dehn had no idea that anything premeditated was happening. It seemed a perfectly natural thing for Birley to be doing, and equally natural that he should explain to him why he was wrong about morality and instruct him to read *Antigone* in the next holidays. It was just the right illustration of why the boy's view of morality was inadequate. But it was only very many years later, when some papers came to light after his father's death, that he discovered how it had come about.

This delicate touch with which Birley strove to inculcate Christian morality is aptly conveyed by Simon Raven in *Fielding Gray*. The Headmaster, an obvious portrait of Birley, has an extremely talented boy in mind for the house captaincy but is not sure about his morals. He summons the boy to his study, where he tries to discover what the code is that he lives by. There follows a sparring match in which the boy declares his adherence to the Greek view of what is pleasant and seemly 'and therefore right', while the Headmaster upholds the more fastidious morality of Christianity.

> There was a long silence between us.
> 'The Greeks stood for reason and decency,' I said. 'Isn't that enough?'
> 'Reason and decency,' the Headmaster murmured, 'but without the sanction of revealed religion. . . ? No, Fielding, it isn't enough. What you ignore or tolerate, I must know about and punish in order to *forgive*. Please bear the difference in mind.'
> 'It is a radical difference, sir.'
> 'Let us hope it will not divide us too far. . . . Will you come,' he went on abruptly, 'and stay with us in Wiltshire? Some time in September?'

Behind the discussion of course lurked the spectre of homosexuality, which emerges from the shadows sooner or later in any discussion of morality in public schools. What is nowadays scarcely seen as a shameful problem was at that time a sporadic hazard attended by grossly disproportionate punishments. For all his scrupulousness in moral matters Birley took the view that homosexuality was not totally unnatural or invariably catastrophic. While he was concerned about the danger that it might make heterosexual relationships less easy in later life, and about the possibility of older boys leading younger ones astray, he did not see the offence as being necessarily against a moral code. It was not easy to make this explicit, however, and when boys were caught, the public schools were in no position to be more enlightened than society as a whole. Flagrant flouting of the conventions had to be punished. For Birley, if this meant expulsion, so it had to be, but this was a desperate last resort after a whole repertoire of other measures and subtle warnings with moral overtones had failed.

After all the frenzy of the early preparation, it was some time before the war intruded much on life at Charterhouse. The most conspicuous new precaution was the 'black-out', for which the Bursar and the Clerk of Works had managed in the holidays to obtain six miles of dark cloth. Bit by bit economies began to be introduced, above all the closing of one of the houses. The boys could not join the services till they were nineteen, and in the first year or so there was little in the way of visits from Old Carthusians in uniform. The OTC turned out enthusiastically once a week, its training largely and somewhat irrelevantly centred on the parade ground. There was a certain incongruity about the fact that Birley, a thoroughly unmilitary figure, had, in taking over Saunderites, found himself presiding over a house that was fanatically keen on the Corps. The more senior NCOs wore leather belts which were frenetically buffed up with a delicate mixture of boot polish and red ink. In the house drill competitions Saunderites were consistently victorious. Birley was of course gratified by their success, little as this particular ethos bore on his own way of life.

But while in normal circumstances the OTC would have been one of the last aspects of school life to claim Birley's active interest, he recognised of course that it had now become extremely important. And when it came to the point, he showed his characteristic flair for finding the right person to provide a source of inspiration. Already in the years preceding the war he had been somewhat worried by the pacifist following which a rather unconventional master called Harry Iredale had gathered round himself in his Literary and Political ('Lit. and Pol.') Society. Iredale was one of those stimulating people who are a confounded nuisance to headmasters but keep a school intellectually alive. It was important to Birley that the pacifist argument should not prevail on any extensive scale. An opportunity had come with the discovery that every third year the Headmaster had the right to appoint the inspecting officer for the annual OTC parade. Birley's enquiries indicated that General Sir Archibald Wavell was the man, and he managed to see him to explain what he wanted. Wavell carried out the inspection, which culminated in a powerful address to the school on the need to defend freedom. Thereafter he and Birley struck up such a remarkable rapport that he was prepared to come along on field days and watch the ritualised platoon attacks on the defensive positions of the Aldershot training area. It impressed the OTC no end to be taken seriously by such a famous general, and this in turn helped to put the school as a whole on the path that Birley wanted.

Another stroke of luck was that Major-General Sir John Davidson, formerly of the 60th Rifles, was Elinor's uncle. Instead of getting boys into a good College at Oxford or Cambridge it was now a matter of getting them into a good regiment. Through the Davidson connection a steady trickle of Carthusians found themselves on the King's list for the 60th Rifles, predominantly an Etonian regiment. And when towards the end of the war there was the risk of becoming a 'Bevin boy' instead of going into the armed forces, Birley, who had brought Labour MPs from mining constituencies down to visit the school, was reputed to say to those threatened with that alternative form of service: 'I think I can get you into a good mine.'

The non-military side of the war effort began in 1940 with the digging up of part of the Northbrook field for potatoes. In due course it became the aim to grow all the school's potatoes and green vegetables on the estate. In the holidays camps were organised in Somerset to enable groups of boys to work for local farmers. From crops the school effort moved on to livestock, permitting a blossoming of talents not normally fostered in orthodox public schools. James Prior kept pigs and nursed them through the infectious disease known as swine erysipelas with consummate skill. The eccentricity of this activity appealed to Birley, but it was rather more than a hobby, for the pork was a significant addition to the school's rations. Not only that, it was the first source of a decent supply of cooking fat they had had for some time. On these counts there was much rejoicing when the first pig was ready for slaughter – until to everyone's alarm it was learnt that a whole week's worth of school meat coupons would have to be surrendered in lieu. With the help of one of the governors, Birley discovered the identity and whereabouts of the man in charge of such matters and telephoned him. In the course of a vehement argument he elicited from this testy official the ineffable remark, 'Oh all right, all right! . . . Granted you can't eat the snout.' It was grudgingly agreed that on this occasion the House need not give up the coupons but the Head Pig Man, as Birley called him, insisted that the concession could not be repeated. Shortly afterwards a small boy in the House who was about to be confirmed asked if his godfather could come to the service. The godfather was Lord Llewellin, the Minister of Food, and Birley asked him to tea. A well-primed James Prior was placed beside him and encouraged to take his opportunity. Several weeks later the rule was changed and the requirement to surrender coupons in such circumstances was withdrawn.

As to the specifically defensive preparations, Birley wrote in his letter to the Carthusian Society of September 1940:

> I have been unable to discover any evidence of Carthusians taking part in the preparations to resist invasion in the time of Napoleon, and I think it is probably true to say that this was the first time in the history of the school that its members formed part of an actual military organisation, equipped for active service, in time of war. One hundred and thirty members of the school, besides members of Brooke Hall, were enrolled in the Home Guards, and over sixty came back for a week during the holidays to do duty here. Of the work done by the school as a whole on military defence works no details can be given now, but it can be said that Carthusians, perhaps for the first time since the school came down to Surrey, learnt something about mud. They could hardly have learnt about it more thoroughly, well up to the knees.

It was from now on that the impact of the war was beginning to be more and more obvious. In the summer of 1940 eight of the staff had left for military service and older men who had recently retired came back to replace them.

September 1940 brought the invasion crisis, which had its amusing side. A staff officer came over to the school with the instruction that if the Germans landed, Birley was to march the boys to Aldershot. 'And the wives and children?' was the reply. That was the end of the suggestion. On another occasion there was a visit from representatives of the Admiralty who were contemplating requisitioning a school. Charterhouse was, they said, ideally situated and equipped – 'with ink in the inkwells'. The discussion was highly confidential but the Admiralty officers agreed to allow Birley to inform the Chairman of the governors. Unfortunately for their plans this was the Archbishop of Canterbury who, by immediately getting in touch with Anthony Eden, saw to it that no more was heard of the idea.

The work of the Home Guard gradually became more time-consuming, for in addition to the parades there was liaison with the Godalming ARP and the enforcement of a curfew after dark. On one occasion a night patrol arrested a young Austrian girl who had been taken on by the Birleys as governess for their two young daughters. Not yet having become a well-known figure about the school she was not recognised and was brought before the officer in charge. Asked who she was, she declared in her shaky English that she was the Headmaster's nursemaid – a reply that was savoured long afterwards. Checking the black-out was the most important task and two masters were on duty each night for the purpose. They wrote their report in a book kept in Brooke Hall where everyone could see it. One night Birley looked in and read the report which said that all was well with the black-out, and he wrote underneath 'for there is nothing left remarkable beneath the visiting moon'. It was the night before the first and only bombs fell on the school.

They came as a timely warning. Given normal precautions, there had been no particular reason for the school to be vulnerable until a searchlight was sited, near Hurtmore. Soon after this came the bombing incident. It was a narrow escape for Saunderites. The first bomb landed twenty yards or so from the House, and all the boys, who were doing their prep in the dining room at the time, dived under the tables. Birley and the Head Monitor were in the Housemaster's study and also dived under a table. Fortunately the bomb missed the tarmac road and fell on soft grass which greatly limited the damage it could do. According to the local newspaper it was a matter for general rejoicing that the founder's statue had not been hit 'though some dirt was cast on to the pedestal and the dignified carved figure'. Two hours after the raid Birley received a telephone call from the Godalming ARP – 'was there any truth in the story going round about bombs at Charterhouse?' It had been the duty of R. L. Arrowsmith, a master attached to the Godalming Home Guard for liaison purposes, to report such incidents. He had however forgotten to do so, being totally preoccupied with the more serious business of making sure that the cricket pitches had not been hit.

Birley then went into action on behalf of the school. With the help of Sir George Schuster, one of the governors, he was able to meet the War Office official in charge of the siting of searchlights and ask if the one at Hurtmore could be moved. This, he was told, was not possible as it would upset the complicated geometrical pattern according to which the siting had been arranged for the country as a whole. But Birley persisted. If Charterhouse were a factory with a lot of people working at night, would he put a searchlight there? The answer was no, probably not. In fact, factories did not work at night because of the vulnerability of large numbers of people closely grouped together. But if factories could close down at night, boarding schools could not, Birley insisted. The point was finally taken and shortly afterwards the searchlight was moved.

As the war progressed, so the spirit of self-help flourished. The farming activities and the Home Guard were only two of a whole variety of National Service organisations of which probably the most exciting was 'Pioneering', the estate work carried out under the buccaneering leadership of Jasper Holmes, Housemaster of Verites. Huge trees were felled and logged up, tracks cut and maintained, pits dug and sheds erected in what Gerald Priestland later described as 'a Five Year Plan atmosphere'. In the anthology *The Charterhouse We Knew*, published in 1950, he recalled Pioneering as the most egalitarian of institutions, attracting 'the unorthodox, the rebel, the naïf communist, the misfit – in short, the controversial characters of the school'. Holmes was in fact the most radical reformer on the staff, with a touch of William Morris about his ideas on democracy and the value of practical skills. In his

House he conducted progressive experiments, such as having the boys elect their own monitors. Birley was not greatly interested in this brand of radicalism, and indeed appointed as Head of the School William Rees-Mogg who had been the ringleader in seeking to thwart Holmes's democratic initiatives and had therefore not been made Head Monitor of the House. It was not that Birley was against the participation of boys in school affairs. He saw it as important that the place should be a training ground for democracy, but he was not prepared to surrender to them the right to make decisions.

Birley's own radical inclinations showed themselves much more in his growing preoccupation with the problem of independent education as a whole. When in 1942 the President of the Board of Education set up a Committee under Lord Fleming to look into the relationship between the public schools and the general educational system, Birley was the nominee of the Headmasters' Conference. He demurred at first because of his lack of experience but the colleagues responsible for the nomination insisted, and so began his initiation into the world of national committees on education policy. There were two other headmasters and two headmistresses on the Committee, but Birley was in a key position as Head of a major boys' public school and it was he who emerged as the most forceful personality among them. A small drafting committee was set up under the chairmanship of A. W. Pickard-Cambridge, who had been a Balliol tutor when Birley was an undergraduate and had later become Vice-Chancellor of the University of Sheffield. Birley was a natural nominee for this committee, and when its report was published in 1944 he was credited with having written a good deal of it.

At the fringes at the very least, the report was pure Birley. One of the trades unionist members of the Committee had wanted to know the reason for the use of the term *public* school, that perennial source of puzzlement and irritation. Birley's response to this, as to most of the conundrums of English social life, was to plunge into the Middle Ages. And so in an HMSO publication dealing with the problem of associating the independent schools with the state system of education in the mid-twentieth century, one reads (albeit in an appendix) about King Canute. In the *Opus de Miraculis Sancti Ædmundi* it was recorded that he had been 'so pious, so charitable, and so great a lover of religion, that he established public schools in the cities and towns, appointing masters to them, and sending to them to be taught well-born boys of good promise and also the freed sons of slaves, meeting the expense from the royal purse'. This, the report noted, was the earliest recorded example of the use of the term public school and had been written about 1180, probably by Abbot Samson of Bury. There followed twenty-odd pages of erudition, tracing the use of the term through conflicting definitions up to the present day. The central point was of course that a public school was so called in order to distinguish it from a private school. In establishing this distinction which crystallised in the sixteenth century, the report quoted a letter from the Privy Council to Archbishop Grindal in 1580, declaring that increased corruption in religion 'proceedeth of lewd schoolmasters, that teach and instruct children as well publicly as privately in men's houses' and requiring all schoolmasters to be 'examined touching their religion' by the Bishop. It may be that some of those who chuckled at this missed the real mischievousness of the quotation by not realising that at this time 'lewd' simply meant not in holy orders. Further engaging quotations followed, which Birley, with the help of Bob Arrowsmith, had dug out to illustrate the pros and cons of a public and private education. From Fielding's *Joseph Andrews* came the passage in which one of the characters maintains that 'public schools are the nurseries of all vice and immorality', whereas from an essay by Oliver Goldsmith came the pronouncement that 'a boy will learn more true wisdom in a public school in a year, than by a private education in five'. And so the anthology continued with Boswell, Jane Austen, Coleridge, Steele, Gibbon, Sydney Smith, Dickens and Matthew Arnold among the authors upon whose wisdom and wit Birley drew for the benefit of this government report.

The main body of the report was also strong on background research, with two chapters which traced the history of the public schools accounting for about a third of the text. Again it was Birley who did the academic spade-work but the historical scholarship was not merely an adornment. Rather it grew out of the belief that the Committee's activity constituted 'a unique opportunity for incorporating the public schools with their distinctive characteristics into the general system and of helping to close in the world of schools a social breach that follows, if it does not actually cause, the more serious divisions in society at large'.

To make the most of this opportunity the Committee set out to examine the historical causes of the modern relationship between the independent and state systems. Their thesis was that the class distinctions with which the schools had become associated were only really firmly established from the eighteenth century onwards and that when they did become established they were not the fault of the public schools. Rather were the schools called into being to meet the demands of a society already deeply divided. However, once the division in education had been effected, it made the breaking down of class distinctions much more difficult. The point of seeing the problem in the full sweep of history lay in one fundamental conviction. This was that to find a workable association between the two sectors would be to pick up the threads of an older tradition than that of the class-conscious development of the eighteenth and nineteenth centuries, one in which the central and overriding principle had always been the gradual extension of opportunity.

To do this required some honest thinking about the orthodoxies which tended to set the public schools apart in the public mind. For this Birley again made a major contribution, which perhaps reflected his first-hand experience of Charterhouse. The house system and the loyalty it engendered was described as having 'led too often to a narrowing of outlook and interests, a further parochialism within the parochialism inevitable in any school, and more especially a boarding school'. Here a footnote referred to an early – and extreme – example at Harrow in 1757 when a pitched battle was fought between Hawkins's and Thackeray's houses. On the subject of games it was suggested that at many schools they occupied an undue place in the boys' interests, and 'elevated to a quite disproportionate degree of importance in their lives certain qualities, in themselves of great value, and it depressed the regard which should rightly be paid to the intellect, and to the talents of the boy who is artistic, musical or skilled with his hands'. But in the matter of both the house system and the games cult the report insisted that the orthodoxy was much less rigid than in the early years of the century.

The section dealing with the prefect system came closer to the fundamental social problem. 'It must be agreed', the report declared, 'that if this training was valuable, to confine it to those from a limited social class meant that it was missed by many boys who would have gained from receiving it. And, further, this restriction was to some degree positively harmful, as it upset the balance of educational experience which should be found in all classes of a democratic community'. This was one of two passages subsequently quoted in the House of Commons as having been written by Birley. The occasion was when the Chancellor of the Duchy of Lancaster, John Hynd, was called upon to defend his appointment of a public school headmaster to the post of Educational Adviser in Germany in 1947.

For all the critical tone of some passages in the Fleming Report the general tenor of the analysis was even-handed, praising the benefits of house loyalty, organised games and the prefect system, pointing out the advantages and disadvantages of day and boarding schools respectively, and recognising that there was no one type of school to meet every need. The aim therefore was to make the range of choice between day and boarding education a wider one, in the conviction 'that this most important of all educational choices ought not to depend, as it does now, on financial considerations and that the issue ought not to be confused by the social distinctions, real or imaginary, which divide the two types of schools.'

Birley himself became firmly committed to the Fleming proposals. From the schools' point of view he believed it to be important to come to terms with the state while they were in a strong enough position to safeguard what seemed to them the essential features of their independence. At this time the state was not particularly hostile, whereas in fugure generations it might be a different story. The other strand in his attitude was more idealistic. As he wrote in one of his end-of-term letters to the Carthusian Society, the problem should be looked at not merely from the point of view of the survival of the public schools but rather from the point of view of what they could contribute to the good of the nation. The onus was on them to take the initiative with what he called 'bold and sensible experiments'.

With the benefit of hindsight the Fleming Report appears naïve in its assumption that local authorities would be prepared to buy large numbers of places at expensive boarding schools. In fact Birley and his fellow committee members were well aware that the scheme would have much better prospects if it were financed centrally; apropos of this a Chief Education Officer had repeated to him the famous remark that people pay their taxes in sorrow and their rates in anger. But politically it was never a real possibility at a time when so much money was needed to build up the new state system established by the Butler Act of 1944. It is true that, as Minister of Education, Ellen Wilkinson was better disposed towards the proposals than the committee expected, and some local authorities did try to make a success of it. But in most cases the initial momentum petered out when other calls on expenditure proved more pressing. It was an enduring disappointment to Birley, who for long afterwards continued to advocate links between the public schools and the state system and to defend the direct grant scheme for free places at leading grammar schools.

The Fleming Committee came on top of the rather more than a hundred and one other things a headmaster had to think about or contend with in wartime. There were the increasing demands of liaison with the armed forces; the recruiting methods of the different services being somewhat competitive, it was important to help the boys who were leaving to make the right choice. There was the strain of keeping things going on the domestic side, living up to the Charterhouse grace which reads: 'Good Lord bless us, and these Thy good creatures, which Thy bounteous liberality has provided for us, and mercifully grant that we, by them being healthfully nourished, may be the better enabled to do all duty and service due unto Thy divine majesty'. Perhaps it was the shortage of domestic staff that prompted one waggish young Carthusian to venture that 'these Thy good creatures' were the insects that had not been removed from the salad. In the matter of food, various ways of making savings had to be organised. When oranges were provided at meals the boys were instructed to pass all the peel to the end of the table so that it could be saved for making marmalade. (On the great day when bananas reappeared after the war they dutifully passed the skins to the end of the table in the same way). Then there were the various kinds of invasion exercises, one of which took up an entire week-end. The account which Birley wrote of this for the Carthusian Society bears repetition:

> This entailed, for one thing, a whole night's duty for the Home Guard of the School, who incidentally did not have the satisfaction of resisting an attack next morning. Perhaps the sector of the line defended by Charterhouse was regarded as *ipso facto* too strong. During the afternoon some forty Carthusians were given the part of a body of famished refugees from Midhurst, flown with insolence and beer from The Squirrel Inn, which they were held to have looted. Their duty was to test the organisation of Wardens in the Borough, and to insist on being taken in at rest centres. In the words of the Chief Umpire, 'The refugees may be said to have gained a complete victory. They defeated the Wardens everywhere and in all cases reached their objective, namely, tea and buns.' The Charterhouse ARP services were subjected to an elaborate test, devised with great cunning by Mr Lovell. The most dramatic incident was the discovery of an unexploded bomb outside Crown (the tuckshop), necessitating its immediate evacuation at a moment when it was doing brisk business. The ARP services, especially the Charterhouse Fire Service, were warmly commended by the authorities. The exercise taught us some very useful lessons about the liaison with the Borough ARP, and the links are now being strengthened.

Towards the end of the war came the unpleasant novelty of 'flying bombs' or 'doodlebugs'. The school was fortunate in escaping being hit; as one Carthusian put it, they were troubled only by 'long hops very wide on the off'. But the noise was menacing and sometimes necessitated diving for cover. On one of these occasions a small boy emerging from shelter piped up for the benefit of Jasper Holmes, in the RAF slang of the time, 'Wizard doodle, sir!' The remark was relayed to Birley who enjoyed it hugely and remembered it many years later in the address which he wrote for Holmes's memorial service at Charterhouse.

The worst feature of the war by far was the periodic news of Old Carthusians killed in action. Birley used to read out the list in Chapel on Saturday mornings, and as the hostilities dragged on it became more common for it to include some that he had known personally. It was the poignancy of this that made the school seem to him and Elinor more than ever one family. This was certainly how they viewed Saunderites, and the peculiar conditions of war resulted in their taking under their wing various boys whose parents were in difficulties of one kind or another. A good example was the case of Otto Fisher, the son of an Austrian diamond merchant who had come to the school in January 1938. Very soon after this came the *Anschluss*. On the day that the news arrived Otto was in despair. He knew that his parents were going to be arrested. Birley realised that the British Consul-General (the Ambassador had been recalled some time earlier) was an Old Carthusian. He wrote immediately, saying that if he was really quick the authorities could probably be prevailed upon to let the Fishers go if he gave them a visa for England. The Consul-General was more than ready to help. Otto's father, who as a prominent figure in Vienna had been one of the first to be arrested, obtained a visa in 1938, and his wife was able to follow the next year. When Dunkirk came Mr Fisher resolved that the family should go to the United States. Otto refused to go with them; his loyalties lay entirely with Britain. It was up to Birley to mediate and he arranged for father and son to meet, the most convenient place being the platform of Woking station. There they walked up and down for half an hour, with Birley talking to one or the other separately on either side of the buffet. There was no breaking Otto's resolve, and in the end Birley told Mr Fisher that he had better give in. Otto was then more or less adopted by the Birleys for the remainder of his time at Charterhouse, going with them on summer holidays as one of the family.

A more unusual case still was that of Omar Pound, whose father Ezra was very rarely able to visit him at the school. The boy was so homesick that his Housemaster, Walter Sellar, scarcely knew what to do with him. The Birleys took him into their family for a time in order to ease him into school life. A later part of the story illustrates the sense of responsibility and solicitude that senior boys were capable of showing. It was a Sunday morning when it was reported in the newspapers that Ezra Pound was working for the Fascists. First to spot it was the Head Monitor of Daviesites, a boy called Lester. He immediately hid all the papers under his bed and told the rest of the House that they had not been delivered. 'Give me twenty-four hours', he said to Sellar – the time he thought he would need to ensure that when Omar did learn the news he would not be the object of hostility. The self-contained nature of boarding school life, together with some skilful prevarication, enabled Lester to be as good as his word. Incidents like this can only begin to convey the shock of learning of the death of such boys. Lieutenant Derek Lester of the Welsh Guards, was killed in August 1944, aged 20.

The peculiar atmosphere of wartime somehow quickened the pulse of Charterhouse. There was a heightening of the intensity with which any good housemaster becomes involved in the community he leads. Birley's interest in the boys was all-embracing. He was as proud of the glittering success of round pegs like P. B. H. May as he was concerned to accommodate the square ones.

When he came to Saunderites Peter May was twelve and by the following summer was thirteen. Birley noticed him in the nets on the first half-holiday and asked Bob Arrowsmith to come along and look at him. He mentioned that there was a rule in Saunderites according to which no boy could play in the House XI in his first year; this was because Birley wanted them to play with boys of their own age at this stage. 'I shouldn't worry about that,' said Arrowsmith, 'concentrate on keeping him out of the School Eleven!' The following year May played in all the First XI matches. Against Harrow, he faced Alastair McCorquodale, one of the fastest schoolboy bowlers ever known (and later an Olympic sprinter) and made 109 in 90 minutes. He was fourteen and a half. If anyone can be said to be responsible for either 'discovering' or fostering such a remarkable talent it was Bob Relf, who after leaving Charterhouse had spent a short time at Westminster before going on to the Junior School of Leighton Park, which was Peter May's prep school.

In a paper which Birley gave on Christian education at one of the Worth Conferences he recalled the case of a boy at the other end of the scale of adjustment to conventional public school life.

It was not long before the beginning of the Second World War, when I was Headmaster of Charterhouse, one of the senior boys in the school was reported to me for having cut the weekday morning service on three days running. I summoned him and said that, while, if he had missed one service I should just have assumed that he had been late, and I might have done the same if it had been two, I could not think this was the reason when it happened three times. 'No, Sir,' he replied, 'it was not that I was late. The point is that I have just become quite definitely a Communist. As a Communist I do not believe in Christianity and I feel, therefore, that it would be quite wrong for me to go to Chapel.' Now, I realised that I had about 30 seconds, at the most, to make up my mind if I thought he was pulling my leg or not. (I may say that one of the reasons why the life of a schoolmaster is such a pleasant one is that one does have every now and then very exciting decisions, such as this one, to make). I decided that he was not pulling my leg and I was quite right. 'Yes,' I said, 'I see that this is really quite an issue. We ought to spend a good deal of time discussing it. To give us time, I give you leave off Chapel for a month.'

Now, I make no claim to any credit for what happened. I understand that if a monkey is placed before a typewriter with all eternity to type in he is bound eventually to type out the complete works of Shakespeare. I was like that monkey. During that month I seemed to do very little else but discuss Christianity and Communism with this boy. And then one day I said to him, 'Supposing you and I were in Moscow together on May the First, do you think that Stalin would have the right to insist on our attending the May Day Parade in Red Square?' 'Certainly he would', he said. 'But why?' I asked. 'Because the Russians believe that in Communism are to be found the solutions of the problems of the world and the May Day Parade is an expression of that belief. So I think he could certainly insist on our attending it.' 'Well', I said, 'I am very sorry. But Charterhouse is a Christian school and that means it believes that in Christianity are to be found the solutions of the problems of the world and the Chapel service is an expression of that belief. So I think I have every right to insist on you attending it.' 'That's all right,' he said. 'That I can understand. That's the first reason for the Chapel services I have ever had which seems to me to make sense. All right, Sir, you won't have any more trouble with me. I shall go to the services.'

When he went out, I felt very elated. My elation lasted for not more than two minutes, for then it suddenly became apparent to me what a shocking thing I had said. 'Charterhouse is a Christian school and the Chapel Services are an expression of this.' What a monstrous claim to have made. What right had we to hold Chapel services if we were not a Christian school? And how very far we were from really being that.

Birley's involvement continued when the boy had left school and, on being called up, embarked on a running battle with the Durham Light Infantry. He managed to get himself court-martialled twice for mutiny, and it was only through his old Headmaster's intervention with the War Office that he was allowed to spend the rest of the war working on a farm.

Now and again there would be a boy with whom Birley could share the bibliophilia that had been stimulated by the Eton College Library. Though Charterhouse had nothing comparable, there was some scope to pursue this growing interest. The library of an eminent eighteenth century antiquary called Daniel Wray had been bequeathed to the governors of the school. A later generation of governors had decided that boys do not read old books and that most of them should therefore be sold. Some however had survived and were kept in the Daniel Wray Room, and Birley suspected that there were other uncatalogued books in a mysterious adjoining room where among other things the librarian J. L. Stokes kept his bicycle. This room was always locked and for a long time, try as he might, Birley could not cajole Stokes into parting with the key. Eventually he extracted a promise that he could have it one Field Day. Since William Rees-Mogg was a budding bibliophile, Birley arranged for him to miss the military exercises in order that they could explore the librarian's intriguing sanctum together. Stokes however managed to slip away without surrendering the key after all. With a delicious feeling of complicity Elinor managed, with Rees-Mogg's help, to get in through a skylight; there was another door which was bolted only on the inside, and Stokes's treasures were at their mercy. They were well rewarded by the discovery of one volume dated 1502, rarer than many incunabula, and another book with a class list inside it which included the name of John Wesley.

The community of boys was one thing, the community of masters another. So as far as the loss of staff went, Charterhouse came off better than it had done in the First World War, and better than many schools in the Second. There were a number of recently retired masters living nearby who made very reasonable replacements for the younger men who left. And there were of course figures of fun, who were not altogether capable of keeping track of what went on. At one point boys were reputedly inviting their friends to those classes where the fun was greatest, rather as one invites people to cocktail parties.

But a large proportion of the regular Charterhouse staff stayed at the school throughout the war. Birley's way of winning their loyalty was by the same industry and enthusiasm that he displayed in his history teaching. His scholarship earned their respect. Perhaps too it was scholarship that earned him the nickname 'Bags' among the boys, for the time that he devoted to reading showed unmistakeably under his eyes. On one occasion he had preached a sermon about what the old moralists had called *accidia*, that peculiar blend of bloodymindedness and boredom for which there is no word in English but which schoolmasters recognise as all too familiar in some of their more troublesome pupils. Jasper Holmes happened to remark after Chapel that it had been an interesting sermon, and a subject that he would like one day to learn more about. The following day he found awaiting him in Brooke Hall a handwritten dissertation following on from where the sermon had left off. Walter Sellar, another Housemaster, had the same experience. He had chanced to remark that he would like to get up to date with what was happening in the national education system, and Birley took him on a walk to explain. Sellar then went off to teach his afternoon classes. When he returned to his House, a long handwritten essay elaborating on their conversation was waiting in the letterbox.

Indeed Birley was an indefatigable writer of letters, not only to the parents of boys but to a whole host of acquaintances in the academic and clerical world. While staying with the Sellars one Christmas he was writing furiously at a desk, oblivious to the chatter going on around him, when he suddenly broke off and remarked: 'I do think this is one of the most delightful addresses I know – The Very Reverend the Dean of Durham, The Deanery, Durham.' It was a letter to Cyril Alington. During this same stay the Sellars' younger daughter, aged five, bumped into Birley on her way to the bathroom, stark naked, whereupon they had a long conversation. This was interrupted by Mrs Sellar who was afterwards rather embarrassed. Birley's reaction was to be 'so delighted to find that someone else's daughter behaves like mine do'.

Sellar was one of the masters with whom Birley had a special bond. When he came to Charterhouse he was just making a name for himself as the author, with Julian Yeatman, of *1066 And All That*. Sellar and Yeatman had been at Oriel College, Oxford together, and the idea of the book originated one evening after dinner at Marlborough College, where they had stayed en route for a walking tour of North Wales. The jokes over the port crystallised into the book during the time when Sellar was teaching at Canford and Yeatman was advertising manager of Kodak. It was a great stroke of luck for Charter-house that this celebrated humorist should be driven out of Canford by the controversial cleric, Percy Warrington, who was at that time at the peak of his career causing havoc in the schools that he and his evangelically-minded associates had acquired. Birley gave Sellar somewhat accelerated promotion to the housemastership of Daviesites, and it was a tribute to Sellar's talent and popularity that this caused no acrimony in Brooke Hall.

If one effect of the war was to draw the Charterhouse community closer together, the other was to slow down the pace of change. So much energy went into simply keeping the place going that there was not much to spare for thought of reforms – particularly since there were so many masters still

As Educational Adviser to the British Military Government, Birley with
a group of German colleagues; Adolf Grimme, Minister of Education for
Lower Saxony, is on his immediate left

T. S. Eliot lecturing in Germany in 1948. The formidable Frau Teusch,
Minister of Education for North Rhine-Westphalia, is on the extreme left

A day out from a Königswinter conference. Birley's passengers include Nigel Nicolson, Lady Violet Bonham-Carter and Jo Grimond

Elinor Birley with Gräfin Marion Dönhoff, Editor of *Die Zeit,* at a Königswinter conference

around whose loyalty was to the ethos of an earlier era, and there was no possibility of bringing in new blood. Perhaps the one thread that remained unbroken from the progressive start that Birley had made to his headmastership was his enduring concern to keep the school abreast of what was going on in the outside world. The steady succession of visitors continued throughout his time there. Nikolaus Pevsner came to speak on architecture long before his books made him famous. T. S. Eliot gave a talk when he came to visit his godson Omar Pound. One of the highlights, shortly after the debate on the Fleming Report, was the visit of a group of Labour MPs. They stayed for several days in the Houses, had meals with the boys and observed all the activities of the school. The *Daily Mail* reported that they were impressed by the 'fine community spirit' and that they did not find any class antagonism. Afterwards they got themselves into hot water with their colleagues in the Party by writing a letter to *The Times* saying that the public schools should not be abolished but made more widely accessible.

As the war neared its end Birley had become very interested in ideas of reconstruction. In the Long Quarter of 1943 a series of lecturers came to the school. Sir Fred Clarke of the London University Institute of Education spoke on educational reconstruction; J. L. Brierly, Professor of International Law at Oxford, on international organisation; W. G. Holford of University College London, planning consultant to the City of London, on town planning; Sir Giles Gilbert Scott, who had designed the school's War Memorial Chapel, dedicated in 1927, spoke on the Royal Academy Plan for London; and Harold Nicolson, who had been Parliamentary Secretary to the Ministry of Information from 1940 to 1941, on foreign affairs.

The interest in reconstruction tied in with some of Birley's other contacts. His Oxford pamphlet on Czechoslovakia had gone down well with the members of the Czech government in exile, especially the final paragraph which read:

On 15 March 1939 a free and independent State was destroyed. The conqueror held that its independence could only be ephemeral, that historically the State was destined to be subject to its stronger neighbour. This has demanded investigation, a study of the history and the culture of the

State subdued. But no Englishman can consider this question and weigh the claims of the Czechs to be a free people
without feeling that he is guilty of impertinence. One who
has heard the men and women of this race speak of their
national history, who can read of Charles IV and John Hus
and Palacky, who has stood in St Vitus' Cathedral by the
tomb of St Wenceslas, who has watched the flowing Vltava
and heard Smetana's Symphonic Poem to the river, where
the songs of the people mingle with the surge of the waters,
such a one *knows* that the Czechs are a nation and that their
greatness through ten centuries of history is their own.

As a result Birley had been able to meet Eduard Beneš and Jan
Masaryk from time to time in London. This ensured that after
the war he would be one of the first to pick up contacts again. In
1946 he was sent out by the British Council and visited schools
in Brno and Bratislava.

The most significant thing to happen for Birley personally
after the end of the war was the decision of the governors that he
should have a term off to recharge his batteries after the heavy
drain on his energies during the decade of his headmastership.
John Maud, the Permanent Secretary of the new Ministry of
Education, got to hear of this and asked him if he would spend a
month looking at education in Germany as a kind of *ad hoc* HM
Inspector. It was too tempting an opportunity to miss. When he
had finished his tour Birley wrote a report for the Ministry
which greatly impressed Maud. Thus when the time came later
for the Foreign Office to appoint an Educational Adviser to
General Sir Brian Robertson, the Deputy Military Governor,
Birley's was among the most obvious names to come up for
consideration. For someone who had been a civilian throughout
the war, the attractions of a post-war job in the field of
reconstruction were strong. Birley was offered the post and
asked Charterhouse to release him.

The governors may well have rued their decision to give
Birley a sabbatical term. They were additionally sorry to lose
him because the task of taking the school through the war had
fostered a particularly good rapport at governors' meetings.
Nothing interfered with the seriousness with which they put
their minds to the affairs of the school. In *A Charterhouse*

Miscellany, compiled by R. L. Arrowsmith and published in 1982, Birley recalled the scene at one of their wartime meetings:

> There was a meeting of the governing body, held at the London Charterhouse, just before Dunkirk. Before the meeting began, the Archbishop of Canterbury, who was Chairman, drew me aside. 'I have just been having lunch with Anthony Eden,' he said. 'You know the situation is desperately serious. It looks as though the British Army may well be surrounded. It will be like Sedan, only worse. Don't talk about it. We must get on with the business.' We then met for some two hours, discussing, I remember, among other things the water supply in Bodeites. Among those present at the meeting were some with very responsible positions. Seven years later I was talking to some young Germans in Hanover about English education and they wanted to know about the public schools. How are they organized? I explained to them the institution of governing bodies. How much are the members paid? 'They are not paid anything.' 'Why do they do it?' 'Often they were at the school themselves and want to help it; sometimes it is because they are very interested in education.' And then a young man said, 'Do you know what I was doing then? I was typing out the orders for Operation Sea Lion. Now I know why we hadn't a chance.'

During Birley's stewardship the governors of Charterhouse were remarkable above all for their farsightedness. The key man in this was Sir George Schuster, who had been Financial Secretary to the Sudan Government from 1922 to 1927 and Finance Minister in India from 1928 to 1934. At Birley's first governing body meeting Schuster took him aside. The school's finances, he said, were in a deplorable state, with the endowment money being wasted. He pointed out that there came a time with buildings when the cost of renovation became so prohibitive that it was better to scrap them and start again. 'That time is roughly a hundred years and will come in 1972.' This accurate prediction was the beginning, under Schuster's guidance, of a new financial policy. The endowment money was set aside to pay off the debts into which the school had run, a separate building fund was started and quickly grew by dint of skilful investment. In the later 1960s, when Oliver Van Oss was Headmaster, the wisdom of having acquired the Northbrook estate in Fletcher's time became apparent. The time for rebuilding had come, and it was possible to sell off the existing boarding houses, so that new ones could be built in which each boy could have his own room. This vast project, unparalleled in the public schools, became a lifelong interest of Birley's. As Chairman of the Building Committee which met regularly for five years, he was in his element at the occasional celebratory dinners when old sites were sold and new houses finished. He became Deputy Chairman (and, effectively, Chairman) of the governors in 1967, resigning in 1972 when his son-in-law Brian Rees became a candidate for the headmastership. But he could never bring himself to resign altogether and he remained on the governing body till his death. It was for him a great triumph when for the first time one of his ex-pupils, Roger Hunt, was elected a governor and it seemed perfectly natural to Birley that at the age of seventy-eight he should stay on for another year or two – just to help him get established.

This enduring loyalty is hardly surprising when one considers not only that a first headmastership is something very special but also that Charterhouse was the scene of Robert Birley's transition from a gifted teacher of history to a nationally known figure. For the appointment as Educational Adviser to Sir Brian Robertson did cause a mild stir. First of all Sir Waldron Smithers, Old Carthusian doyen of right-wing backbenchers, ensured that the announcement did not go unnoticed. He made it very plain to the House of Commons that in his view the one good thing about the choice of Birley for the post was that he would thereby cease to be the Headmaster of Charterhouse. Soon afterwards the whole business got another, longer airing in the House. Squadron-Leader Ernest Kinghorn, MP for Great Yarmouth, after declaring that no personal attack was intended, spoke at great length about the inappropriateness of Birley's qualifications for the job – as opposed to their appropriateness for other pinnacles of achievement such as Head Master of Eton or Harrow. The two points of substance were first that what was needed was someone with wide experience of the state system of education, which was more similar to what was being rebuilt in Germany, and secondly that the job 'was given out on an old school tie basis'.

The old school tie theme was taken up by John Corlett, Member for York. Both MPs had had their suspicions aroused by a profile in *The Observer* of 30 March 1947, the opening paragraph of which read:

> The Headmaster of Charterhouse will shortly leave his study with the great desk, the well-chosen prints and paintings, and the glass dome enclosing a landscape model with figure which, when tampered with, proves startlingly to be a Swiss musical box. Released as from the end of the present term, he will take up new quarters, for a period not yet determined, among the rubble mounds and calcined stumps of Berlin as Adviser on Education to Sir Brian Robertson, Deputy Military Governor of the British Zone, who is also an Old Carthusian.

In those days of the first post-war Labour government, when the privileges of a public school background were under fire as something to be lived down, the phrase 'who is also an Old Carthusian' was just too much.

In defence of the decision John Hynd avoided the old school tie accusation by making great play with Birley's associations with the criticisms of the public schools in the Fleming Report. To the charge that it was more appropriate to have someone from, say, His Majesty's Inspectorate he pointed out that, in addition to the incumbent Director of the Education Branch in Germany, a number of HMIs were already serving there on secondment. The appointment of Birley had much more to do with the handing over of responsibility for education to the governments of the individual *Länder*. To follow this new trend in British policy the man they were appointing was, he maintained, eminently well qualified.

If there had been any doubt about the daunting nature of the job that was now to be undertaken, it was dispelled in this parliamentary debate. If there was something for Robert Birley to live down, there was a good deal more for him to live up to.

CHAPTER EIGHT

Post-War Germany

Robert Birley's appointment as Adviser to the Deputy Military Governor signalled a turning point in the way the British approached the problems of post-war German education. Nearly two years had elapsed since the early chaotic months that followed the final surrender. At that time the importance of education had lain first and foremost in its value as a means of destroying National Socialism. The Potsdam Agreement of August 1945 summed up the general aim in its forthright declaration that 'German education shall be so controlled as completely to eliminate Nazi and militarist doctrines and to make possible the successful development of democratic ideas'. If it was not exactly clear what was meant by democratic, there was little doubt about what lay behind the rest of the wording. The elimination of Nazism meant a thorough purge of teachers and textbooks. Control meant giving the British officers complete authority over every sector of the education service. The point of departure was a profound distrust of everything German; the destination was the 're-education' of a nation.

On the ground it did not work out quite like that. The education officers found themselves every bit as preoccupied with devastation as with denazification. In the cities they were faced with unimaginable ruins out of which they had somehow to conjure up the wherewithal to provide enough makeshift accommodation and materials to enable the schools and universities to get going again. Policy guidelines were largely irrelevant; improvising on the spot was what mattered. Those recruited for this odd postscript to the colonial tradition had to be above all resilient. At his interview Geoffrey Bird, the officer sent out to take charge of the University of Göttingen, enquired what his job would entail. 'For Christ's sake, man, find out when you get there,' was the reply. What the education officers found out when they got there was that, by and large, any authoritarian preconceptions they may have entertained simply dissolved in a commitment of energy that soon made nonsense of non-fraternisation regulations. Alongside the Germans from the so-called White List – those 'whose character, professional standing, experience and political reliability render them especially suitable to be placed in positions of special responsibility' and who were appointed to leading posts – they had to roll up their sleeves and set about the very elementary and very daunting business of making basic material provision for the three million or so young people in the Zone.

By the time Birley came on the scene, first during his short visit in the autumn of 1946 and then as Educational Adviser from April 1947 onwards, the most exacting of the practical tasks had been carried out under Donald Riddy, the first Head of Education Branch. Having taught modern languages at Felsted and then gone on to be a member of His Majesty's Inspectorate, Riddy was an accomplished linguist and knew a great deal about German education. Many years later at a conference at St Edmund Hall, Oxford, Birley paid tribute to his achievement in the early days of the occupation. 'It was not a matter of my coming and finding the foundations of our educational work very well laid. What I did was to come and walk into a fully built house, and one very well built too and very well furnished.' Indeed Riddy had seen Education Branch through the whole period of its formal control over education in the British Zone. Towards the end of this time the atmosphere had begun to change. As denazification became less of a preoccupation, so the importance of the British control of education declined. The time was coming for the idea of re-educating a nation to be quietly abandoned, in the recognition that the Germans themselves should play a much bigger part in reconstruction than had been envisaged at the beginning of the occupation. Now it was no longer control that was appropriate but advice.

When Birley arrived in Berlin in April 1947, his first fortnight was a bewildering one. First he had to get his bearings in the amorphous organisation of the Internal Affairs and Communications Division from which Education Branch was now to be hived off. Next came ten equally busy days in England which included two meetings with Lord Pakenham, who had replaced John Hynd as Minister with special responsibility for Germany, and visits to Oxford and Cambridge with the purpose of arousing interest there in the problems of reconstruction. He had, too, a long talk with George Tomlinson who had succeeded Ellen Wilkinson as Minister of Education, but a meeting with the Foreign Secretary, Ernest Bevin, had to be put off. It was rapidly becoming clear that the job was bigger than Birley had bargained for, in view of the politically delicate nature of the problems.

Out of the early bewilderment a critical attitude soon began to emerge. The metaphor in his later public tribute to Riddy was well chosen, for what had been done up till then had more to do with bricks and mortar than with long-term policy. 'We are, I believe, setting about education in the wrong way,' he wrote to his father after the first month, 'trying to influence every branch of it, and so doing very little, instead of concentrating on the points where we really *can* make a difference. But all of this will take a great deal of working out.' The first part of the working out had to do with the staffing of Education Branch. Those at the top were not congenial to him. While he respected Riddy's encyclopædic knowledge of the German education system and his capacity for hard work, he considered him lacking in imagination, inclined towards bureaucracy and not good at encouraging initiative among his staff. Co-operation would not be easy. As it happened, the Ministry of Education wanted Riddy recalled to his inspectorial duties and his departure was arranged for the beginning of September. Replacing him was the first important appointment that Birley had to make in Germany and it had interesting implications.

The existing arrangement was that Riddy was the head of Education Branch in the Zone, while in Berlin where the four-power control called for a separate and independent organisation, the man in charge was Tom Creighton, who before the war had been doing research at Trinity College, Cambridge. Both spheres were to come under Birley. His first idea was to replace Riddy with the Berlin man, with whom he had immediately struck up an easy rapport. When the proposition was unofficially put to him, Creighton protested that he could not really think of himself as a good administrator. Birley's rejoinder was telling. 'I think that Education Branch could profit from some really bad administration,' he said, whereupon Creighton declared himself ready to take the job on if that was what his superior officer really wanted. It had however been a somewhat impetuous choice and Birley realised soon afterwards that it was wrong. He was honest enough to say so to Creighton, who was quite happy to remain as his deputy in Berlin.

Within the Zone the natural successor was Riddy's deputy, a sometime Home Office official whom Birley described as 'a nice chap, but without the least bit of drive or leadership'. He would probably have been prevailed upon to appoint this man if General Robertson had not insisted on his choosing the best of the contenders. This was Rex Hume who was at the time Regional Governmental Officer for Lower Saxony and could not be released to join Education Branch till January. The resentment that this delayed outside appointment caused did not make life easier. As Birley wrote to his father:

> The Deputy Director is very offended indeed at what he considers to be his supersession. What is more, a good many of the Headquarters staff support him. It is all most unfortunate. The personnel of the Headquarters are, on the whole, a second-rate lot of men and women, and if some of them were to resign I should not be sorry to see the last of them, though I should be hard put to it to find any successors. I don't suppose they will, though, when it comes to the point. I am afraid I shall have a very uncomfortable time until next January. After that I feel quite confident. This kind of thing is very unpleasant, and it is very wearisome, but it is what one must expect, I suppose.

The opportunity to reject the principle of Buggins's turn was welcome. But it was the first time in Birley's life that he had to face such an uncomfortable decision and such personal unpopularity. Charterhouse had not, any more than any headmastership, been altogether plain sailing, but there had never been any serious dissension in Brooke Hall. Throughout his time as Headmaster, Birley had been on the whole popular as well as respected among the staff. He was now facing the problems of a new kind of leadership, drawing on his reserves of patience and tolerance in order to disguise, if not overcome, a certain irritability and unwillingness to suffer fools.

Fortunately there was little time in which to dwell on the tension in those early months. There were meetings with Education Branch staff in all parts of the Zone as well as in Berlin; periodic trips back to England for consultations; surveys of repositories of the contents of museums and art galleries; formal occasions when exhibitions had to be opened and speeches made; broadcasts on British Forces Network; and dealings with the American, French and Soviet administrations. To facilitate all this activity there were travel arrangements so privileged as to be mildly embarrassing. Whenever Birley left his office he was driven in a magnificent Lagonda by a smartly turned out soldier called Maden, a fanatical supporter of Derby County, who had played for the Colts XI of the Club. This was the Derby County of Raich Carter and Billy Steel, for whom a record transfer fee had been paid. The one time when Birley's car was never available was Saturday afternoons. For then Maden was invariably to be found in the kitchen with the German staff, listening to football commentaries on the wireless. His other passion was the Lagonda. On one occasion they were called upon to drive to Holland and Birley suggested that Maden might enjoy getting out for this jaunt. 'Oh, I don't know about that, sir,' was the reply, 'but it's nice for the car.'

For journeys out of Berlin Birley always had priority for a place on an aeroplane. When he travelled by train in the Zone his 'equivalent rank' of Major-General entitled him to have a whole sleeping compartment to himself. What really mattered, however, was that he had direct access to General Robertson, the Deputy Military Governor, and Robertson for his part was glad to have an Adviser who was not paralysed by deference. It was an astonishingly high level for a total newcomer to the world of military administration to find himself in. But the fact that it had suddenly become part of his normal duties to be meeting Government Ministers, Bishops, Ambassadors and Chiefs of Staff – other than merely socially – bore its natural fruit in a rapid growth of authority and self-confidence. This made it easier to ride over the internal difficulties in Education Branch, as did, even more, the arrival of Elinor and the children to join him at the beginning of September.

This was an especially exciting moment for the two girls, as it was the first time that they had been out of England. By now Julia was already boarding at her mother's old school, St Leonard's, and although Rachael, at eleven, was a year below the normal age for being sent away, it proved possible to get her into the nearby Junior School for a couple of terms before she went on to join her sister. To begin with they all had holidays together in much the same way as they had done at Charterhouse. But as conditions became more difficult, straightforward family life had to go by the board. Elinor spent a good deal of time staying with her parents-in-law in Bournemouth and for some months, too, was able to take a flat in London which a cousin was vacating. The reason for the disruption was partly that it seemed unwise to have the family in Berlin once the blockade began, and partly that in any case Birley was simply enormously busy.

From the start there had been a very great number of people and places to get to know. It was the Adviser's responsibility to make formal visits to educational establishments all over the Zone and Birley soon came to realise just how formal such occasions could be. If he visited a university, for example, he was quite likely to find all the professors lined up outside, as though for military inspection. The officers of Education Branch were therefore generally primed beforehand to ensure that such visits would be as low-key as possible. But even if there was no parade outside there would generally be a line of faces peering out of every possible window of the building outside which he was to arrive. On one occasion when the grand visit was awaited at the University of Cologne, there was some uneasy surprise when the only vehicle to appear was a tiny Volkswagen Beetle. There was not even an accompanying motorcyclist. Never the most nimble of men, Birley had some difficulty in levering himself out of the back seat where he had been happily wedged, in conversation with another officer of Education Branch. The entire university watched in bemusement as first an arm appeared, then a leg, and then, after a pause to prepare for the fully glory of the anti-climax, the tall shambling figure of the 'equivalent' Major-General finally unwound itself from the minute car. It was pure accident that on that particular day the car pool at Düsseldorf had had no other vehicle available. But as an unpremeditated symbol of the resolve to rid the education system of militaristic attitudes it could hardly have been bettered.

As well as getting to know the Education Branch people Birley set about cultivating prominent Germans who had been opposed to the Hitler regime and who could be expected to play a leading part in any national revival. These were by no means confined to the world of education and politics. It was a great stroke of luck to receive a letter from Max Beerbohm telling him about a German lady he knew who was working as an interpreter in the British Zone. This was Elisabeth Jungmann who had been secretary to Gerhardt Hauptmann during his years as the grand old man of the German theatre and who had a vast range of acquaintances in the literary and artistic world. Birley sought her out and instructed her to travel all over Germany making contact with people of influence who tended to keep out of the public eye. She was never expected to write a report, but simply to come and see him from time to time and relate what she had been up to. She spoke both English and German, with cavalier disregard for precise translation. Once they were driving through the ruins of Pforzheim where the workforce had little in the way of equipment. 'What they really need here is some buggers,' declared the outraged Elisabeth. 'They haven't got a single bugger,' she went on, warming to her theme, and there was a good deal more talk of buggers, which seemed to her a reasonable translation of *Bagger*, the German for bulldozer. The efforts of Elisabeth Jungmann, who later became Max Beerbohm's second wife, were complemented by those of Guy Wint, a figure of bizarre brilliance who had been recommended to Birley on the strength of his success in political intelligence in India during the war. Like the future Lady Beerbohm, Wint was given no formal duties but was simply expected to bummel around Germany, indulging his uncanny knack of assessing political attitudes and advising on how to influence them.

These two imaginative appointments – which could hardly have been made by bureaucrats disposed to measure work in terms of office hours – had far-reaching consequences. Gradually Birley gained a feel for the new networks of influence that were being stitched together among prominent former opponents of the Nazis. His house became a centre for week-end gatherings of Germans from all spheres of public life. One of these discussions, which was to be on the refugee problem, had a particular long-term significance. Having been told by H. J. Walker, a prominent officer of Education Branch in North Rhine-Westphalia, of the activities of a certain Frau Milchsack, Birley invited her along. Granddaughter of the celebrated lexicographer Konrad Duden, she had married a successful Düsseldorf businessman and her introduction to Birley was the beginning of the friendship which later bore fruit in the foundation of the Anglo-German Association and the Königswinter Conferences. From 1950 onwards Lilo Milchsack directed and stage-managed this imaginative exercise in informal international diplomacy, cajoling leading figures in every walk of life in Britain and Germany to give up several days to hold joint discussions in the relaxed senior common room atmosphere that she was able to create. Birley himself seldom missed attending, usually as chairman, and the remarkable 'hostess on the Rhine' – Dame Lilo as she subsequently became – never ceased to acknowledge the debt that her particular brand of diplomacy owed to him. As she wrote to *The Times* apropos of his obituary, he was 'the midwife, godfather and guiding spirit of Königswinter'.

The business of reviving intellectual life in Germany was stimulated by a succession of prominent visitors from Britain. A. D. Lindsay and Richard Crossman had been the first two, and among those who followed them over the years were T. S. Eliot, Herbert Read, Harold Nicolson, Stephen Spender and Vera Brittain. During Birley's time as Adviser Berlin had the lion's share of these visits and life there reached a pitch of intensity. When, in the summer of 1948, the Russians severed all road and rail links with the Western Zones, it became imperative to convince the German intelligentsia that the Western Allies had no intention of abandoning their sectors of the city. The point was very firmly made in one of Ernest Bevin's Foreign Office telegrams and it was Birley's responsibility to do something about it. Some kind of cultural diplomacy was clearly called for. It was a moment created for the admirable Creighton who as an undergraduate at Cambridge had known 'Dadie' Rylands and Boris Ord, two luminaries of the cultural life of the University. Now he lost no time in making arrangements for Rylands to bring his Marlowe Society and Ord his Madrigal Society to perform in Berlin.

That was only the beginning. Guy Wint suggested broadening the enterprise into a full-scale Elizabethan festival and soon there were six people working flat out on the plans for an 'Elizabethan month'. Birley would return from his trips to the Zone to find his office commandeered by these enthusiasts who were always running out of space but never out of ideas. Not only did the two Societies give their performances but academics came to deliver all manner of lectures and a full-scale exhibition of Elizabethan life was mounted. The whole affair had a certain undergraduate intoxication about it. Birley himself had a ready-made personal contribution to make to these *Elizabethanische Festspiele*. This was the 'Shakespeare Gruppe' which he had formed to conduct play readings and debates in English at his house. These went on after the festival was over, too, and always had the highest priority in his engagement diary. With a soupçon of perverse showmanship he would say, 'I can't go to the Military Governor's for dinner tonight, it's my Shakespeare Gruppe.' One particularly gratifying feature of the meetings was that a number of people came over from the Russian sector to take part in them. It so happened that the last day of the blockade was one on which the group was due to meet. It was an obvious occasion for a party and Birley undertook to provide the food and drink. But that was not quite all that they wanted – they insisted on celebrating by reading *Hamlet*, without a single cut.

The propaganda value of the Elizabethan festival itself was prodigious. Nothing would have been better calculated to give the lie to any anxiety about Transport Command's ability to keep the air lift going than the notion that they could spare planes to bring in material for exhibitions and troupes of actors. Berlin was impressed. The choice of plays, too, made people sit up. *Measure for Measure* was not the most obvious Shakespeare to do, and *The White Devil*, Webster's portrayal of 'the famous Venetian Curtizan' whose scandalous licence was the talk of Rome at the end of the sixteenth century, was really rather too much for the more staid elements among British and Germans alike to swallow without protest. There was much disputation about what the play meant, and notices after the first night under headlines such as *Englische Neurose?* implied that only a sexually perverse nation would put on such a piece in such circumstances. What mattered above all else, however, was that the people of Berlin were left in no doubt about the determination of the British to stay. The policy of gaining their confidence was reinforced by one particular piece of luck. The performances of the Marlowe Society were to be announced on the *Litfasssäulen*, the advertisement pillars dotted about the city. Birley had not realised it, but these were controlled by a single company which had a monopoly. So the advertisement appeared all over the city including the Eastern sector. This made the Russians furious, driving them to retaliate with cultural events of their own.

The peculiar status and atmosphere of Berlin created awkward problems in the organisation of the schools. By virtue of having been the first to arrive in the city in 1945, the Russians had been able to steal a march on the Western Allies and ensure that the most influential posts in the education service were filled with communists or communist sympathisers. This radical disposition was confirmed in the elections to the legislative assembly and six months or so after Birley's arrival a law was passed which had three controversial features: the elimination of religious education; the abolition of private schools; and the introduction of a comprehensive system with no selection of any kind up to the age of fourteen, which for the majority of children was the school leaving age. Before all this could be implemented however the law had to be ratified by the occupying powers.

This was a ticklish problem for Birley. It was one of the fundamental principles of Education Branch that it should not become embroiled in German party politics. So although the British may not have liked the legislation, they acknowledged that it was the work of a democratically elected Assembly and did not feel that they could oppose the general way in which it was proposed to introduce comprehensive education. But for someone of Birley's background and convictions it was unthinkable to acquiesce in a ban on religious education or private schools. This, he maintained, was removing fundamental freedoms that transcended party political controversy. There ensued what he described as 'a most prolonged game of diplomatic chess'. Eventually, however, the Western arguments somehow carried the day, and the Russians who had been firmly supporting the law in its entirety gave way. A compromise was reached which safeguarded the right to religious and private education, and so in 1948 the Berlin School Law could finally be ratified.

The other major confrontation was over the university. The Russians had to all intents and purposes commandeered the Humboldt University by putting it under the administration of their Zone and not of Berlin. The British responded to this illegal act by keeping under their control the Technische Hochschule which was in their sector of the city, and by reconstituting it as the Technische Universität. Despite the discouraging attitude of the university authorities, Humboldt students came over to the Western sectors from time to time to attend cultural events. Some took part in the play readings of Birley's Shakespeare Gruppe. But as tension grew in 1948, things were becoming increasingly difficult for them and it was evident that the only answer was a new university. It so happened that on the eve of the blockade Birley and Creighton had dinner with the four leading city politicians to discuss its foundation. It was the evening of the announcement that the new West German currency was to be introduced in Berlin, and Birley suggested that they break off their discussions to listen to the broadcast about it. The Germans declined to do so, being much more concerned to talk over the foundation of what was to become the Free University of Berlin.

With this incident began the most fascinating episode of Birley's time in Germany. It was obvious that the city was going to be split. The educational administration was situated in the Eastern sector. At issue was whether the officials and inspectors would stay put, or move over to the West. The culmination was an astonishing confrontation. Birley's own subsequent account of it, in *The British in Germany*, published in 1978, ran as follows:

From that moment I had no doubt that we in West Berlin would win. It is not always appreciated that for five months after the blockade began Berlin still remained an administrative unit. Towards the end of November we became fully aware that the Russians would soon split the city. It was one evening at that time, just before six o'clock, that I was rung up at my office in the Fehrbelliner Platz by a lady, Frau Dr Panzer, who was responsible for the secondary schools of Berlin. She spoke from her department's headquarters which were in the Russian sector. 'Mr Birley,' she said, 'the most dreadful things have happened today. May I see you at once?' This was awkward as at half-past six I was due to read a paper at my house to a Berlin Literary Society on the third scene of the fourth act of *Othello*. However, I suggested that we should both go straight to my house, where we might have a few minutes together before the meeting began. Unfortunately she was delayed and arrived at the same time as my guests. I still feel appalled at the thought that she had to sit through my paper, the discussions which followed it and then wait until we had refreshments. It was nearly half-past nine before the last guest left and I was able to ask her what had happened.

A few days previously we had invited to Berlin Mr Lester Smith, one of the leading figures in English educational administration, to look at the schools and then give a talk on what to do with a new school law once there was one. All the officials in the education administration of the *Magistrat* and all the school inspectors had been summoned to listen to him. When he had finished he left to catch a plane at Gatow and then, immediately after, before the meeting broke up, in stalked the Russian Deputy-Military Commandant of Berlin, with a revolver in his holster, and addressed the meeting. His speech was very violent and full of threats. He said that the Russians knew quite well that money which should have been spent on education was being used instead for the so-called *Luftbrücke*, the new air station at Tegel and the *Sturmpolizei*. He added that the Russians knew quite well who were the supporters of educational reform and who were not and that the latter could expect no mercy.

She had taken shorthand notes of the speech and as she read them to me it became quite clear what it portended. The Russians had made this violent demonstration in order to frighten the educational administration to remain with them when the split we were all expecting took place. 'And then,' she concluded, 'came the most Nazi moment I have known since the end of the war.' I asked her what she meant. 'A complete silence.' The remark was significant. What happened after that I learnt later on from others who were present. The silence was broken by Frau Dr Panzer who got up and made a reply which from all acounts was a magnificent performance. She began by telling the Russian general that he had no right, even if he was a representative of an occupying power, to bring his revolver into an educational meeting. She went on to tell him that he was lying, that he knew that he was lying, and what she said was particularly insulting was that he knew that they knew that he was lying.

The effect of her speech was to ruin completely the effect of the general's intervention. A few minutes later he left the room leaving the arguments to be continued, rather miserably, by the Communist members of the administration. It did not last long. I have no doubt at all that the future of Berlin education depended on that moment when she broke the silence and answered. If she had not done so, I do not believe that most of the educational administration and the school inspectors would have come over to the West, when the split came three days later and with them 800 of the 1100 students and all but two of the professors and lecturers of the *Pädagogische Hochschule*, which, as it was attached to the Humboldt University, was under the control of the Russians.

My first action was to summon to my house members of the Education Branch in Berlin to inform them, as we had certain prepared steps to take immediately the split took place. It was not until after midnight that I was alone with her again and able to ask her the question I had been wanting to put to her ever since I had heard her story. 'Why did you do it?' The answer was immediate and may seem surprising. 'St George's in the East, Stepney.' She was referring to a secondary modern school in a very poor part of East London, a very remarkable school under a very remarkable headmaster. We had arranged for her to spend four weeks in England a few months before. She had visited this school and been deeply impressed by it. When she had returned to

Berlin, she said to me at once, 'If I could have in Berlin three schools like St George's in the East, Stepney, I could revolutionise the education of this city.' What it meant, of course, was that at that moment of crisis she felt that she could not cut herself off – not from anything so grandiloquent as Western Civilisation or the Free World – but from a particular school in London and the friends she had made there.

I have related this incident in some detail because it seems to me to sum up well our educational policy in Germany after the War. First, this lady had been chosen by us for an important educational post because we knew that she had shown herself staunch in resistance to the Nazis. She had been caught distributing underground Social Democrat leaflets and had been condemned to a concentration camp, from which she had escaped during an air raid. At the end of the War she was in the British Zone. She had become the personal friend of members of the British Education Branch in Berlin. We had been able to bring her in touch with British schools and teachers so that she really felt that she was a member of the same family. What we had never attempted to do was to 're-educate' her, to teach her democracy. That would have been an insult.

The episode was characteristic of Frau Dr Panzer, one of the most rumbustious – and hard-drinking – characters associated with Education Branch. After she had managed to escape from the concentration camp she had been tracked down by guard dogs unleashed in pursuit. The story went that she put her arms round the dogs and whispered, *'Bellt nicht, bellt nicht, seid lieb'* ('Don't bark, don't bark, good dogs'), whereupon they did indeed trot off without barking, so unused were they to this kind of treatment.

The story of Frau Dr Panzer was, too, a glowing illustration of how Birley wanted the work of Education Branch to be interpreted. At the heart of British policy was something which defies analysis in the conventional categories of educational history. Scholars subsequently engaged in research into this period and accustomed to thinking in terms of structures of education systems, have found it tiresomely evasive to be told that such structures were for the British education officers largely irrelevant. Their concern was overwhelmingly with individual pupils, individual teachers and individual schools, and only minimally with the formulation of policy statements about systems. This collective attitude was not by any means all Birley's doing, but he did set an example which impressed those who worked under him. On one occasion the Branch had with great difficulty secured Plön Castle for use as a boarding school for children orphaned by the war. To her distress, a few days before the school was to open, Edith Davies, the Education Officer in Kiel, learnt that a British Army unit was making preparations to move into the castle. Birley protested at once but to no avail, until he found an unexpected card up his sleeve:

> And then I made a discovery. As a young man the headmaster of the school had taught for a short time at an English public school called Tonbridge and the British Military Governor, Marshal of the Royal Air Force Sir Sholto Douglas, had been a boy there. So I wrote the Marshal a letter in which I stated once more all the arguments against the closing of the school and ended by saying that it was particularly unfortunate because the headmaster had been for a time a master at Tonbridge and he was proving successful in spreading the ideas he had learnt there throughout the schools of Schleswig-Holstein. (I may add that I told Herr Möhlmann of the Education Ministry in Kiel that he must support me in this.) The next thing that happened was that I was summoned to a meeting of the Chiefs of Staff at Hamburg. The Military Governor was not used, he said, to having his orders questioned after they had been issued. 'However, gentlemen,' he said, turning to his Chiefs of Staff, 'I have heard recently that this school is in the position to make a unique contribution to German education. I have decided, therefore, to change my mind. The Sappers will go to Flensburg.'

Incidents of this kind convey the flavour of Birley's leadership more vividly than any statement of policy about, for example, the age at which children should transfer from primary to secondary education.

It was not that Birley was oblivious to the political battles over issues of this kind. He had a certain historical feel for the various traditions of German education, in particular the religious ones. But he was bound to be somewhat at sea over the intricacies of the politics. Fortunately it was quite apparent that the variety of tradition simply made nonsense of any idea of imposing a uniform pattern of education on the schools of the Zone as a whole. There was for example the traditionalist view that in education the two most powerful bulwarks against a recrudescence of Nazism were Christianity and the classical tradition, and that this meant restoring to their former importance the denominational elementary schools and the classical grammar schools. In the Catholic Rhineland such a course was never in doubt. At the other end of the scale was the impulse to jettison tradition, do away with privilege and build up a secular comprehensive system. This was the road along which Schleswig-Holstein set out, and in Hamburg too there was a strong faction in favour of comprehensive schools. In Lower Saxony, the fourth *Land* under British jurisdiction, the situation was different again, for there the more balanced mixture of traditions called for some kind of compromise between the traditionalist and progressive extremes.

Faced with these contrary currents, and the many undercurrents that they concealed, it is hardly surprising that Birley and his colleagues kept out of the politics of educational reform. The elimination of Nazi elements was of course another matter. Much of the denazification of the teaching profession had, it is true, been accomplished before Birley's arrival. But this was the negative side of the extirpation of Nazi ideology; the positive side lay in giving help to those teachers who were restored to their posts, above all through the provision of appropriate textbooks. This was a task which appealed all the more to Birley for the fact that the most difficult problems were in the teaching of history. He took an intense interest in the work of Hedley and Kathleen Davis in the Textbook Section of Education Branch and in one especially remarkable group of German writers led by Professor Georg Eckert in Braunschweig. This group published, at their own expense, a series of small handbooks on German history. The first of them was printed on scrap paper discarded by the local newspaper. The reason why Birley supported this project so enthusiastically was that it was fully in line with his policy 'to do everything possible to give the German teachers responsibility and to avoid the temptation to tell them what to do and then expect them to do what they were told'.

This home truth was applicable in every sphere of educational activity in Germany. Some of the most striking examples were in youth work, where it was vital to fill the vacuum left by the Hitler Youth, and in adult education. Birley had a particularly soft spot for an extraordinary establishment called St Michael's House at Blankenese near Hamburg. A kind of informal centre, it had an obvious appeal to someone who never felt obliged to do things by the book. As he later wrote:

This had nothing to do with the Education Branch of the Control Commission, nor for that matter with the Control Commission itself. It was, in fact, wholly illegal. It was paid for out of occupation costs, although it did not fall into any category covered by the arrangements about them. At this place all rations between Germans and English were shared equally, which was also illegal. We were supposed to be neutral in religious matters; nothing less neutral than St Michael's House could be imagined, for it was a definitely Christian institution, run by an English priest (now a bishop of the Church of England) and a German Evangelical Church pastor. But let me make it clear that there was nothing emotional or 'pentecostal' about it. Those who went found they were taking part in really serious discussions on fundamental political questions. We invited all the young ex-Nazis, now free and, to use the common phrase, 'category six ex-Nazis,' that is, allowed only to do manual labour. A great many accepted the invitation and came and I have good reason to believe that many were deeply influenced by it. Of course, we could not talk about it. One day the Chief of Staff in Berlin asked me to come and see him. 'I say,' he said, 'can you tell me about a place called St Michael's House? I have just heard of it. It seems to me wholly illegal.' There was nothing for it and I told him all about it. Now, this Major-General was a devout Roman Catholic. After a moment's silence he said to me, 'Do you ever take any people from our side of the house?' 'Well,' I said, 'you don't make it very easy for us. But I can assure you that there is not a Catholic bishop in West Germany who, if he knows of some ex-*Gruppen-führer* who he thinks might benefit from a visit, will not send him to us.' 'Really,' he said, 'that's very interesting. All right, don't worry. You'll hear no more about it.' And it went on for another six months. Then in changed conditions it was clear that it could not be paid for out of occupation costs any longer and it had to be closed. But the young men who had been there, many of them ex-Nazis, got together and raised money which they sent to us and this kept it going for another month. No Old Boys ever paid their place of education such a tribute as these young ex-Nazis paid to St Michael's House.

This remarkable centre was only one of a number of places whose essential purpose was to enable the Germans to find their own way towards a democratic future.

The sphere of education which Birley found personally the most rewarding was probably the universities. For one thing he had more experience of them through having visited Robson-Scott in Berlin between the wars and given some lectures there on English education. For another, true to his Balliol back-ground, he believed that it was from the universities that the new generation of political leaders should be drawn. Demoral-ised and badly in need of reform though they were, their traditions made them potentially one of the most powerful forces for restoring self-respect to German life. They were a focus of ideological interest in British universities where there were a number of dons keen to investigate how it was that they had abdicated their responsibilities during the National Social-ist era, and what should now be done to put them on a more sound footing. This interest led to the appointment of a delegation of the Association of University Teachers which visited Germany in January 1947. For the German academics whom they met, it was the first major formal international contact after thirteen years of isolation. Its purpose was twofold, to give advice on reconstruction and to explore ways of resuming links between British and German universities.

The delegation's report was published a few weeks after Birley's arrival as Educational Adviser. It was perceptive and well-written, but without much appreciation of the delicacy of the practical business of guiding the German universities towards reform. It did, however, have two major constructive ideas and Birley lost little time in seizing on these as the basis of his policy. The first was for an international commission to be set up to look into the German education system, after the style of a Royal Commission in Britain.

The crucial point, Birley decided, was that the commission should be composed of Germans, with only token foreign representation. The second idea was to take positive steps to satisfy the 'burning desire for contact with Great Britain' which the AUT representatives had found in all the universities they had visited. The support and help of the British universities was clearly essential to finding good people to strengthen the staff of Education Branch and to building up a programme of exchanges.

Birley was soon able to get Bevin and Pakenham interested in these ideas and towards the end of November 1947 the three of them met a group of Vice-Chancellors at the building in Gordon Square now known as John Foster House. Professor Hughes Parry of London presided and the others were Dr Priestly of Birmingham, Dr Evans, Principal of Aberystwyth, Dr Stallybrass, Principal of Brasenose College, Oxford and Canon Raven, Master of Christ's College, Cambridge. Bevin spoke of the 'great missionary effort' which he was asking of the British universities, and Birley outlined the specific ways in which he wanted them to help. Apart from the 'missionary' side of things, it was an opportunity to explain his plans for the university commission. It was to consist of six Germans, one Englishman and one member of a neutral state, preferably Switzerland. The German *Land* governments were, he went on, delighted that his Branch was taking this initiative because they knew that they could not have done it themselves. It would be essential to find a really good man from the British universities.

No names were canvassed at the Gordon Square meeting, for Birley had already made up his mind to invite A. D. Lindsay to serve on the commission. The opportunity came when he visited Balliol two days later. He had been asked to dine with the Fellows, as a prospective candidate to succeed Lindsay who was shortly to retire from the Mastership. To add to this excitement, the following evening he dined with the Provost of Eton, his erstwhile mentor Henry Marten, who, it turned out, was very keen to have him as Head Master in succession to Claude Elliott. It seemed likely that either position was his for the taking and, once back in Berlin, he confided his thoughts on the matter to Tom Creighton. It was Eton that he really wanted. The main reason was his belief that, with a Conservative government likely to be returned at the next General Election and to have two terms of office, the Head Master of Eton would be well placed to influence national education policy for a decade. Birley's membership of the Fleming Committee, followed by his experience in dealing with Education Ministers in Germany, had led him to cast himself in the mould of liberal-minded adviser to a Tory administration. It was one of his more extravagant flights of fancy that the Head Master of Eton would be 'virtually the Conservative Minister of Education'. For the moment, however, the whole thing was shrouded in uncertainty. As he wrote to his father, 'it is a very confusing position to be in, but perhaps it is fortunate that I have been so busy that I have hardly had time to think about it'.

From then on there was even less time. There was all the work of getting the University Commission going. Characteristically, he adopted an informal approach, setting out, in the words of the celebrated aphorism, to know everybody rather than to know everything. And he was splendidly equipped for pursuing such a line. The house in the Grünewald was virtually a small *Schloss*, with servants galore. Although his own German was shaky, he had constantly at his elbow Berta Hochberger, who later became the wife of George Humphrey, Professor of Psychology at Oxford, and who as an interpreter had a sixth sense of what, in the interests of diplomacy, should be translated and what should not.

It would have been odd if Birley had not revelled in his seigneurial position. But it was not the luxury that constituted the attraction. Indeed this made Elinor in particular somewhat uncomfortable, and on those occasions when she accompanied her husband on tours in the Zone she was keenly aware of the privations of families struggling to educate children. In the course of a visit to the University of Münster Barbara

Perraudin, one of the Education Branch officers, spotted her discreetly handing over a parcel for the student welfare service which turned out to be one of her husband's few suits. The privileged grandeur of their position never ironed out their wrinkles of personal asceticism in the otherwise lustrously smooth life in the highest echelons of the Control Commission. They were oddly impervious to the delights of good food and wine. At the dinner to celebrate the conclusion of the work of the University Commission Birley was at the head of the table, with General Robertson on one side and Henry Everling on the other. When the wine was served Everling whispered to Berta Hochberger who was beside him that it was undrinkable. The crestfallen waiter said that whatever else they had was worse. Birley's reaction was to giggle in huge amusement; it was not remotely important to him.

It was the scope for exerting influence rather than the gentle living that intoxicated Birley, an influence very much in keeping with his schoolmasterly instincts. He loved creating an atmosphere in which problems could be seriously studied, and generally encouraging others to take the initiative in solving them. He enjoyed his dealings with the Education Ministers of the four *Länder* which together made up the British zone, and ensured a congenial atmosphere for their discussions by inviting them once a month to spend a couple of days at his house. The Minister with whom he had the most natural rapport was Adolf Grimme who was being particularly imaginative in reorganising the schools of Lower Saxony. Anything but a narrow party politician, he was sensitive, charming and lovable. So lovable in fact that when his own political frustrations were getting on top of him, he eloped with the wife of the Prime Minister. It was by virtue of Birley's tactful work behind the scenes that he was spirited away forthwith to a new career in broadcasting as Director of the Nordwestdeutscher Rundfunk.

Another of the Ministers, the redoubtable Christine Teusch of North Rhine-Westphalia, was one of Birley's greatest admirers. Frau Teusch had started her career as an elementary school teacher before turning to politics and entering the Weimar parliament at the age of thirty. She was a deeply devout Rhineland Catholic but very fair to the Protestants. She had a formidable intellect but could be extremely emotional with her friends. She fascinated Birley and her fellow Education Ministers. Part of the lighter side of discussions among the men at one of the week-end gatherings was speculation on whether she was the kind of woman who wore pyjamas or a nightdress. One evening after she had retired to bed, they drew lots to decide who should be deputed to find out. When the Minister who had drawn the short straw went to Frau Teusch's bedroom on a trumped-up pretext, she appeared in a dressing gown so voluminous as to conceal any trace of what she wore underneath.

During one of these memorable stays in Berlin it was discovered that all the guests would have to have an extra day there because there were no sleepers available on the overnight train. It was the day on which the English boarding school children were to go back for the beginning of term, and anyone British had priority over anyone German. No one minded, except Christine Teusch who insisted that she simply had to get back. Birley gallantly undertook to get a sleeper for her, only to be told that there were none available, even for anyone British – below the rank of Major-General. A sleeper was accordingly booked for Major-General Teusch. It was a story which spread like wildfire in the various Education Ministries, and which Frau Teusch did not easily live down. It reflected a certain bond between her and Birley. Asked in a radio interview whether it was difficult working under an occupying power, she replied that she could never have done her work without Mr Birley and Lord Pakenham. Many years later when the Queen and the Duke of Edinburgh visited Germany, Christine Teusch was one of those introduced to them. She took the Queen's hand in both of hers and talked with such animation that the officials had difficulty in moving Her Majesty on. When they did manage it, Frau Teusch started on the Duke in similar fashion. Afterwards she telephoned her friend Luise Bardenheuer, another prominent educationist, to say, '*Ich habe der Queen alles von Mr Birley erzählt!*' (I told the Queen all about Mr Birley!')

In the cordiality of Birley's relationship with so many of the Germans with whom he came into contact lies the key to his achievement as Educational Adviser. It was more than just

charm. He drove himself hard. At his house in Berlin he would
be up talking till late into the night with Ministers or officials
and then, when the others had gone to bed, he would be spotted
tiptoeing downstairs to get on with his work. He would never
have broken up the conversation to do so. He was always
approachable, bubbling with interest in everything that went
on, and no detail was too small for him to attend to it personally.
It was not efficient administration in the normal sense. Birley
had never been a very organised person and to some of those
who worked under him in Education Branch it appeared that he
simply did not have his feet on the ground. When he burnt the
midnight oil it was more likely than not that he was preparing a
paper for his Shakespeare Gruppe, or an address for one of the
many functions he was invited to attend. His skill as a speaker
was an invaluable asset in the public relations side of his work,
which always pushed routine administration into the background. He used his talents to bring about a simple but
profound change. Education Branch had begun by pouring
enormous energy into helping the Germans. Birley's shrewd-
ness lay in putting across the idea that it was not he who was
helping them but they who were helping him.

The idiosyncratic lead which Birley gave makes it difficult to
draw up a balance sheet in the normal categories of educational
politics. Ideas about school reform – largely for and against
early selection for grammar schools – gave rise to impassioned
controversy among German teachers and administrators.
Birley himself could never get very concerned about this. As he
said in an address at Chatham House shortly after his return to
England, 'I do not want it to be thought that I believe that the
reform of a school system necessarily changes the nature of the
schools, what is taught in them, and how it is taught. In fact, I
regard the very prevalent modern view, that such reforms,
especially when they are essentially social and not educational
in their intent, will of themselves alter or improve the nature of
a country's education, as a formidable modern heresy.'

As for the universities, the Commission completed its report
within just over six months of beginning work. At the heart of
its range of recommendations was the idea that the universities
should cease to be under the control of the Ministry of
Education but should be governed instead by a body represen-

tative of the community as a whole. The influence of Lindsay
was obvious in what was for Germany a revolutionary proposal.
But the report soon began to gather dust on Ministry shelves
and within twenty years or so was almost completely forgotten.
Soon after the riots that caused such havoc in the German
universities towards the end of the 1960s, Birley – to his wry
amusement – was asked by a prominent German educationist
whether he had heard of a report which had come out in 1949.
With a twinkle in his eye he said he had heard of it. 'If only we
had followed that report', was the response, 'we might have
saved ourselves many hectares of broken glass.' But if little
came of the recommendations of the Commission, a lot came of
the policy of building up links between Britain and Germany.
In 1949 a professor at Münster told Birley that a quarter of the
students there had been abroad since the war. By contrast he
himself had been one of the first party of German students to
visit England after the First World War, and that was in 1926,
eight years after it had ended.

Many tributes have been paid to Birley's work as Educational
Adviser. Even outside the field of education he gained a
reputation for resourcefulness in guaranteeing the restoration
of important buildings like the Marienkirche in Lübeck or
Schloss Brühl near Bonn. It would be only too easy to
exaggerate what he did for Germany. It would be less easy to
exaggerate what Germany did for him. His time there was a
unique opportunity for a headmaster to find himself at the
centre of the national stage, a unique opportunity to prepare
himself for a prominent position in British public life. What
that position was to be was already settled by the end of 1948.
The Fellows of Balliol had still not made up their minds on the
Mastership, and in fact Birley had become marginally the least
likely of the three candidates. It was just as well therefore that
he preferred Eton. On 18 December his appointment as Head
Master was announced in *The Times*. He had achieved what he
most wanted. The German friends with whom he had worked
were delighted for him. But when one of them was heard to say
that he was going to be headmaster of a grammar school, Frau
Teusch would have none of it. She declared stoutly that Mr
Birley was going to be Head of the University of Eton.

CHAPTER NINE

Head Master and Bibliophile

The headmastership of Eton is the highest peak of school teaching. Or rather of public school teaching. When the day comes for the position to be filled by someone from a State school, it will be like Reinhold Messner reaching the summit of Everest without oxygen. Robert Birley's own equipment for the ascent had been good. Apart from his impeccable academic credentials, his eight years on the staff in the inter-war period had been successful and happy, and had marked him out as a future headmaster of distinction; furthermore, to have been considered already during that time as a candidate to succeed Alington was really quite remarkable. It was a natural progression to have now reached the point of taking charge of a school whose idiosyncrasies he knew so well and of which he was so fond.

This familiarity was not in itself a recipe for success. For a headmaster to know and understand the various groups that have a finger in the school pie is no guarantee of ability to harmonise and advance their interests. Leadership is another quality altogether and there can be few places where it presents such a challenge as at Eton. For one thing, there is no other school in which the headmaster has his Chairman of Governors, the Provost, as his next-door neighbour. Furthermore, the Fellows over whose meetings the Provost presides are men of daunting distinction. Other forces are daunting too. As well as being the most illustrious, Eton is the largest of the leading public schools. Nowhere else is there quite such a formidable body of parents keeping a watchful eye on how the headmaster is directing the education of their sons, nor quite such a large number of influential Old Boys, running as it does into many thousands. Within the school itself there is the job of handling a staff of over a hundred, including twenty-five housemasters enjoying substantial independence, not to mention some 1200 boys drawn from among the most sophisticated and independent-minded families in the country. What is more, to preside over this most obvious symbol of privilege in education is to be in the public eye more than any fellow headmaster. Journalists of the popular press scan the pages of the *Eton College Chronicle* regularly in their search for exciting copy. The headmaster has a public relations job of great delicacy.

In the nineteenth century it had been commonplace for a retiring Head Master of Eton to be made Provost. In the present century the practice was abandoned. The nearest thing to a reversion to the tradition was the appointment to the post of Henry Marten who had taught for many years at the school and been Lower Master under Alington. As Provost, Marten was the prime mover behind the selection of Birley as Head Master in the autumn of 1948. However, he did not live to see his protégé take up the position in the following year, so that, as well as a new Head Master, a new Provost was needed. Thereupon the Fellows reverted to the nineteenth-century practice by appointing Claude Elliott, who had stayed on as Head beyond his normal term until Birley was free to leave his post as Educational Adviser in Germany. The potential disadvantages of such an arrangement are obvious – few head-masters are likely to relish having a predecessor constantly in the background. But experience had shown that it was just as possible for a Provost who had not been Head Master to interfere in the day-to-day running of the school. Other considerations were more important.

Claude Elliott had come to the headmastership from Jesus College, Cambridge. At the time it was a puzzling appointment for the whole of his teaching life had been spent in the University and he did not have much interest in wider educational matters. Dryly humorous, with a good measure of cynicism in his make-up, he was not the man to pioneer exciting new ideas. It is unlikely that in normal circumstances he would have been judged a successful headmaster. But at the time of his appointment circumstances were far from normal. The school's finances were in disarray, and as the shadow of war deepened, the prospects for setting things to rights were far from buoyant. As the situation became more difficult, so Elliott's stature increased. It did not matter that he made no fist of teaching boys and that, after acquiring a reputation for giving lessons of monumental dullness, he was not averse to giving it up. When the time came to make the really important decisions, he did so in an imperturbable way that commanded increasing respect. And they were generally right. His judgment showed itself above all in his refusal to have the school evacuated. The pressure to do so had been strong, not least from the Provost, Lord Quickswood, whose view of the matter arose out of a curious conscientious objection to air raid shelters. But, with the invaluable support of Lord Halifax, Elliott had stood his ground. His most convincing argument was that Windsor and Eton were not an evacuation area and that it would be ill-judged for a privileged community like the College to be seen to be scuttling to safety. To his lasting dismay there was one master who sent his children abroad. But with this exception Elliott brought the Eton community through the adversity of the war years intact, earning widespread admiration for his resolution.

Towards the end of his headmastership Elliott had set about the very considerable task of rebuilding the school's finances. When he took advice about this it emerged that the management of the properties which the College owned in North London was in a woeful condition. The need for renovation of buildings and negotiation of new leases were pressing and at Elliott's instigation a complete review was put in hand. The other idea which emerged from his consultations was the Eton College Appeal. It was quite evident to the Fellows that Elliott was the man to see these financial undertakings through and that as Provost he would be in an ideal position to do so. He did indeed prove to be admirably suited both to the management of the properties and to the business of guiding the efforts of the Old Etonians who undertook the bulk of the fund-raising. In his second year as Provost the project took off. Within six months they were a third of the way to their target, six years later nearly half a million pounds had been subscribed. From then on the Appeal became a continuing fund to which successive generations of Etonians were asked to contribute.

With Elliott – one of nature's bursars – thus occupied in the affairs to which he was temperamentally so suited, there was little serious danger that he would inhibit the work of a successor who was of such a very different stamp. Perhaps indeed the most important thing of all was this difference. The new inspiration that Birley brought to the position lay above all in the extraordinary combination of scholarship and teaching which he had developed during his early years at Eton and his headmastership of Charterhouse. To some degree the originality lay in being able to make such a contribution possible at all. In Germany he had seen the principles of military administration in operation and he resolved to adapt them to Eton in, so to speak, a staff officer approach. The technique was to delegate the background work on a problem to one of the masters – who was then expected to prepare a short paper setting out the pros and cons of the possible solutions. This was supposed to enable the matter to be resolved after twenty minutes or so of discussion. Business was to be conducted briskly and without fuss.

In practice things were rather different. No one who worked with Birley is likely to remember him as conducting business briskly and without fuss. However straightforward the matter to be settled, he could fly off into ever more convoluted illustrations and analogies. The saving grace of this way of complicating the business in hand was that it was generally very amusing and instructive. Birley displayed the same astonishing intellectual energy as at Charterhouse. If one of the housemasters sent him a note asking for a ruling on a routine matter, he was likely to receive in reply eight, ten, twelve pages of closely packed handwritten argument which had strayed off the point and more often than not failed to answer it. But despite the immediate frustrations it caused, the enduring impression of this uncontrollable enthusiasm was its engaging charm. However odd it was as a way of doing so, it established as good a rapport with the housemasters as most headmasters ever manage. Few were entrenched diehards of the kind that he was wont to dub barons and for the most part they were only too ready to co-operate with him.

Somehow, with the help – or toleration – of his housemasters Birley managed to keep routine administrative pressures sufficiently at bay to be able to put teaching in the very forefront among his priorities. To have become, like Claude Elliott, totally immersed in organisation would have been unthinkable. Indeed 'Birley's Law' stated that the larger the school to be administered, the *more* the headmaster should teach. Otherwise he would only get to know those at the top of the school and the criminal classes. In fact he managed to teach about ten hours a week. He taught history, not only to the historians as he had done during his earlier time at Eton, but also to a heterogeneous non-historian groups known as CLMS (Classics, Languages, Maths and Science). This was important to him for he regarded history as an indispensable element in every Etonian's education; and to ensure that what he did was taken seriously, he would sometimes set an examination on it at the end of the half. His lessons went off at all sorts of tangents, like demonstrating for the particular benefit of the scientists how to do mathematical sums in Roman numerals – including long division. One subject that went down especially well with this group was Byzantine history, with Birley revelling in his explanations of the bureaucracy of those times.

The other subject which he taught was Divinity, in celebrated mass lessons conducted in School Hall. In the first half he took Genesis; the second he devoted exclusively to the twenty-four hours of the Passion; and in the third he gave an *explication de texte* of the hymns and psalms which would be coming up in Chapel in the following week. To make the task even more demanding he sometimes set an examination which entailed looking over some hundred scripts. The purpose of this was not solely to ensure that Divinity was taken seriously, it was also an unobtrusive way of keeping a headmasterly eye on the quality of the English in the school. But it was above all an opportunity to make the boys think about moral issues, in a way which was very much in line with modern thinking about a moral education based on consideration of other people's interests. The Divinity classes were occasions which stretched to the limit his ability to hold the attention of an audience, and there were a good many toffee papers on the floor at the end. 'Feeding the five thousand, I call it', was how it was once summed up by the custodian who had to sweep them up afterwards.

The pace that Birley set himself told in a lack of personal organisation which endeared him to his pupils in one particular respect. There was a convention at Eton known as a 'run', rather similar to the *akademisches Viertel* ('academic quarter') in German universities. If a master was late for a class, the boys were expected to wait for fifteen minutes; once that time had elapsed they were at liberty to return to their Houses. Birley was mostly late, by either fourteen or sixteen minutes. Consequently, in the hope that it would be sixteen rather than fourteen, his pupils were generally speaking poised to dash off in their various directions. It was characteristic of his unwillingness to let formal organisation interfere with the interesting things in life. When he was late, it was more than probably because he had stumbled on some interesting idea and had been looking up the background to it.

The other, and more important, side of this coin was that his teaching continued to be invariably fresh, repeatedly enlivened by some new book he had been reading. He could come into some early morning lessons looking like death, and his more perceptive pupils would know that he had spent most of the night engaged in his secret vice, the study of ancient books in the College library. This pursuit of knowledge, now if anything even more voracious than at Charterhouse, gave to the school an intellectual weight that is more commonly associated with a university. Frau Teusch had not been so far off the mark after all. It was not the scholarship in itself that was the most important thing. Some of what Birley published in these years contained mistakes which would have embarrassed a university historian. Rather, what was important was the way in which this scarcely exhaustible appetite for learning carried over into his teaching. His supreme gift was not as an original researcher but as a teacher, with an extraordinary capacity to make knowledge positively exciting. After he had been in a classroom one could follow, via the mine of antiquarian information on the blackboard, the course that this excitement had taken.

Birley set out to make the thrill of learning the cornerstone on which the academic work of Eton was supported. He created an aura in which respect for scholarship took precedence over respect for persons. The smallest boy was every bit as important as the most senior master, indeed a good deal more so if he had scholarly leanings. Birley would show a fifteen-year-old round College Library with the same seriousness of purpose that was appropriate for a visiting headmaster or university professor. The difference lay in the reactions of his guest. Tom

Howarth recalled staying with the Birleys when he was temporary Head of Winchester in the interregnum before the arrival of Desmond Lee. The occasion was the Eton-Winchester cricket match, and when rain stopped play they had to find some other way of passing the day. Birley of course suggested a look at the library and proceeded to expose his visitor to a dazzling display of erudition. Howarth, himself no mean scholar, was by the end, as he said, quite deflated at having been intellectually upstaged in this way.

Birley did indeed enjoy showing off but there was one occasion when the boot was on the other foot. Elinor had a brother Philip who was a highly successful London solicitor. On one of his brother-in-law's visits to Eton Birley proudly showed him the Gutenberg Bible, of which there are less than fifty in existence. Philip was able to remark with the air of an experienced book collector, 'Oh! I've got one of those!' His host did not know that in fact he was not a real book collector at all. He had simply bought a part share in a Gutenberg Bible as a financial speculation. So it was Birley's turn to be put out of countenance. But it was rare indeed for one of the Head Master's aces to be trumped or appear to be trumped in this way. Most of his contemporaries shared something of the feelings of Tom Howarth on the day of the cricket match.

For a young pupil, on the other hand, with no pretensions to competition, but, rather, an awesome astonishment at being taken so seriously by an otherwise olympian figure, the sensation was quite different. The real point was that Birley's antiquarianism was quite inextricably bound up with teaching. The one derived its raison d'être from the other and Eton provided an unrivalled opportunity for the two to proceed in tandem. Yet the gift for teaching was not dependent for its flowering on the favourable cultivated atmosphere of Charterhouse or Eton. Birley's headmastership of England's most famous school provided him with opportunities to visit and teach an occasional class in other less famous ones. At Highbury Grove, the comprehensive school in North London brought into the public eye by its ebullient headmaster Rhodes Boyson, he was one of only two visitors that Boyson could recall having the instinctive capacity to command instant and total attentiveness once he had taken charge of a class. It may be glib to talk of teachers being born, not made, but flair of this kind is the most precious of all qualities in the instructing and influencing of young people.

Perhaps the most impressive thing of all was that teaching from his position as Head Master was not, as one might have expected, some kind of distillation of the work he had done before, but a succession of new discoveries fed by his consuming love of College Library. The library was the very model of a retreat for the eighteenth century gentleman with ample leisure and bookish inclinations. But for Birley it was not merely a private indulgence of this kind; as the years went by he managed to make it more and more accessible to bibliophiles both inside and outside the confines of the school. In May 1954 he arranged an exhibition of printed books and manuscripts on the occasion of the visit of the Bibliographical Society to Eton. One of the high points of the visit was the paper he read in Election Hall on the history of the library. It was a connoisseur's address packed with the detail that excites the bibliophile, and relieved here and there by occasional twinkling comments that conveyed the gentle amusement which he derived from his researches. His favourite character among his predecessors as Head Master of Eton was William Horman, a notable benefactor of the library who died in 1535 reputedly aged nearly 100 and whose *Vulgaria Puerorum*, as Birley explained, 'must be one of the most charming textbooks ever written and is an important landmark in the humanist revolution in English education'. The fact that four of Horman's books were in their original form was a convenient pretext for a preliminary digression on the ornamentation of stamped bindings, culminating in the information that Horman, himself a book binder, left his binding tools in his will to the College Butler. 'I give this piece of information without comment, but it seems to me to give rise to some interesting speculations.'

In the address there followed other idiosyncratic facts that had come to light in Birley's perusal of the audit books. During an unhappy period in the history of the library

it is rather mysterious to find that a good deal of unspecified work was carried out in the Library in July 1552, and that a workman, Trodd, was paid 'for ii dayes workynge and a half

abowte the Cariage of Rubbish out of the liberarye'.
Although eleven days' work 'careying rubbyshe out of the
Churche' in the previous year may well have referred to the
clearing away of altars and ecclesiastical ornaments, I cannot
believe that Trodd, however methodical a worker, could
have taken two and half days removing superstitious books
from a Library that cannot then have held as many as a
thousand books. It almost looks as though the Library was
moved again three years after it was turned out of Election
Hall, but probably there had been some delay in fitting up its
new home.

Another reference was to a moment of intense activity when

in the summer of 1561 we read that the wives of two of the
College workmen, Mrs Spens and Mrs Bolton, were paid a
shilling 'for maikynge clene and swepinge ye Librarie, 20*d*.
was spent on 'ryvetynge the cheynes in ye Librarie', and 10*d*.
on 'iii dozen of Chaines', while 7*s*.4*d*. was paid to 'Shepherd
the Carpenter and his fellows for takinge downe desks and
settynge up ye same in the Lieberarie for 4 daies at XI^d a peece
a day'. There even seems to have been some attempt to
restock it. In the British Museum is a fifteenth-century
manuscript of the *Opus imperfectum super Matthæum* and
other works of Chrysostom with the inscription, 'Thomas
Valentius Etonensi collegio dedit biblothece restituende
ergo, 20 Augusti, 1561'. Thomas Valence was Headmaster
from 1555 to 1561.

Anyone with a knowledge of schools can guess what was
the cause of all this activity. There was going to be an
inspection. And, in fact, on 9 September of the same year,
1561, a long postponed Visitation of the College took place,
conducted by Archbishop Parker – hence, no doubt, the
concern for the Library – assisted by Robert Horne, Bishop
of Winchester, and Sir Anthony Cook.

One of the most interesting puzzles in all of this was the losses
which the library had sustained, summed up by a sad comment
written in one of the margins in a seventeenth-century hand:
'Ubi sunt?' Birley had established that these losses owed
nothing to any desire to have a purge of popish books but that
the books had rather disappeared because they had been

superseded and were no longer wanted. Or 'from what might be called natural causes', demonstrating that the problems of librarians are as old as libraries themselves:

> For, whatever else may be said about the Library during this gloomy period, the books were read – or at least were taken out. (As so often, the practice of chaining the books seems to have been a very futile protection.) For this there is singular evidence in a list entered in the audit book, headed, 'Certayne Bookes of the Colledge found in Mr Belfeldes Chambre after his death and delyverd to Mr Smith and Mr Kyston Bowrsers by Mr Hargate the VIIIth of December A° D¹ 1558 as followeth'.
>
> It was a notable haul. The list begins with 'Opera Chrisostomi in 5 volu [minibus]', in all probability from Longland's bequest, and contains no less than twenty-two more books. John Belfelde had been at Eton and King's and a Fellow of Eton since 1536. Anthony Allen, in his manuscript Catalogue of the Provosts, Fellows, and Scholars of King's College, written about 1750, spoke of him in enthusiastic terms. 'Went from College when Fellow and was after chosen Fellow of Eton College from whence (indeed it is a most desirable Retirement) he would not be prevailed to remove for any much better Preferment. . . . How amiable appears this Character! in what a beautiful light is this rare self-denying Divine placed to our View! Can we forbear envying him, who it seems envied no man.'
>
> Be that as it may, and assuming that Mr Belfelde was just a careless borrower who forgot to return the books which he had never entered, I am glad that Mr Hargate retrieved the books. For they included some very interesting volumes, among them four of Horman's and three of Lupton's.

Some of the investigations had a flavour of detective work. The audit book for 1596–7 had this startling entry, 'Item to Plumer ridding the haye out of the liberarie ii dayes *XVId*'. Birley's theory ran as follows:

> It has always been inferred from this that the Library in use since the middle of the century had come to be used also as a store-room for hay. I am extremely sceptical. The amount of

hay which it would take a workman two days to remove would surely have filled the room to the ceiling. The Fellows of the time may have neglected the Library, but I do not believe that they would have allowed the books to disappear from view altogether. After all, the Provost, William Day, though the *Dictionary of National Biography* says that his 'contributions to learning were of the scantiest', was spoken of in his own day as 'noted for learning and piety', while among the Fellows were John Chamber, to whose remarkable manuscript work on astrology I shall refer later, Adam Robyns, who in a few years' time was to make a notable gift of books to the Library, and William Whitaker, the Calvinist Regius Professor of Divinity at Cambridge and undoubtedly one of the most learned Englishmen of the time, whom Bellarmine, of all people, admired so much that he kept his portrait in his study. In 1594 Whitaker had presented to the Library a copy of his *Adversus Thomæ Stapletoni Anglopapistæ Defensionem*.[1] I cannot believe that he did so knowing that it would be buried in hay.

It is surely clear that the Library was moved again. This time we can tell where it was, for in the audit book for 1678–9, three years after it had been moved once more, we find the entry, 'More allowed Mr Roderick [Lower Master] for the furnishing of the Chamber in the Old Library under ye Long Chamber'. Savile's Library must have been where the Master in College's Pupil Room is now, on the north side of School Yard. No doubt the room had previously been used for storing hay, and, by the time the audit book was made up, had become the Library.

The interest in binding was heightened by the fact that in the early seventeenth century there was a well-established practitioner of the art at Eton. An item under the heading of 'Reparaciones' in 1599–1600 refers to one of the College workmen, called Skydmore, being paid *XIId* for one day 'about the bookbinder's work'; thereafter there were frequent references in the audit books to the 'Boke bynder', leading to the assumption that it was Skydmore's job to get the workshop ready. One of the decorations used in the bindings had two heads in medallions, inscribed HERCVLIS and VELIA. This was copied from a roll which is quite a common one, 'but the engraver altered the name of the goddess, presumably feeling that a feminine ending was more suitable for her'. 'It is pleasant to think', commented Birley, 'that the Fellows allowed their manuscripts and oldest printed books to be decorated with a roll which perpetuated so magnificent a howler'.

The first bookbinder to be named was Goodman Williamson whom Birley described as 'the constant companion of my odd moments for the last two years' and 'a very real figure to me'. Williamson was brought to life for the purpose of the paper by a letter written by Sir Dudley Carleton, son-in-law of the Provost, from Eton on 15 December 1608 to a friend in London who had consulted him about the binding of a Bible:

> I doe understand that the goode workemen in Fetter Lane are some of the godly brethren, and that theyr exterordinary skill they learnt at Geneva, by which they presume in Bibles that are putt to them to leave out the Aprocripha. We have here a goode workeman, but he hath commonly his hands full of worke, and his head full of drinck, yet I had as leve venture my worke with this goode fellow that is sometime sober, as with them that are allwayes mad.

As Birley's account of the history of the library continues, so the interesting vignettes follow one another. There is a tantalisingly incomplete entry about 'the books of the Marchioness of Newcastle', better known as 'Mad Madge' or the Duchess of Newcastle, poetess, dramatist and biographer. There is the visit of the great Uffenbach in 1710. 'Unfortunately,' writes Birley, 'he visited only the School Library, which then had about fifty books, and he left under the impression that the School was called Cato's College. I have my suspicions about the age of his guide.' And there is Rowland, the Surveyor of Windsor Castle, who in the 1720s put up the present library building for which the College had received donations from thirteen subscribers, including six Fellows and the Lower Master, 'but not, I regret to say, the Head Master.' Birley described Rowland's building thus:

> Rowland's Library, seen from the Cloister outside, is a dignified but not a very inspired piece of architecture: it is

well proportioned, but rather heavy and unadorned to the point of grimness. But the interior is masterly, the vista through the rooms being particularly striking. As Dibdin said, 'As you enter, you catch the whole vista-like view of the three divisions.' Above all, the Library is in every way convenient for its purpose. The plaster work of Worrall and the woodwork of Richards, though not particularly original, are very effective. The Library contrives to produce an atmosphere of warmth, richness, and practicality.

These words unwittingly summed up Birley's own contribution to the library. He appreciated to the full its warmth of atmosphere and he exploited its richness. Carrying on the tradition of Monty James who had catalogued the manuscripts, he was the first to set about cataloguing the printed books. In her recent biography of P. G. Wodehouse, Frances Donaldson relates how Birley sent Plum a copy of his catalogue, in which item 17 reads:

17 The Gutenberg Bible or 42-line Bible. Fo. Mainz c. 1455: The first printed book, of which 48 copies (if some seriously imperfect examples are counted) have survived; twelve of them printed on vellum.

Having described in some detail the Eton copy, the catalogue continued:

To the recorded copies of the Gutenberg Bible should be added one in the library of Blandings Castle.*

It was Birley's fond hope that someone, perhaps a German professor, would swallow the bait and ask him how to get to Blandings to inspect the book. 'I shall, of course, suggest to him that he catches the 11.18 or the 2.33 p.m. train from Paddington Station for Market Blandings, having secured a room at the Emsworth Arms Hotel and making use of the services of Mr Jno. Robinson and his station taxicab,' he wrote

*In the museum at Blandings Castle you might find every manner of valuable and valueless curio. There was no central motive, the place was simply an amateur junk-shop. Side by side with a Gutenberg Bible for which rival collectors would have bidden without a limit, you would come across a bullet from the field of Waterloo, one of a consignment of ten thousand shipped there for the use of tourists by a Birmingham firm. Each was equally attractive to its owner.' *Something Fresh*, Chapter 3.

in his letter to Wodehouse. Although he did not trap a German professor he caused a great deal of worry to the great New York bookseller Mr H. P. Kraus. And a great deal of amusement to P. G. Wodehouse who wrote to him: 'I wonder if the Gutenberg Bible is still at Blandings. Surely one of the many Blandings impostors must have pinched it by now, and Lord Emsworth would never notice.'

The serious fruits of Birley's work in College Library included a number of significant contributions to bibliographical studies. Notable among these were 'Roger and Thomas Payne: with some account of their earlier bindings' and 'The Library of Louis-Henri de Loménie, Comte de Brienne and the bindings of the Abbé du Seuil', published by the Bibliographical Society in 1960 and 1962 respectively. Still more significant perhaps was how Birley made the library a practical tool for his teaching. It was the perfect legitimation of an apostolic succession from Monty James who had, all those years before, introduced him to the delights of bibliophilia.

The practical value of the library lay above all in the realisation that one of the best guarantees of kindling the interest of boys and girls is to put the emphasis on people and things before launching into ideas and theories. At Eton it was possible to show the boys a Gutenberg Bible before discussing the importance of the invention of printing in European history. It was possible to show them a book which had belonged to Robert Boyle while he was at Eton – with the names of two previous owners scored out and 'Boyle' scribbled in the margin – before discussing the significance of Boyle's Law for the development of science. All of this had of course its element of one-upmanship. It impressed the boys and conveyed an air of superiority to the staff, in that it was coupled with an ability to dominate conversations with an astonishing repertoire of recondite fact.

It was not the same as conventional scholarship. The exuberant pursuit of detail was too much an end in itself for that. The cliché is not seeing the wood for the trees, but the title of one of Birley's lectures published during his time as Head Master, *The Undergrowth of History*, tempted the facile *bon mot* that he did not see the trees for the undergrowth. Perhaps the title of another collection published in 1962 is a more appropriate metaphor to characterise his researches. This was the series of Clark Lectures, delivered at Trinity College, Cambridge, in which, under the title *Sunk Without Trace*, he salvaged six submerged literary works and attempted to refloat them. What the lectures demonstrated was that his interest lay in what was rare rather than what was seminal, although they did throw up occasional gems, such as in Nathaniel Lee's *The Rival Queens* the origin of the phrase 'bit the dust':

> sunk to the blushing Earth
> To plough it with his teeth.

The Clark Lectures are, it must be confessed, rather heavy going and were a disappointment to his audience. The review in the *Chronicle* loyally declared that 'Dr Birley's style illuminates the submarine gloom', pointing out in one case how 'we are made more critical of our own literary fashions, more tolerant of the non-conformers'. But if in conception these were characteristic projects for Birley to undertake, they were so heavy as to all but smother the natural mischievousness which was the most engaging quality in his research and his writing.

The Undergrowth of History on the other hand was such a success that it was the quite genuine wish of the Historical Association, before which it was delivered, to have it published. In it Birley examined, with a soupçon of nostalgia, the evidence for the great but now unfashionable legends of English history, among them Alfred burning the cakes, Drake playing bowls on Plymouth Hoe, Sir Philip Sidney offering the cup of water to the wounded soldier at Zutphen and the drowning of the Duke of Clarence in a butt of Malmsey wine. His commentary on the way in which attitudes to history change was a spirited rearguard action on behalf of the preservation of traditional stories:

> More and more the historian has to concern himself with what is regarded as the essential substructure of society. He tends to become more and more like the archæologist, who has the good fortune to have only the material of the substructure to deal with. And I suppose that the 'milk' for the future student of the substructure should not be the story of Alfred and the cakes, but rather some information about

the life of the ninth-century peasant in Somerset, the way in which he constructed his dwelling and baked his cakes. And yet Life, the actual life of individuals, goes on in the despised superstructure. Its twists and turns produce dramatic episodes, tragic or comic, pathetic or just plain exciting, and moments which test men and women so that their true character is displayed. These make good stories, which men feel instinctively to be significant, and much of the significance of History will be lost if they are ignored.

These were observations which conveyed something of the secret of his own success in teaching the history specialists of Charterhouse and Eton.

Perhaps the most entertaining use that Birley made of his array of sources in the library was the information that he unearthed about the history of Eton College itself. This enabled him to take a mischievous delight in recounting the less dignified features of its otherwise distinguished history. When Richard Austen-Leigh's occasional publication *Etoniana* was revived, Birley contributed two articles in which he explained that at the time of the foundation, Henry VI had really been thinking of a church, which, following the granting of indulgences by the Pope, would become a centre of pilgrimage. It was only when things did not work out as intended that the idea of a school emerged. Birley got much fun out of pointing out that Eton was thus founded on the failure of a quite different venture. 'It is the purpose of this paper to show that it was the Eton Parish Church which caused Eton College to be founded, that Henry VI's decision to build the new Parish Church, which we now call College Chapel, had nothing to do with the school, and that, if it had not been for its connection with the parish, Eton College before long would have ceased to exist.'

The role of Eton in the Civil War was another subject that fascinated him. He claimed to have discovered that there were more Etonians on the Cromwellian than on the Royalist side. Such evidence as he had gathered supported his feeling that there had always been something disputatious about Eton and it was important to him to be able to prove that this was historically so. He was himself nothing if not a questioner. Why should this, that or the other literary work, famous in its own day, have sunk without trace? Why should the legend of the burning of the cakes have grown up around Alfred? If Dante were writing now, whom would he have placed lower down in Hell, Hitler or Quisling? The excitement about knowledge was fuelled by the need to answer questions. If Birley was right in his intuitive feeling that Eton had been historically a questioning school, then he was himself, as it were, ur-Etonian. For if one side of his personality as Head Master was nurtured by his immersion in scholarship, the other was his capacity to link this with direct involvement with the affairs of the day. It was a fittingly 'balliolesque' reliance on sound learning as the foundation of successful participation in national life. It provided the intellectual weight with which Robert Birley put his stamp on the Eton of the 1950s.

CHAPTER TEN

Into the Modern World

'How nice to have a Head Master who is cleverer than oneself,' observed one of the housemasters shortly after Birley's return to Eton. 'How nice to have a Head Master who is not interested in drains,' remarked another. Birley's scholarly values were apparent from the beginning, and as time went on, increasingly influential. But if his strenuous intellectual activity was admirable as a way of creating an ethos, it carried with it certain disappointments for the staff. Between the wars Eton had been the most sociable of schools. The atmosphere had been such that one of the most consistently frequented gatherings was to be found not in any House Master's drawing room, but in the Head Master's house where the Alingtons' butler held court over coffee every morning. Anyone could attend this salon- below-stairs, masters, their wives, trades-people who supplied the school, Dames – as the ladies who preside over the domestic arrangements in the Houses are called – and other non-teaching staff. It was a relaxed conviviality which symbolised the absence of conventional snobbery at Eton in those days. Behind it lay the deft hand of the supremely generous-minded Mrs Alington, revered by those around her as the epitome of all that the wife of a Head Master of Eton should be.

To follow the Alingtons was therefore a formidable assignment. Even if the Elliotts had been disposed to take the same path, things would very soon have had to change with the austerity that the war years brought. When the Birleys arrived in 1949 those who remembered the style of the Alington era were rather hoping to see it revived. After all it was in that atmosphere that the new Head Master's own professional style had developed, and Elinor Birley had herself been devoted to Mrs Alington. But the situation was not quite so straightforward as that. Certainly Birley was in some ways more approachable than his predecessor had been and in due course his enthusiasm for teaching was to bring more warmth into the atmosphere. In this respect there was perhaps some similarity to his taking over at Charterhouse in 1935. And whereas the Elliotts had seen the opportunities for entertaining severely curtailed, under the Birleys it was possible for the Head Master's house to become a centre of activity once more. But those in the Eton community who envisaged a new Alington era were misjudging both the mood of the time and the extent to which the Birleys were in tune with it. The days when a relaxed and carefree penchant for social life blended easily with the more fundamental aims of an Eton education were over. While someone who had remained cocooned in the public school world might have been tempted to put the clock back, Birley, with the wider experience of post-war attitudes which he had gained in Germany, was not.

So while the Birleys were anything but withdrawn in a community which after all contained so many old friends, they displayed little of the panache which some of the more socially inclined of those friends had been hoping to see. It was not to be a return to the days when the way to respond to an unexpected call to entertain was, in the memorable phrase of Hubert Hartley, to 'get them all strawberries and Fuller's cake'. That could only have appeared inappropriate to a couple who had seen at first hand so much devastation and hardship in the schools of Germany. Quite apart from this deep-seated sobriety, the conditions of the time did not lend themselves to any kind of lavishness. It was not just that the doctrine of austerity, brought home by the realities of rationing, continued to hold sway. Public school masters were quite simply less well off after the war than they had been before it. This was more true of the Birleys than of most. Faced with a Head Master's house which had been designed for grander times, and which they could scarcely afford to furnish, they needed to simplify the domestic arrangements.

The nature of this simplification was significant. Beneath the enormous and magnificent first-floor drawing room was an equally enormous dining room which the Birleys felt would have to be abandoned as impractical. The Provost and Fellows were not however prepared to let them convert the audit room, which was also on the first floor, into a dining room. So, stuck

with the anachronistic layout, they showed a touch of stubborn-
ness in taking the unprecedented step of using the drawing
room for a double purpose. One end became a dining area,
while the other served as a sitting room. This manifestation of
the disinclination to entertain too lavishly did not of course go
unremarked. In the way that small communities have of getting
things out of proportion, the domestic rearrangement, which
had a very practical justification, contributed to the Birleys'
leftish reputation. One wag called it the Soviet living room.

Outside the school the impression of left-wing sympathies
was greatly magnified by the nickname 'Red Robert' which
Birley very soon acquired. It was entirely fitting that the myth
of his dangerous radicalism should derive from a case of
mistaken identity. The origin of the phrase was this. Elinor's
sister-in-law was a member of a very superior bridge club in
London where the news of the appointment of the new Head
Master was greeted with some dismay. The reason was that
another member of the club had been to Berlin and afterwards
confided to fellow bridge-players that Birley had a picture of
Karl Marx hanging in his office there. The grounds for this
piece of gossip were delicious. In the next-door office to Birley's
worked a man called Armitage who was responsible for travel
arrangements. As a result, many visitors had occasion to go to
this office without ever going through to see Birley himself. It
was above the travel desk that the bridge player had seen the
shocking picture. The explanation lay in Armitage's passion for
music and the visiting bridge-player's inability to distinguish
between a portrait of Marx and one of Brahms.

The absurd Red Robert label being in fact the invention of a
group of Old Etonians, it was more commonly as the Head Man
that Birley was known to the boys at the school, while to the
masters he was either 'R. B.' or 'The Sage'. It might have been
more appropriate to carry on the Charterhouse nickname of
'Bags'; because he was not nightly either host or guest at a
dinner party he was able to spend even more time in College
Library. The late hours he kept there made the celebrated bags
under his eyes increasingly obvious. In this element of
solitariness lay his particular release from the pressure of an
otherwise intensely busy life and his way of keeping above the
petty tensions of an enclosed community. With his experience

in Germany he had grown beyond the total involvement that characterised his Charterhouse days. As Head Master of Eton he was something of a national figure with more and more external public speaking engagements for which College Library was proving an inexhaustible source of information and inspiration. If all this made him appear remote and aloof at times it also had the effect of channelling his energy into a number of major priorities which he pursued singlemindedly: a fitting way of going about things in a post where an eye for strategy rather than a taste for tactics was the overriding requirement.

The strategy became apparent in the transformation heralded by Birley's headmastership. First there were the buildings which had suffered substantial war damage. On a return flight from a night raid a German aircraft had jettisoned surplus bombs on the College. One had exploded immediately in the Precentor's dining room in Savile House. The other was discovered in the Head Master's schoolroom next to Upper School, where the Provost, Lord Quickswood, is remembered as having poked it with his umbrella, declaring, 'Its a dud, I'm sure it's a dud.' Mercifully it was somewhat later that it, too, exploded. The one redeeming feature of the damage that was done was that most of the Chapel's stained glass was shattered. It had been hideous and the organist was instructed to play the loudest possible chords with the object of bringing down the remaining bits. In *Eton Repointed*, published in 1970, James McConnell looked back at what it had felt like to survey the situation twenty-five years earlier:

The war had not only put a stop to plans for improvement. It made nonsense of all financial calculations and provisions. When it was over the financial position of the College was alarming. The reconstruction, which after six years of enforced neglect had now become urgently necessary, was likely, at a conservative estimate, to cost many times more than the assets available. To begin with, the historic buildings had been standing for periods ranging from two to five hundred years. Apart from about £30,000 spent on the buildings in School Yard between 1874 and 1933 no major work of restoration had ever been undertaken. An eminent architect described them as 'hulks'; they were crumbling into decay, eroded by the ravages of weather and time, knocked about by enemy action, and enclosing within their massively strong outer casings a pest of notable potency, the death-watch beetle. Equally pressing was the problem of the boarding houses. Quite apart from any structural weakness the living conditions for boys were in many houses old-fashioned and unhygienic. The accommodation for domestic staff and the conditions in which they had to work were often lamentable. Under the prevailing circumstances it was a very real question as to whether the boys' houses could be made workable at all. These were formidable problems for a school with little in the way of funds for current expenditure, struggling to secure its independence. To look back twenty-five years from the point we have reached now is to appreciate the tremendous faith which was needed to envisage the restoration of Eton.

For the first few years after the war it was a case of make do rather than mend. Birley was fortunate to come back at a time when the school had begun to pick itself up and set about preparing for the major restoration that was needed.

With Elliott beavering away at the Appeal in the background, maintaining, in his shy and modest way, that all he had achieved was to give things a push in the right direction, Birley was able to pour his energy into what was to be done with the money that was being raised. Soon after he came, building restrictions were lifted and the business of eliminating the shabby reminders of war could begin. If Eton's spectacular buildings of today have a *soigné* look about them, the foundations of that care were laid during Birley's headmastership. The challenge to the imagination of reconciling the preservation of a national heritage with the expansion of facilities called for in a modern school was one that he relished. On the one hand he was a passionate conservationist; he got very worked up about saving the Victorian pillar box in Eton High Street, and could say exactly where to find the best manufacturer of wrought iron to restore Victorian lamp posts. On the other hand he had the imagination to put the artistic above the conventional when the occasion presented itself.

One such occasion arose within months. The first piece of restoration to be undertaken in the Chapel was the east window, the dominant feature of the building. The situation invited controversy. At the centre of it was the Irish artist Evie Hone. Her Celtic style of work had caught the imagination of Sir Jasper Ridley, a prominent Old Etonian, and it was he who was instrumental in seeing that she was one of those competing for the commission. Her chief rival was someone whose designs were unexceptional but more likely to blend with the perpendicular gothic of the building. Ridley's great ally was Lord Crawford, an accepted arbiter of taste at the time, who declared that her glass was far and away the finest that he had seen. To Birley's delight it was the Evie Hone faction which won the day.

When Miss Hone came over from Dublin to size up what needed to be done, she was accompanied by several Roman Catholic priests whose disapproval of the Protestant edifice was evident. The Head Master took charge of the situation. While the artist was in conference with the architect, he led her retinue to the nave where he was able to show them the fifteenth-century wall paintings which had survived an attempt by the Reformers to have them effaced. Among these he could show them various pre-Reformation images of saints and of the Blessed Virgin. The spirits of the Irish Fathers were revived. Evie Hone's design, unveiled in 1952, was a striking Crucifixion in which the elongated arms of Christ seemed, as she told Birley was the intention, 'to stretch over every boy in the congregation'.

Evie Hone died before she could carry out any further commissions. To follow her was a tall order, especially in designing the windows to go on either side of her work, in the chancel. The artist chosen was John Piper and Birley was very much to the fore in the choice of the subjects to be portrayed. James McConnell quotes Piper's own comments on the origin of the pictorial windows that were executed, four representing parables and four miracles:

Inserting modern glass in an ancient building is 'always a problem, and a responsibility; but to a large extent it did not arise here as it had been faced in the biggest possible way by Evie Hone with her east window, and it was for me only a question of making a satisfactory marriage in the N. and S. walls between Moira Forsythe's heraldic glass and Evie Hone's work. This was largely a question of colour and tone transition; the more easterly windows had to be much darker than the more westerly ones – which is convenient anyway, as the sanctuary end needs less light and perhaps richer colour. And the transition had to be undramatic.' The problems dictated by the structure of the windows 'seemed to demand by their design some kind of (i) proposition (ii) resolution. Hence the Parable and Miracle scheme. . . . Robert Birley was of the greatest help and spent a long time, on many occasions, in discussion with me about possible subjects and interpretations. Most of the solutions (translations into possible visual terms that might be acceptable – especially by boys) stemmed from his ideas. His understanding of the demands was remarkable and any credit here should be entirely his.'

What had mattered to Birley above all was that the pictorial representations should be such as to be directly comprehensible and appealing to the boys.

The heraldic glass which had been done in the period between the restoration of the east window at the beginning of the decade and the chancel windows at the end of it had had an appeal for Birley too, this time an antiquarian one. These windows were to portray the coats of arms of various benefactors of Eton. He was fascinated by the case of John Reynolds, uncle of Joshua, who was a Fellow and had previously been headmaster of a school in Exeter. It was Birley at his most characteristic. His researches had revealed that Reynolds was the editor of a standard edition of the geographical works of Pomponius Mela, widely used in schools in the eighteenth century. Mela's studies apparently led him to the conclusion that the language which Adam and Eve spoke in the Garden of Eden was Basque. Equally striking was the account given in the book of how, before the time of Columbus, some people had set out from America and were washed ashore on the coast of Holland; Birley had a theory that this might have been the source for Canning's remark about 'calling the New World into existence to redress the balance of the Old'. Scarcely anyone at

Eton could make head or tail of the story as Birley related it, but there was no doubt about Reynolds's right to feature in one of the windows. He had been a prodigious benefactor who gave his entire library to the school and endowed a number of scholarships. The problem was that he had no coat of arms. It was the occasion of one of the periodic disagreements between Head Master and Provost. Elliott was for simply using Joshua's arms. Birley protested, threatening to tell Anthony Wagner, the Richmond Herald. To this Elliott replied: 'If we have a visit from the College of Heralds, Birley, you and I will meet them at the top of the Chapel steps. With halberds.' In the event John Reynolds was commemorated by means of the heraldic device of making a pun on his name. One of the windows shows a fox holding a globe, in one corner of which the continent of America can just be seen.

A further aspect of the transformation of Eton which began in Birley's time had to do with the academic life of the school. It comprised two interrelated quiet revolutions, one of which he accepted with some reluctance, the other of which he embraced with enthusiasm. The first was the academic competitiveness induced by the expansion of the public examinations system. The second was the modernisation of the curriculum, success in which was more and more to be measured in terms of these same examinations. When he became Head Master in 1949 little had changed since his previous time there. The curriculum of the specialists was largely determined by the requirements of Oxford and Cambridge, and the national examination system was not particularly relevant. The main targets were the entrance scholarship examinations of the various Colleges, which encouraged a pretty free hand in the range of subjects taken. Those who did not aspire to these heights of scholarship became educated in a leisurely, unruffled atmosphere which put personal cultivation above the acquisition of formal qualifications.

When O and A level were introduced in 1951, it was with the liberal-minded intention of releasing boys and girls from the straitjacket of the old School Certificate, which had caused Birley himself such problems, so that they would be able to pursue what interested them and would be rewarded with something to show for it. What happened in the event was that the teaching in individual subjects became correspondingly more earnest and competitive. The high fliers reached O level standard younger and younger, and the low fliers flapped harder and harder to avoid crashing. The competition sharpened still more at the A level stage as the arrangements for admission to the universities and the professions became inexorably more stereotyped. During the early 1950s there was no overwhelming desire in Eton to join the A level lemmings, but eventually it became evident that the growing prestige and recognition of the examination made it equal folly to stand aside. The days of the Grand July, Eton's own private examination set and marked by Oxford and Cambridge dons on a syllabus devised by the school, were numbered. The fact was that Etonians were being obliged to think about their future prospects in much the same terms as sixth formers elsewhere. It was not only the end of the Grand July, it was the end of the days when higher education meant almost exclusively Oxford or Cambridge. With county grants making it possible for most families to afford university education for their children, a degree was becoming a desirable preliminary to more and more careers, and Birley saw that the Etonian net would have to be cast wider. To each one of a group of masters he gave the job of discovering all that they could about one of the provincial universities. He himself was especially keen on Keele, with its innovatory foundation year in which arts and science subjects were studied in combination. Whenever he mentioned the provincial universities he would invariably add 'such as Keele', to the point where it became the last place that masters could bear to hear about.

Birley viewed these developments in the national educational system with mixed feelings. On the positive side was the enrichment of opportunity which resulted from the growth of science. Like many other schools at the time, Eton benefited from the Industrial Fund, which had been set up to foster science teaching in schools. A generous grant helped to provide magnificent new laboratories to replace the existing ones. A number of these had been among the most advanced for their time but had since become outdated. It was for the science specialists above all that A level brought a new earnestness which was at first not easy to reconcile with Eton's style. Birley saw the shift in this direction as being long overdue, realising that too few of the more able boys had in the past acquired the kind of educational background that would enable them to succeed in industry and commerce. The future lay more and more with science and technology and it was necessary to come to terms with the hard work that they demanded. But at the same time it was important not to allow these pressures to destroy the unique quality of the school's life. His own erratic experiences with public examinations contributed to the scepticism with which he viewed the new developments and he strove to ensure that they were never able to dominate the curriculum totally.

So although Birley acknowledged and to some extent sympathised with the general mood which, at Eton as much as anywhere else, was broadly in favour of the changes that were taking place, he foresaw more clearly than most other headmasters the over-specialisation towards which the whole development was tending. He put up stout resistance, seeing to it that all the specialists kept up some kind of extra studies which lay outside the normal span of their A level work. There was a vast range of these activities – as far as Birley was concerned, the more off-beat the better – and they produced some of the best work in the school. Among the languages taught was Hebrew, and there were also modern subjects like accountancy. The most impressive advice was there for the asking. When the teaching of economics was suggested and there was some uncertainty about what to do, Birley as usual went straight to the top. He consulted Maynard Keynes, who turned out not to be in favour, taking the view that it was much more important to concentrate on mathematics. This advice was followed until, in 1957, an Old Etonian master who was a keen economist persuaded Birley otherwise.

There was another notable illustration of going straight to the top in order to ward off the advance of specialisation. Civil servants in the Admiralty had devised a scheme to base the entrance qualifications for officer training at Dartmouth on science A levels. Birley was appalled at the idea and, when a conference was held to discuss it, he sent as his representative one of his housemasters, Peter Lawrence, who had been in the Royal Navy during the war. Lawrence discovered that the admirals – some of whom were men with whom he had served – were also appalled at what the Civil Service was hatching. When he reported back, Birley observed thoughtfully: 'There are two ways in which we can do this. Either we can go through the proper channels . . . or go straight to Burma.' To Burma he went, inviting Lord Mountbatten to lunch at the Travellers' Club, along with Desmond Lee, Headmaster of Winchester, and Deric Holland-Martin, the Second Sea Lord. No more was heard of the plan.

Birley's stand within Eton helped to offset the narrowness into which a curriculum dominated by A level was being drawn. Indeed occasionally there was a boy who made use of the examination system to go further in the other direction than his headmaster could bring himself to approve of. There was the case of a classical scholar who had taken A levels in Greek, Latin and Ancient History and gained an Exhibition at King's. He had two more terms at Eton and asked Birley if he could take A level in Chemistry and Italian – the latter from scratch – in that time. He wanted to be a scientist but did not want at this stage to attempt Physics – that, he felt, would come in good time. Birley agreed, whereupon two weeks later the boy came again and asked if he could do A level Divinity, since one of the set books was the same as for Greek. With rather more hesitation Birley once again agreed. Several weeks later the boy wisely did not consult his Head Master when he resolved to work for English A level too. In the summer he passed in all his subjects, and so left Eton with seven A levels.

In grappling with the onset of the public examinations obsession Birley was preparing for a new era in the academic life of Eton. When he had taken over the headmastership, the school's reputation for scholarship was already second to none. A month after Birley's appointment Canon Raven, the retiring Vice-Chancellor of Cambridge, gave a talk which attracted much press coverage and in which he made a characteristic calculated indiscretion. Comparing the standard of the 1949 entry with that of a decade earlier he remarked: 'In Classics, with the sole exception of the boys from Eton, the standard is not so high as it was before the war. I think the same is probably true of some of the other literary subjects'. He went on to speak of the rise in the standard in science and engineering.

It was for the remarkable rise in the level of achievement in scientific subjects, for which A level was to be the pacemaker, that Birley was laying the foundations for the rise in the general level of academic achievement reached under his successors, Anthony Chenevix-Trench, Michael McCrum and Eric Anderson. But at the same time he was concerned that those foundations should not be too narrow. If the greater academic competitiveness was to be welcomed, it was to be with no more than two cheers. It was for him just as important to protect what was unique in an Eton education. To many of those who remembered the earlier, more leisured days it must have seemed a close run thing, but by the end of Birley's time as Head Master it was, on the whole, acknowledged that somehow he had managed it. His achievement was summed up in an eloquent valedictory profile in the *Chronicle* by Crispin Haseler and William Waldegrave:

His greatest achievement has been to bring Eton into the modern world without destroying her traditions. The coming of A level has challenged the somewhat leisured ideals of education so long and so excellently practised at Eton. It was, of course, out of the question to remain outside the national system. Yet, on the face of it, A level could not be adopted at Eton without revolutionary changes in the lives of all specialists. Especially was this true for science specialists, whose numbers have so greatly increased in the last fifteen years. It would have been all too easy to throw the old style of life at Eton to the A level vultures. To many it must have seemed inevitable that everything should be rearranged to fit the new quantity of work and the demands of a system not designed with Eton in mind. How natural it would have been to reduce games, societies and half-holidays to be the slaves of the new dictator. But, in fact, we have the best of both worlds and somehow life goes on as before, even for the scientists in their gorgeous and, incidentally, up-to-date new buildings. If life is at times very gruelling for the most versatile, the compromise is a marvellous boon for the vast majority – a piece of modern revolution for which we must all be admiringly thankful. Of course it is to Dr Birley that the thanks are mainly due. It is through his restrained realism that we have shed the deplorable attributes of the charming backwater, while preserving its unique delights. He has achieved that most uncommon thing – revolution without destruction.

The academic changes precipitated by the introduction of A level and its importance for university entry were making Eton less remote from education in the country as a whole. This was something which Birley not only welcomed but sought to accelerate by making the place less exclusive. Between the wars the staff had been made up almost entirely of public school men, a large proportion of them Old Etonians. To bring about a change required a deliberate policy to cast the net more widely. This Birley did, finding in the process candidates of outstanding academic merit. He was anxious to cast the net equally widely as far as the boys were concerned, striving to maintain the declining momentum of the Fleming Committee's proposal for the admission of state scholars. Every housemaster was urged to keep a place on his list for one of these. If the local authorities could have been persuaded to take up the offer in full, theoretically there could have been twenty-five state-sponsored boys entering each year, and before long over 100 in the school at any one time. Indeed it need not have stopped there, as there was some support within Eton for broadening the entry further in this way. The fact was, though, that the local authorities were never really likely to feel they could justify the cost of sending their best boys to schools like Eton in sufficient numbers for the scheme to make any great impact.

At the other end of the scale the old style continued. Parents either knew or got to know a housemaster, put their son's name down, usually within six months of birth, and chose a prep school largely on the basis of personal recommendation. But at the same time competition was ceasing to be confined to the King's Scholarship examinations and beginning to make Common Entrance less of a mere formality. Connections survived and the established prep schools such as Summer Fields and Sunningdale, Cothill and Hawtreys, went on sending more of their boys to Eton than anywhere else. But with Birley's encouragement a wider range of schools now came into the reckoning. He devised a new approach to Common

Entrance in which no marks were given for the examination papers except in Latin; for the other subjects there were merely symbols α, β, γ to indicate which class the candidate seemed suited for. There were further symbols to denote such things as 'not a good paper but well written' and the decisions on admission were made by a committee of four masters. When prep school headmasters rang up asking to know the marks their boys had obtained, as was the frequent practice, they were met with Birley's reply, 'I'm afraid we don't give marks.' It was in fact much better simply to tell them that if a boy wanted to try again next time round, they would have to do something about, say, his maths or his French. At the same time there was a rule that if an aggrieved headmaster was adamant that a mistake had been made, the boy could be brought for a day to Eton where he could join in all the classes to give the masters an opportunity to judge for themselves once again. Whether it was ever actually put into practice is doubtful.

The fact that it was gradually becoming less of a formality to get into the school was not lost on those Old Etonians who found that the offer of a place was delayed, sometimes until the last minute. For those who passed Common Entrance at the first attempt, however, there was never any need to worry and towards the end of Birley's time as Head Master a survey showed that sixty per cent of the boys were sons of Etonians. Although he made as much as could be made of the state scholarship scheme, and was very proud of those who came to Eton by means of it and flourished there, it was not substantial enough to transform the school in the way that Birley had hoped. There was little in the way of a social transformation to accompany the academic one behind which Birley had put his weight.

Hand in hand with Birley's concern to build up the academic life of Eton went the same benign interest in sport which he had shown at Charterhouse. Considering his reputation as a non-sportsman, his knowledgeability about individual games would frequently take young masters by surprise. It might be some unusual feature of the history of the Boat Club which would crop up in conversation, or the awareness that the Third VIII was causing friction with other schools by winning too many races. What was important to him above all else was that there should be plenty of variety. Not only were all the now commonplace minority sports increasingly encouraged, but he made sure that Eton's two unique ones, the Field Game and the Wall Game, were preserved. The eccentricity of the Wall Game had a particular appeal for Birley and he enjoyed taking visitors to watch the famous sprawling, wriggling, muddy mass of Etonian bodies. It was a particular pleasure to inform them that, contrary to all appearances, there were in fact two sides.

Another idiosyncratic game which Birley enjoyed encouraging was Eton Fives. Among the group of schools which played this version of Fives, Eton was one of two that were dominant at this time. The other was Aldenham, and during Birley's fourteen years as Head Master each of these two won the annual championship five times. Beyond this conventional competition there was another, unusual, outlet. Birley was delighted to learn, from an article in *The Times* in 1957, that in Sokoto in Northern Nigeria 'curiously Eton Fives is popular'. The curiosity was explained shortly afterwards in a letter:

TO THE EDITOR OF THE TIMES

Sir, – My Councillors and I were recently delighted to meet your Special Correspondent, and to see the news of this Emirate in your issue of October 28, together with pictures of our girls' school, the river ferry in Argungu Town, and the fives court.

Beneath the picture of the fives court you write, 'Curiously Eton Fives is popular.' You may be interested to know that fives was introduced here by Mr S. J. Hogben, an education officer and author of *The Mohammedan Emirates of Northern Nigeria* in the early 1920s. From Sokoto Province it spread all over Northern Nigeria, and has remained popular.

We are very glad that your newspaper has brought news and pictures of our country to our friends in Great Britain.

Yours truly,
SARKIN KEBBI MUHAMMADU III,
Thirty-first Emir of Argungu.
The Emir's Palace, Argungu, Northern Nigeria.

Two years later came a reminder when in the championship final the Eton pair, T. C. Pilkington and J. R. Smithers, lost to D. R.

Barker and U. Muhammadu of Aldenham. Mohammadu had played Fives in Nigeria before being sent to school in England and coming under the wing of Geoffrey Bolt, the master in charge of the game at Aldenham.

The Nigerian schools which played Eton Fives counted a number of cabinet ministers among their alumni, and it was not long before one of these prominent personalities – the Sardauna of Sokoto – paid a visit to Eton. Clad in tribal costume and attended by an imposing retinue, he was shown the buttress of the Chapel where the game had originated, and the courts where it was now played. After watching the proceedings for a time he asked if he could play. Then, looking like Saladin, as one of the boys later put it, he gathered up his robes in his left hand and played a vigorous and skilful game with his right. Birley seized the opportunity of the visit to foster links with Northern Nigeria and the master in charge of Fives, Stephen McWatters, took a team of Eton boys to play there in 1961. Some Nigerian boys returned the visit two years later. Birley's subsequent correspondence brought in the Commonwealth Relations Office and in 1965 a full Eton Fives Association side, led by another Eton master, David Guilford, went out at the invitation of the Northern Nigerian Government. The visiting English teams discovered to their surprise that the Nigerians played the game with a tennis ball.

As he had done at Charterhouse, so again at Eton Birley set out to give religion an important place in the life of the school. He took Confirmation very seriously and found time to give almost individual attention to every candidate. His sermons were occasions for surprise more often than for the boredom customarily associated with such addresses. The connoisseurs would catch one another's eye as he found some excuse for a digression on medieval stained glass, or frescoes, or other religious decoration. For his religious conviction was sustained above all else by his interest in Christian art and history and the sense of continuity and constant renewal that it gave him. The replacement of the stained glass in the Chapel was an apt expression of this theme of renewal. The windows by Evie Hone and John Piper were a favourite source of inspiration for sermons, such as the last one that Birley preached as Head Master, which began:

Those of you who are leaving Eton will, I know, be looking back now over the four or five years that you have been here. Most of you – I am sure I can really say that nearly all of you – will be feeling, though you may not be able to explain it, that your life here has had some meaning, that there was some point in your having been at Eton. You will certainly have many memories.

I want first to ask you to remember, among many other memories, no doubt, one of the new windows in this Chapel, the one depicting the miracle of the Loaves and Fishes. Perhaps the story of that miracle in the Gospels is an exaggerated version of some story of a common sacramental meal, shared between Christ and his disciples and the crowd that followed him. But the story has a message all right and I think it is very well told in this window. Notice first the hands, grasping, violent, nightmarish. I happen to have known what happens to a people when food and other necessities of life are very scarce. Do not think it ennobles them. It makes them grasping and violent, like those hands. I never look at the window without thinking of one of the most horrible scenes I have ever witnessed, the subway of the station at Hanover in Germany at night, in the years just after the war when there was a great scarcity. It was one of the centres from which the black market operated. I went there once or twice to see if there was any way in which one could keep young men, of about the age of some of you, out of this utterly corrupting place. It was hardly lit at all, and in the darkness you could see hands moving, very like those hands.

The answer is in the top half of the window – a generosity in giving which does not mind at all if it gives more than is necessary. There are no grasping hands in this part of the picture.

It is in ways like that that you should face the problems of the future. Never despair of them. Never be shocked by them. *Never* ignore them. Great difficulties and great dangers can only be met by giving much.

It was in this line of interpretation of Christianity that Birley was at his best, conveying his admiration for those whose convictions enabled them to overcome privations and despair. What he tried to show in his sermons was that the example of figures like Dietrich Bonhoeffer could inspire a crusading Christianity expressed in positive action. 'Great difficulties and great dangers can only be met by giving much.'

It is not often that ideals of giving even little are uppermost in the minds of boys at school. Birley's original wish on becoming Head Master had been to encourage more of them to be ordained. But if this proved unrealistic as a way of stimulating a sense of service in a larger number of those who were leaving, other more immediate possibilities did present themselves. Birley was one of the first to be involved in the Ockenden Venture, Joyce Pearce's imaginative scheme to provide holiday centres for children of refugee families, first of all from Germany and later from South America, Africa or the Far East as the need arose. Over the years a succession of Eton boys worked for the remarkable Miss Pearce.

The second opportunity came when in 1958 Alec Dickson founded Voluntary Service Overseas. In the early days when he was struggling to get his scheme financed, his reception at the hands of ministers and civil servants alike was – with the honourable exception of Alan Lennox-Boyd, Secretary of State for the Colonies – uniformly apathetic. The two headmasters who had the imagination to share Dickson's vision were Kim Taylor of Sevenoaks School and Birley. Both of them saw from the beginning that this was a new way for those brought up in privileged circumstances to have an opportunity to give something in return, and both thought hard about how to ensure that the volunteers were as equipped as their schools could make them to handle the situations they were going to face. Dickson's achievement was remarkable. With the help of his wife he ran the whole organisation from a one-room office at his home in Mortlake. The story went that all the records were kept under the bed. It was just the sort of flair and inspiration that appealed to someone of Birley's temperament.

There were moments of delicious eccentricity. A letter once arrived from an Old Etonian volunteer in Papua who was urgently in need of three mules. Birley proceeded to track down a retired archdeacon in Ilfracombe who was able to tell him the price of mules in Papua. Then he read out the letter in College

The Provost and the Head Master at the Eton Wall Square on St Andrew's Day 1954. The 'eleventh men' are making notes for the *Eton College Chronicle* report

Royal Visit to Eton, July 1956. The Duke of Edinburgh talking to the
Head College Waterman, Chief Petty Officer Barnes, who had served
with him in the Royal Navy

Nigerian visitors playing Eton Fives

Chapel, adding that the sum required was £150. Masters were told not to subscribe, and he wrote to parents asking them not to do so either. What he wanted was a spontaneous response from the boys themselves. Within a week £840 had been collected.

The apathy of officialdom towards Dickson's initiative persisted until, a few years after the foundation of VSO, the idea of a US Peace Corps received the backing of President Kennedy. Attitudes changed overnight at the thought that the Americans had stolen a march. The Cabinet took an interest. Treasury money materialised. VSO was poised to change gear. At this point Dickson was invited to spend a month in the States sharing his experiences with Sargent Shriver who had responsibility for the Peace Corps. At the same time the internal politics of VSO became correspondingly complicated. Shortly after his return, and despite pleas from Birley and others, Dickson resigned. The venture was on the brink of collapse. The early months of 1962 were critical and Birley was given leave by the Provost and Fellows to spend a great deal of his time helping to keep the organisation going. It survived and prospered.

After leaving Eton to become Professor of Education at the University of the Witwatersrand Birley had an opportunity to see some of the fruits of his work at first hand. In a letter to *The Times* he described how he 'found two young men, both aged nineteen, each in charge of a camp of Rwanda refugees, the number of which had been swollen, as a result of the recent tragic happenings in that country, to thousands. They were surmounting immense difficulties with astonishing success. In one school of 150 boys, one with a considerable reputation, two boys of eighteen have recently been for two months the only teachers. I was told on good authority that they had saved the school from having to be closed.'

This was, in very practical terms, a re-definition of the tradition of public service in which Birley himself had grown up. It had been for him of great consequence that Eton of all schools should be on the crest of this new wave of idealism.

CHAPTER ELEVEN

Head of Heads

The idea of public service was close to the centre of Birley's life as Head Master of Eton. At Charterhouse he had sought to take a very self-contained school out of its seclusion and make it more aware of public life. At Eton he had a more natural place in the public arena. In consequence it was not possible to be so happily singleminded about school affairs as he had previously been. The problem of how to reconcile the effort of keeping a firm hold on internal matters with that of meeting outside commitments is one which it is common for headmasters to face towards the end of a successful tenure, and they are generally carried through by the momentum of the authority acquired in their earlier years. This had been so for Birley at Charterhouse when he became a member of the Fleming Committee. At Eton the reconciliation was needed from the very beginning. To his Fleming reputation had been added the name which he had made for himself in Germany and it was only natural that he should be greatly in demand. Above all there was the Headmasters' Conference. In the 1950s he seemed to be an omnipresent member of its Committee and by that token a continuing influence on its policy-making. Towering over the great majority of his fellow-members, he was indisputably Head of Heads.

These outside commitments were bound to be a strain in two ways. In the first place they entailed a good many public appearances as a speaker with a reputation for originality. The source of this originality lay in his scholarship. As well as being a haven of escape from the day-to-day tensions of school life, College Library was a source of inspiration for his addresses to learned societies, his sermons as visiting preacher and his innumerable after-dinner speeches. It was an achievement in itself to meet the punishing schedules that all this entailed, but the challenge of doing so and at the same time holding the reins of the most complex of the English public schools was very much greater.

That Birley relished the challenge and rose to it, and that Eton did not become a runaway horse was due more than anything else to his relationship with the staff. He was accessible and approachable at the times that really mattered – when encounters were unexpected and tense. If a housemaster had some frightful drama and came to his study at eleven in the evening, he could generally manage to look up as though the caller was the one person in the world he wanted to see. He was able to make the most difficult, awkward or inconvenient situation appear as though it were a welcome social engagement. He had a nose for tenterhooks and would instinctively act swiftly to dispel uncertainty or anxiety.

Although some of the staff may have found the Birley ménage more austere than they might have wished, they were impressed to a man by the phenomenal energy that R. B. displayed. It was a feature of Eton life that masters and their wives coming home from a party in the early hours of the morning would look up at the window of College Library and invariably see his light burning. Elinor, it was well known, would have gone to bed long since and left her husband to his books. Even so, they found it hard to conceive of how he managed to read quite so much. Asked on one occasion how he did manage it, his reply was, 'I read while I'm dressing', which led to all kinds of speculation about books propped up alongside the shaving mirror or on the dressing table. Perhaps indeed there was some extra reading time to be created while he struggled into his famous cassock and bands.

It was not however the erudition in itself that earned the respect of the Eton staff, rather it was the way Birley had of being scholarly without being in any sense remotely or ineffectually donnish. If his extensive reading was something of an indulgence for someone whose job is the very practical one of running a school, it was an indulgence that was crammed into the hours when lesser people dally over dinner, watch television or sleep. Birley stretched the day beyond the limits that most men set for it. As a result a disposition which might have diminished his authority actually increased it. For with the scholarship went a presence that in routine daytime hours dominated the school for masters and boys alike. This was where his inclination to take on so much teaching was important. As well as being Head Master he was at the centre of things as a member of the History Department. His frequent absences for outside commitments were of course a potential source of great inconvenience to his colleagues, but he was endearingly scrupulous about making provision for the divisions that he was obliged to abandon, more so than many a junior master under less pressure. Letters to Giles St Aubyn, who towards the end of Birley's time became Head of Department, were always apologetic about being 'an appalling nuisance', with no hint of any assumption that as Head Master he was in a special position and could do as he liked.

The most severe test of relations with the staff came in his handling of mid-morning 'Chambers', the Eton substitute for a masters' common room. Questions could be fired from any direction, and there were times when the exchanges were of an acerbity worthy of Prime Minister's Question Time. On one occasion a master was so positively rude that Oliver Van Oss said to Birley: 'You really cannot allow beaks to talk to you like that'. Birley replied: 'Unless you do, you won't ever get a really good staff'. It was of supreme importance to him that masters should feel that they had the freedom to say what they liked. His strength was his tolerant readiness to argue out any issue. His weakness was a tendency to be longwinded to a point where some in his audience wanted only to get away. But more often they were fascinated at the sight of him excitedly rolling a pencil between his hands, or swinging his spectacles round and round (heaven knows how many pairs he must have broken). He was forever declaring that 'we must get this right', and whenever a compromise of some sort was suggested, there was much talk of 'grasping the nettle'. There was generally a good chance of a memorable moment at some stage in Chambers. Some of Birley's announcements caused great merriment, as when he explained that he would be away for a few days attending a rather unusual conference. 'I must go because they are very keen for me to be Chairman. I think they want someone who will simply sit there and say nothing.' By far the most compulsively loquacious man in Eton, he was not aware that he had said anything funny.

Most of Birley's absences were for short periods like this, above all for the Headmasters' Conference or for his regular appearances at Königswinter where he invariably gave a paper.

But there was one memorable exception at the half-way stage of his headmastership when he and Elinor went to the United States during the summer holidays and did not return until six weeks or so after the beginning of the autumn half. The United States astonished them and in a small way they gave some cause for astonishment in return. For much of the time they were at St Paul's School, about two miles outside Concord, New Hampshire. It was something of a sensation in the school community that they tended to ignore the car that was provided for them, and one master's wife was heard to say to another, 'Do you know, the Birleys *walk* into Concord!' They did however use the car for longer expeditions, one of which ended with dinner with Ogden Nash and his wife. 'Dinner – if you can call it that – took place out of doors and consisted of innumerable beefsteaks cooked by the poet over an open brazier and a great deal of Indian corn finished off with buckets of ice cream,' was how Birley described it in a letter to his sister. The spell of teaching at St Paul's was sandwiched between brief stays in Washington and New York. In the former Birley was greatly tickled by a sign outside the White House which read PARKING RESERVED FOR SECRET SERVICE. In New York he and Elinor were the guests at dinner, first of the American Old Etonians and then of the Grolier Club of bibliophiles. Once again the Eton College library came to the rescue, for on the basis of his researches there he was able to dazzle his hosts with an address about a series of Old Etonians who had been among the earliest settlers in America, and one in particular, Thomas Lynch, who had signed the Declaration of Independence. For their own crossings of the Atlantic, on the *Queen Elizabeth* going out and the *Franconia* coming back, the Birleys had a place of honour at the Captain's table; on the return journey it even turned out to be peppered with Balliol men.

These absences did not ease the task of maintaining contact with the hundred or so Eton masters individually, but there were nevertheless, apart from Chambers, various ways in which Birley made his benign influence felt in their lives. The married ones would for example hear from their wives how he had charmed an audience of Eton ladies with erudite lectures on Dante. His family made their mark too, notably on the occasion when the Birleys' two daughters Julia and Rachael mounted an exhibition of modern art, the work of an imaginary American artist called Hamilton T. Forsyth. Together with various accomplices they painted all the pictures themselves and put one of their friends up to impersonating the artist. Hamilton T. Forsyth was in fact the name that Rachael had given to a hypothetical stick insect which she claimed she kept in her room at Lady Margaret Hall, Oxford. The exhibition was arranged for an evening when Birley *père et mère* were to be out to dinner. The younger Eton masters and their wives were invited, all of them knowing full well that it was a spoof, thought up as a way of promoting a lively party. It was, too, a lively affair and when the Birleys arrived home from dinner they steered well clear, slipping upstairs to bed forthwith. The whole episode became quite a talking point next day, for it was reported in the *Daily Mail* under the headline ETON MASTERS HOAXED – AND THE HEAD KNEW ALL ABOUT IT. Birley was quite angry with Julia who was the ringleader. It was the press incident which annoyed him and made it difficult for him to appreciate the contribution that the party made to the sense of community at Eton.

Birley's own contribution to this sense of community lay first and foremost in his loyalty to staff and boys alike. He could, it is true, be ruthless in his punishment of gross misdemeanours, but within his moral Pale he showed warm understanding as well as loyalty. As David Macindoe, the present Vice-Provost, wrote in the *Chronicle* obituary: 'When a House Master outraged parents by some high-handed action, it was he who accepted the responsibility and the abuse; when a young boy was detected stealing small sums of money twice in a month, it was he who insisted that there was no question of expulsion, but that the rest of the house should be told, in strict confidence, and urged to carry the boy through his time at Eton; it was the making of the boy and the house.'

This loyalty showed itself at its most fierce in the face of any criticism from outside the school. John Wells, who went to teach at Eton towards the end of Birley's time, found himself projected into embarrassing limelight by the popular press. Having done a good deal of cabaret with Richard Ingrams and William Rushton at Oxford, he had joined them and Barbara Windsor for a performance at *The Room at the Top*, a night club

above a furniture shop in Ilford. The show had been devised by
Stephen Vinaver and produced by Willie Donaldson – alias,
much later, Henry Root. The circumstances turned out to be
somewhat seamier than he had bargained for, and Wells
innocently sought an undertaking from a marmalade-haired
press agent that there would be no reference to the fact that he
was teaching at Eton at the time. It was the best way of ensuring
the opposite, a gleeful headline in a popular newspaper
proclaiming ETON MASTER PEDDLES SMUT IN EAST
END. Wells's performance had in fact been a characteristic
product of the satire boom of the time, an impersonation of
Field-Marshal Montgomery, wicked no doubt but innocuously
devoid of smut. Although it was the muckraking, not the
impropriety which was the real issue, the whole shoddy
business greatly upset the Provost and Fellows. Birley took it
upon himself to defend Wells publicly as being a very good
schoolmaster, while privately explaining to him the importance
of using a long spoon when supping with the devil. What was
significant was that he did not let the responsibility fall on his
young colleague but absorbed much of the flak on his behalf. It
was on this loyalty to his staff that his authority among them
was quite naturally founded.

Few things in fact aroused Birley's indignation quite so much
as his dealings with the press. His reaction to the reporting of
his daughters' party was characteristic. In any situation that
involved journalists he was sufficiently nervous to be capable of
losing his bearings, an extraordinary blind spot in someone who
had an intuitive sense of direction as a headmaster. There was
the time when one of the house captains was made, against his
better judgement, to beat a junior boy. The boy then ran away,
the incident got into the papers, with the house captain named,
and his father stormed down to Eton to see Birley. At the end of
the tirade to which he was subjected, Birley looked very
concerned and said: 'We mustn't let this get into the papers.'

It is true that most of the journalistic activity boiled down to a
search for stories about revelries of drunken boys or break-ins
by sex maniacs. But in practice reporters mostly had to make do
with accounts of schoolboy pranks. There was the occasion
when Charterhouse boys daubed an Eton cannon, a revered
relic, with paint and put up signs saying CHARTER-

HOUSE – STRICTLY PRIVATE; and when Eton boys retaliated by painting two equally revered statues at Charterhouse Etonian blue. Although much of the attention of the press was good-humoured, and spitefulness was rare, Birley could never really bring himself to accept it with any sort of good grace. Quite harmless episodes could lead him to overreact with uncharacteristic pomposity. One instance of this was when Lord Snowdon – then the young Antony Armstrong-Jones, a recent Old Etonian – took some photographs for the *Tatler*, provoking a frosty letter, which Snowdon later reproduced in his book *Personal View*.

FROM THE HEAD MASTER

Personal   16th February, 1953

Dear Mr Armstrong-Jones,

I understand that you were responsible for taking a number of photographs at Eton of boys coming back at the beginning of this half. As you were with your half-brother Martin Parsons, whose photograph you took, I take it that the information I received was correct.

I should be glad to have an assurance from you that you will not take photographs again in that way about Eton without obtaining our permission first. I may say that this permission would not be granted for photographs of this kind. We realise that on certain occasions, such as the Fourth of June, the situation is rather different, but we do not want to have photographs taken generally of boys while at the school in the way this was done for the number of The Tatler.

Yours sincerely,
R. BIRLEY

The attentions of the press were unwelcome enough. For an Old Etonian to be involved was, for Birley, adding insult to injury. This paranoid attitude persisted to the very end. In his last year as Head Master he wrote to Giles St Aubyn apropos of an incident involving the press: 'Do be careful about these people. The *only* thing to do is not to trust them an inch'. It was as well that towards the end of his headmastership he was prevailed upon to leave this particular kind of public relations largely to the Lower Master; Oliver Van Oss, himself the son of a press baron, could handle reporters with a skill that the Head Master did not possess.

The edginess with the press was the one exception to the natural sense of authority, physical, intellectual and moral, that Birley exuded. It was as assured with the boys as with the masters. To be sure his shyness did not make it easy, and a fair number of boys went through the school without having any direct dealings with him. But for those who did get to know him informally for one reason or another, his understanding tolerance and concern for their welfare belied the outward signs of aloofness. His awareness of difficulties could astound. Tom Camoys spent his first three and a half years at Eton in the unfortunate situation of having to wear a steel brace because of a back ailment. The resulting exclusion from all games was no joke at that age. In his first term, at the very bottom of the school, he was wandering about looking for some division room or other when R. B., on his way from Chambers, buttonholed him. The small boy was startled at being recognised at all, let alone being told by the Head Master how sorry he was about the back trouble, and how important it was to turn the situation to his advantage by putting the spare energy into his academic work. Camoys very soon leapfrogged into a more competitive division, in what was called a 'double remove'. After that he went from strength to strength, became a house captain and ended up with a place at Balliol. Another Balliol episode demonstrated Birley's ever-readiness to step in when help was needed. The boy in question who impetuously walked out of his entrance examination for the College and was subsequently miserable, was astonished to find himself suddenly taken in hand and driven rather inexpertly to Oxford for lunch, after which the Balliol dons were prevailed upon to give him another chance to take the abandoned papers.

In matters of routine discipline Birley made the fullest use of awe-inspiring ceremonial. When malefactors were hauled before him, no hint of familiarity tempered the terrifying formality of the occasion. This terror being frequently punishment enough, he was able to accompany his bark with a minimum of bite. At other times he could show flashes of imagination in coping with disciplinary problems – as for instance when it had been brought to his notice that a particular master had lost control of a class to the point where the boys were shambling into lessons chewing gum and wearing bedroom slippers, as a way of signalling their intention to do no work. One morning they arrived sleepily in early school in this state and, to begin with, noticed nothing amiss. The master appeared to be at his desk as usual – hidden behind a copy of *The Times*. Suddenly, with a timing worthy of Alec Guinness, *The Times* was lowered to reveal the avenging Fury in the person of the Head Master. None of them ate a hearty breakfast after the lesson was over.

Discipline was, however, only one dimension of Birley's aura of authority, and in the context of Eton life as a whole a comparatively minor one. His impact on the boys was made in a more positive way, both through his teaching and his efforts to build up their confidence and self-possession. He enjoyed making his own contribution to the many ways that Eton has of developing the capacity to speak in public. In Harold Nicolson's *Diaries* the entry for 20 October 1954 reads:

> I go down to Eton to lunch with Birley. After lunch a boy of the name of Shaw appears and does a recitation from Arketall [Lord Curzon's bibulous valet, to whom Nicolson devoted a chapter in his collection of autobiographical sketches *Some People*]. He had chosen the recitation for Speeches, and Birley, in his amused way, had said, 'Well, I have the author coming here on Wednesday, and if you come in after luncheon, he will show you exactly how Curzon talked'. I should have died of shame at his age, but Shaw took it calmly. How wonderful Eton and Birley are at giving self-confidence to a lad!

Building self-confidence in this way has of course been an art in public schools generally, but at Eton it has a particular political dimension. In a book about the school published towards the end of Birley's headmastership, former Conservative MP Christopher Hollis wrote that 'there is no school anywhere in the world which has a record as a nursery of politicians which even begins to approach that of Eton'. It is hardly surprising that this tradition has survived, in view of the magnetic attraction of Eton as a place for leading politicians to have their sons educated. By virtue of its size as well as its reputation it has no doubt been every bit as remarkable as a nursery of prominent figures in many other walks of life. But for all the variety of the flowering of Etonians it was the political orientation that most fully captured Birley's imagination. It was always his unhesitating answer to the question: what is the single most important characteristic of the school? It was one of the biggest factors in his ambition to become Head Master, for he saw the position not only as one in which he could educate future politicians but also as one in which he could himself have an influence in political affairs.

The opportunity to make a start came almost immediately. In his first half as Head Master Birley followed in the footsteps of Bertrand Russell and delivered the second series of Reith Lectures, on the theme of European Union. Though the subject was on the face of it topical, there was something unreal about it. The desire for union which was so evident on the Continent was not shared in a Britain still resting on its postwar laurels of moral superiority over the rest of Europe. It was a point at which the country was in danger of drawing complacent rather than constructive conclusions from the war. The vision that had prompted Churchill to moot the idea of a United States of Europe was still heavily clouded and Birley began his first Reith Lecture with the forthright assumption 'that when we say we have decided to join a European Union, we mean what we say'. But he recognised that it was probably still too large an assumption and that his lectures were really about finding some new path that might lead to a European outlook in Britain, an understanding that unity could be achieved without sacrificing diversity.

Up till then most of the discussion had centred on the economic aspects of the problem and to a lesser extent on the political. Birley turned his attention to the traditional British ways of thought in which political attitudes have their roots. This he called the cultural aspect, in the full awareness that culture had, *pace* T. S. Eliot, 'become one of those words which are used when we want to avoid thinking clearly'. The fundamental theme was that there was no historical inevitability about Britain's separateness from the rest of Europe. In order to put the imperial tradition into perspective he looked back at the mingling of traditions in the Lindisfarne Gospels; he recalled that in the eighth century Wynfrith from Crediton in Devonshire had been chiefly responsible for the conversion of the German tribes to Christianity; and he evoked the homage paid to England in the eighteenth century because its society was founded on principles which writers like Voltaire declared in his *Lettres anglaises* to provide a model for Europe. For if the eighteenth century was the 'French century' in which every ruler of every little principality was building himself a palace on the model of Versailles, 'the original ideas which changed men's views on politics and social relationships and were to cause the great revolutions at the end of the century, came for the most part from this country. These ideas were visible in British society, with its tolerance and intellectual freedom, its insistence on the principle that all men were equal before the law as the best defence against tyranny, and its remarkable parliamentary system of government. And they were expressed by great writers such as Locke and Adam Smith, who were read all over the Continent and were regarded as European figures'.

The point about developing the theme of the enduring principles of society was that any European Union had to stand for something fundamental if it was to be anything more than merely an alliance. There had to be common ideals. The lectures set out to explore the meaning of such terms as patriotism and nationalism, to show that it is possible to reconcile different loyalties – 'no Englishman wants a Scot or a Welshman to "replace" his loyalty to Scotland or Wales or feels that this is incompatible with his loyalty to Britain' – and to suggest three particular contributions that Britain could make to the way of life of a European union. The first was the Disraeli one-nation ideal of social cohesion, the second was the balance between a belief in individual freedom and a sense of social responsibility, and the third was the principle of the rule of law which was endangered by the growth of bureaucracy.

However trite they may since have come to sound, these were fundamental themes, and the erudition and inventiveness of Birley's variations on them added a streak of originality to the national debate on Europe. The fact that the lectures were the first public utterances of the new Head Master of Eton added to the notice they attracted. There were some private tributes but the public response was not especially favourable. The general impression was that the lectures were too much of a history lesson, with Birley's restlessly erudite discursiveness obscuring what he was trying to say. The radio critic of the *Observer* suggested that 'Mr Birley the accompanist was dominating Mr Birley the soloist, so that the melody was sometimes overpowered by the embellishments of the pianist'. Although the lectures made good reading in the *Listener*, he had not mastered the art of writing to capture an audience on wireless. Hence he came off badly in the comparison with Bertrand Russell whose inaugural series had made more compelling listening. The *Spectator* critic summed it up, observing that 'Mr Birley seemed to have composed his lectures for the study rather than the studio'.

The one really controversial point that Birley made was in the third lecture, on the question of the need for a common language. His suggestion that it would be best if this were French laid him open to the charge of superficial thinking. The *Manchester Guardian* asked whether a common language really was a road to international understanding. 'Where one exists – in Belfast and Dublin for example, or in Brussels and Paris – the civil servants and dons to not automatically embrace like long-lost brothers.' And from a listener in Bristol Birley received an eight-page letter filled with quotations purporting to show that there was Biblical authority for saying that the European nations would never unite.

Much more fierce was the reaction from the right-wing journal *Truth* in which an attack on Birley's internationalism became the focus for resentment at his appointment as Head Master of Eton:

It cannot be said . . . that the title of the first discourse was reassuring. If there be, as assuredly there must, an Old Etonian section of Valhalla, its occupants, representing very many generations of men who have striven for the sovereign independence of their land, could only have been amazed and hurt beyond measure to hear a headmaster of their famous college speaking to the world on 'The Problem of Patriotism'. Patriotism for these men, as for millions of others bred in the same tradition, was no more a problem than is breathing a problem to healthy lungs. It was instinctive, as, indeed, it must be in every national community which has not run to seed. Why, then, should Mr Birley find difficulty in it? The answer is that it obstructs the building, and may endanger the maintenance, of the artificial contraption which he and all the other fashionable internationalist indeterminants wish to erect at Strasbourg, or Geneva, or Lake Success, or wherever it may be.

The flow of invective culminated in a denunciation of the whole Federal movement, nurtured by the pinkoes of the BBC, and with the appointment of Birley to Eton interpreted as the ultimate illustration of the rot that had set in throughout British national life.

While it is easy to ridicule the pretensions of the Federalists, one must not forget that the Federal movement is strong and the danger arising from it is real. It has been, in one form or another, the theme-song of the BBC from its earliest days. That the headmaster of our greatest public school should now proclaim his adherence to it shows how low has fallen the star of our nationhood. What was won on the playing fields of Eton, it seems, is destined to be thrown away in the Headmaster's study. Were Mr Birley's views known when he received his appointment? A more awful thought – was his appointment made, in part, because of those views? Queer things happen these days, and answers to such questions are never tendered. His Majesty the King, when at Windsor, may care to take note that his neighbour across the river finds patriotism to be a problem.

Nor did the matter rest there. From the backwoods a number of Old Etonians wrote to the Provost to say that he and the Fellows had made a great mistake in appointing Birley, and that they ought to get rid of him as soon as possible. For one of them this was not enough. He wrote a letter to *Truth* saying that Birley ought to be tried for High Treason. The letter was published. The Head Master of Eton survived.

While the Reith Lectures did therefore arouse a certain amount of controversy and public interest, they were not a contribution sufficiently striking to launch Birley on a path of political influence. If there was any prospect of his following such a path it lay in the oportunities for personal contacts which his position brought him. Many political figures visited Eton, invited by the boys to speak to various societies, and Birley was always ready to help by entertaining them to dinner. On a personal level he became very friendly with Fenner Brockway, the Labour Member for Eton and Slough. When he was elected in 1950, Brockway wrote to Birley to say that, although he did not expect the school to approve of his political views, he was none the less their MP and would be glad to help in any way he could. Birley responded by inviting him to Eton from time to time. Eyebrows were raised when in the spring of 1959 Brockway was asked to judge the Birchall Citizenship Prize competition. The subject was race relations and the recommended reading was *Naught for our Comfort* by Trevor Huddleston. An Old Etonian MP, who got to hear of the invitation, promptly wrote to the Provost, protesting at the choice of someone 'whose own record on the subject is so highly coloured'. Whatever the amusement the letter caused, it was for Birley one of those tiresome incidents that had to be kept quiet, for fear the press would get hold of it and present the Labour Party with an opportunity to make their Tory opponents look foolish.

Not that Birley had much cause for unswerving allegiance to the Conservative Party at this time, for little had come of his ambition to be the *éminence grise* of national education policy. In two two-year terms as Chairman of the Headmasters' Conference he had had a good measure of practical politics during a decade which saw a growing urge in the Conference to make the public schools socially less exclusive. Birley was a natural leader of deputations to the Ministry of Education in Curzon Street. But he had little leverage with a Conservative government. Many fences had been broken by his membership of the Fleming Committee and the internationalism of his Reith Lectures, and there was little prospect of mending them. Among right-wing Tories he was marked down as untrustworthy.

The meeting at which Birley and his colleagues urged central funding for a scholarship scheme was a sad disappointment. The Minister was Lord Hailsham; at the HMC Annual

Meeting of 1957 Birley reported on how he had turned down their proposals. 'He said he could see only four reasons for deciding to send a boy to an independent boarding school. The first reason was that the school might belong to or be connected with a particular religious denomination, to which the boy's parents also belonged. The second was that it might provide a classical education. The third was that it might provide a certain type of discipline – that the boy would be beaten, preferably by other boys. The fourth was that the parents might have a family connection with the school'. On none of these grounds, Lord Hailsham had continued, could public expenditure be justified. If the criterion were to give a better education on other grounds than these, then not more than five public schools would be superior to the average grammar school. In any case, he had concluded, conveniently ignoring the direct grant schools, for the Ministry to administer and finance such a scheme would be an invasion of the rights of the local education authorities, and positively undemocratic. It was not until some twenty-five years later, when the grammar schools had largely been replaced by comprehensives and the direct grant abolished, that a Conservative government was disposed explicitly to reject the argument about local autonomy and introduce the quite differently conceived assisted places scheme. Although this was something on which the Party was reasonably united, the initiative for it did not come from the middle-of-the-road paternalist Tories with whom Birley had most in common.

Birley could indeed be said to have a growing share in the shaping of this moderate tradition. A fair number of Carthusians and Etonians of his time found their way into the House of Commons or became active in the Lords. In a tribute in *The Carthusian* William Rees-Mogg wrote that 'he grounded a sense of historic liberalism in all of us'. While it would be going too far to talk of his exerting direct political influence on future parliamentarians while they were at school, it is none the less remarkable how many of them kept in touch with him in later years.

The great meeting-place was Königswinter where his friends and ex-pupils from all parties could gather in an atmosphere free of the ritualised antagonisms of Westminster; men like

Dick Taverne and Geoffrey Johnson Smith of the Charterhouse generation, Jo Grimond and David Howell from his
earlier and later Eton periods respectively. One of the most
notably Birleyesque pairings was that of Carthusian Jim Prior
and Etonian Grey Gowrie successively at the Department of
Employment and the Northern Ireland Office in Mrs Thatch-
er's first government.

To dwell on Birley's involvement with national politics
would however be to misinterpret what it was that made him a
nationally respected figure. It was on his headmastership of two
great schools that his reputation primarily rested, and among
his peers it was formidable. The network of political contacts
did of course contribute to the aura which surrounded him at
the Headmasters' Conference. He was forever giving the
impression that he knew what was going on behind the scenes.
'Don't raise that now', he would say knowingly in committee, 'I
am having lunch with the Minister on Thursday and I am going
to bring it up then.' Amusing as his fellow Heads found his
conspiratorial manner and the confidences communicated with
the utmost secrecy, their amusement did not diminish their
affection. He was just that bit older and just sufficiently more
experienced than the other leading headmasters of the time to
be able to get away with what in lesser men would have been
regarded as namedropping. To the younger heads he was a
figure to venerate – even more than the other three great
personalities of the Conference in the 1950s, Eric James, High
Master of Manchester Grammar School, or as used to be said,
of Manchester itself, Desmond Lee, the fearsomely clear-
minded Head of Winchester, and the humorously avuncular
Walter Hamilton of Rugby. For a decade or more these four
seemed to take it in turn to be the Chairman of the Conference.
Only Hamilton matched Birley's record of four years in the
chair.

Birley therefore enjoyed as much power in the political forum
of the public school world as any other headmaster of his time.
But unlike normal politics where national prominence has
seldom much to do with local constituency support, the
reputation of a headmaster is not built on his performances on
any national stage. Rather it rests on the sum of countless
relationships in the humdrum everyday life of a school, the

aggregate of debts of the boys and girls that he has taught, helped and guided. These are the 'first things first'. Without them any adventitious national reputation is built on sand.

With Robert Birley, the foundation was solid in a way that makes it no exaggeration to speak not merely of reputation but of renown. His departure from Eton, on his retirement at his sixtieth birthday, was one of the most remarkable sights witnessed there in recent times. It is only on such rare occasions that the entire school is assembled. The Head Master's farewell address was not particularly sparkling, but it was transcendentally genuine, and the boys responded with that cumulative intuition which in some mysterious way draws the experience of earlier generations into the crescendo of appreciation. The applause was ecstatic, lasting for 2 minutes 59 seconds. The familiar shambling figure was overwhelmed. No film director planning a new *Mr Chips* could have dreamt up a more spectacular final shot than the view of R. B., his head and one waving hand just visible above an ocean of cheering boys, against the backdrop of Lupton's Tower, with the pale faces of the Fellows, who had been meeting over dinner, peering out of its upper windows at a demonstration of affection that they could scarcely credit. And, walking away from this magical scene the son of a well-known Irish racehorse trainer, impervious to hysteria, remarked to one of the younger masters, 'What a very tedious episode!'

CHAPTER TWELVE

South Africa

Life at Eton was so full that the Birleys rarely had time or inclination to talk about the future. In the normal run of things the appointment of a new Head Master would be due in about 1964, and it was only when this time was fast approaching that Birley gave any thought to what he should do next. A quiet retirement was difficult to imagine. One problem had been provisionally solved, the mundane one of where to live. The constant flow of visitors to Eton, in holidays as much as in term, was such that by 1958 the Birleys had begun to feel the need of a bolthole to which they could occasionally escape into anonymity. In the course of a visit to some friends in Canterbury they were told of a small Georgian terrace house that was for sale nearby. They arranged to buy it there and then. It was in any case time to face the tied cottage problem and plan for the day when they would no longer have a house provided for them. Although at that time no one had dreamt of a new university being founded in Canterbury, by 1962 when the plans for the University of Kent were well advanced, the coincidence had led to some speculation that Birley would be its first Vice-Chancellor. In the autumn half of that year he found himself repeatedly obliged to dismiss the rumour that he was going to leave Eton early.

As far as Canterbury was concerned, the rumour appeared to be without foundation. But there was some substance to the suggestion that Birley might become a Vice-Chancellor. In March 1962 he received a letter from his old friend John Maud who was now British Ambassador in South Africa. This was to let him know that he would shortly be receiving an invitation from a body calling itself the 1961 Education Panel to go out to South Africa on a short visit. The Panel had been set up as a kind of private commission of enquiry, its main purpose being to marshall opposition to a government education policy which appeared to threaten independent schools. As a well-known champion of the English public schools, on which a number of South African schools were modelled, Birley was an obvious person to consult. In his letter Maud urged his friend to accept the invitation, but his reason for doing so went beyond a mere desire to accommodate the Panel. It so happened that later that year the Vice-Chancellor of the University of the Witwatersrand was to retire and according to Maud 'those with most knowledge and influence desperately want his successor to be a really distinguished one from Britain'. Behind the invitation lay the idea that the Birleys could have a look at 'Wits' without any commitment. Maud was quite sure that if Birley chose to, he could become the next Vice-Chancellor.

The prime mover behind the invitation was Whitmore Richards, director of one of the gold mining houses, member of the Council of Wits, friend of John Maud, and someone who was very conscious of his own English background. Educated at Wellington and Caius College, Cambridge, he devoted a great deal of his energy to the encouragement of English education and the support of the private schools. And he was one of the founders of the 1961 Education Panel. When Birley, having accepted the invitation, visited South Africa in the spring of 1962, a first report on the Panel's deliberations had just been published. It consisted of a brief statement of principles and philosophy, and it was now time to follow this up in a more practical way. The working committee found itself at a loss how to proceed and its members looked to Birley for inspiration. They were not disappointed. He joined in the discussions with his customary enthusiasm, giving them a new and positive impetus. He was just the man they needed.

The Vice-Chancellorship was, however, a quite different matter. Richards's influence, however great it was in the world of independent schools, did not extend to the Council of Wits, which at that particular time could not conceivably have considered anyone other than a South African for the position of Vice-Chancellor. Birley was never seriously considered. In fact the main link which Richards had with Wits was with the Faculty of Education. He had been something of a critic of its work and in order to expand its scope he had pressed for the establishment of a second chair. Although he had succeeded in this, it had so far proved impossible to fill the new post satisfactorily. Birley was well suited to step into the breach and was invited to do so as Visiting Professor. When he returned to England he had the autumn half in which to think it over. At a special meeting early in December he told the Eton masters of the offer, and that he had decided to accept it.

When the Birleys arrived in Johannesburg it was barely three years since the police had killed sixty-nine blacks at a riot in Sharpeville and barely three months since the African National Congress leader, Nelson Mandela, had been imprisoned. During their first year he was tried once again and sentenced for life. What he said from the dock made an indelible impression:

> Above all, we want equal political rights, because without them our disabilities will be permanent. I know this sounds revolutionary to the whites in this country because the majority of voters will be Africans. This makes the white man fear democracy. But the fear cannot stand in the way of the only solution which will guarantee racial harmony and freedom for all. . . .
>
> During my lifetime I have dedicated myself to the struggle of the African people. I have fought against white domination and I have fought against black domination. I have cherished the ideal of a democratic and free society in which all persons live together in harmony and with equal opportunities. It is an ideal which I hope to live for and to achieve. But if needs be, it is an ideal for which I am prepared to die.

This dignified statement expressed the sentiments with which the Birleys identified themselves.

Taking up the post of Professor of Education at such a time was bound to excite the crusading side of Birley's make-up, the same urge to fight intolerance and repression as he had admired in some of the courageous survivors of persecution under Hitler that he had got to know in Germany after the war. There was no question of his sitting idly by and settling for a quiet donnish life aloof from the action. On the other hand, as a newcomer it would have been presumptuous to appear to be setting this very complex world to rights, quite apart from the practical dangers of causing trouble for other people, when he himself would always have a convenient escape route. It was scarcely conceivable that he would be arrested – he was, as he generally liked to put it, 'too respectable'. But he was quite aware that whatever quasi-diplomatic immunity his position gave him, it was wise not to trade too heavily on it.

There were two major tasks that Birley had been set. The first had to do with the transition of young people from school to university. In South Africa admission to the universities was not highly selective. There were few nuances of the kind associated with A level grades in the United Kingdom. Getting a place was, broadly speaking, a matter of passing rather than failing the matriculation examination. The corollary of a large drop-out at the end of the first year was perhaps to be expected. But even so there was at Wits a desire to look for ways of improving the success rate, and it was this that Birley was asked to do. To understand the problem he needed to get to know the schools, something which interested him every bit as much as teaching in the University.

It very soon became Birley's view that the schools were not preparing their pupils adequately. It was not a simple matter of criticising the teachers. They were, he thought, enslaved by a rigid syllabus leading to a matriculation examination which put disproportionate emphasis on learning things by heart. As a result they had little experience of fostering independent thinking among their pupils, who in turn found themselves at a loss when faced with the demands of university study. In short, there was no sixth form on the English model with which he was so familiar. On one of his school visits he came across a most extraordinary lesson in progress during which the boys were told to shut their books, put their heads on the desks and go to sleep. The teacher then put on a record of some music and intoned a list of historical facts, mainly dates. Birley was flabbergasted. The young man doing the 'teaching' told him somewhat sheepishly that sleep learning was an effective technique. They did remember their dates.

All this was a denial of what Birley himself had stood for up till then. In his farewell address to Eton he had said that one of the most important things about the school was that when uncomfortable ideas were put forward, they were met not by raised eyebrows but by vigorous argument. However much learning a teacher had to impart it was, in Birley's view, the argument about what he said that was the real education. South African schools were failing to educate in this way and it was this failure above all that prompted him to try to bring about changes in the examination system. Mischievously – for it was not altogether a fair comparison – he drew on his own lack of examination success at school in advocating reforms. And since examination boards can seldom be the most popular of educational institutions, his protests against their tyranny found a ready echo among parents suffering from 'matric neurosis'.

It was not long before Birley was initiating discussions of how the situation could be improved. He arranged meetings between representatives of schools and universities which were without precedent. Not unexpectedly, some felt threatened. On one occasion he was catching a plane to Bloemfontein to speak at a meeting and at the airport ran into a group of teachers from the Transvaal. One of them told him that they were on their way to the same meeting to support the Orange Free State opposition 'to that scheme of yours for bringing teachers and university people together'. In fact it was in the Transvaal that in due course an experiment was begun whereby in twenty selected schools the external matriculation examination would be replaced by the schools' own assessment of their pupils' abilities. The chairman of the committee responsible for trying out this scheme declared that 'he hoped it would result in making pupils more competent to think for themselves and more likely to adapt themselves to the outside world after leaving school'. Here at least Birley's message appeared to have got through.

The other main assignment was more sensitive. In 1959 an Act of Parliament had withdrawn from the universities their right to take in whatever students they wished, regardless of colour. The intention was – so leading figures in the government maintained – to phase out completely the opportunities for blacks to study at white universities. Before 1959 Wits had in fact had only a small number of black students. The prospect now was that even this number would be steadily reduced and that such links as the University had with black education would be loosened and fall away. Birley was to find ways of keeping in touch. This too meant getting to know the schools, a task hampered by many obstacles and disincentives. He managed however to spend a lot of his spare time slipping off to visit, and teach classes in, the high schools of Soweto. There was a conspiratorial flavour to this which greatly appealed to Birley, particularly as he seldom bothered to obtain the permit that was, strictly speaking, needed. He was not really doing anything illegal. But there was an unmistakeable atmosphere of intimidation in South Africa at that time, arising from a desire on the part of some officials to create uncertainty about what was and what was not allowed. So while teaching in Soweto was not quite the cloak-and-dagger activity that Birley liked to think it was, and there was no real likelihood that he would fall foul of the authorities, he was showing considerable strength of character in doing so. Here was a prominent figure demonstrating a quite unusual disregard for conventional barriers which during that period of exceptional tension could appear just as daunting as legal ones. There was something about it that was reminiscent of A. D. Lindsay's call to Balliol men to ennoble their safe camps by going beyond them.

The simple directness of the young people in the African schools called for a different approach from the one that was appropriate for the history specialists at Charterhouse or Eton. The kind of question he was asked was, 'Is it true that the Nazis killed a great many Jews?' to which he would reply, 'Yes.' 'How many?' 'Well, the most conservative figure I can give you is five million.' Birley would then break the shocked silence by saying, 'If I give you a promise that when there is a massacre in the Congo, I will never say that is what blacks do, will you promise me that you will not say this is what whites do?' This would be followed by a solemn exchange of promises. Birley would then tell the story of the symbol of the 'White Rose' and how a small group of Munich students gave their lives to resist Hitler. This time the silence was expectant rather than shocked. 'Now if I promise that I will not say this is what the Congolese do, but what *some* people in the Congo do, will you promise that you will not say this is what the Germans do, only what *some* Germans have done?' Again there would be a solemn exchange of promises. It was the technique of someone with an intuitive gift for teaching.

The difficulties under which the black schools were working were immense. At the time it was Government policy to regard the blacks in Johannesburg as temporary residents – rather like Turkish or Italian *Gastarbeiter* in Germany or Switzerland – who would all eventually go away. The consequence was to oppose the establishing of facilities which would give Soweto a permanent look. For a residential area of such magnitude, comprising as the acronym indicates the various townships of the south-west, the place was startlingly lacking in shops and recreational and social amenities, even compared with the well-known poor communities of, say, Brazil. Soweto was treated as though it did not exist. There were no signposts to it and it was common practice to leave it off maps altogether.

In such unpromising circumstances the quality of work in some of the black schools was remarkably high. The more ambitious ones, like Orlando High School at which Birley did most of his teaching, subjected themselves to the strongest competition by preparing their pupils for the school-leaving examinations which were thought to be the most difficult, those of the Joint Matriculation Board. The original idea behind the creation of the JMB, on which all the South African universities and education departments were represented, was that it would supersede the four individual provincial examining authorities, so that there would be one national matriculation. The provincial examinations survived, however, and although all five were supposed to be of equivalent status, the JMB was generally thought to be of a higher standard than the others and was the one taken at the white independent schools.

Within the curriculum, too, Orlando High and similar schools chose the most difficult options. English, Afrikaans and the five recognised black languages were all examined at two levels; the higher was intended for native speakers and the lower was for those learning it as a second language. Boys and girls of all races had to pass both English and Afrikaans, and to pass in one language at the higher level. If blacks took their home language at the higher level, they could take both English and Afrikaans at the lower. Schools like Orlando High would not do this. They believed that mastery of English was crucial and encouraged, sometimes even required their pupils to write English at the higher level. Consequently there was a strong flavour of English culture in the education they were providing. As far as literature went, George Eliot was considered patronising, while Shakespeare and Dickens were very popular. 'Dickens writes about us', they would say. On one occasion Birley's heart sank when he discovered that Trollope was among the set books. But this, too, went down very well, perhaps by virtue of its describing a hierarchical rural society.

Such brushes as Birley had with the authorities over his activities in black schools could have an element of farce about them. He had helped to raise money for a new library for Orlando High School. The existing one was a room about sixteen feet square which doubled as a staff room. After it had been opened by Harry Oppenheimer, South Africa's best known industrialist, an extraordinary furore ensued when it became known that the school was proposing to call it the Robert Birley Library. The Secretary for Bantu Education declared that a school library could not be called after a well-known communist who in England was known as the Red Dean. When challenged about this allegation that Birley was Dr Hewlett Johnson, the Secretary revealed the source of his information to be the *Encyclopædia Britannica*. Despite his protestations the name was put up. But when permission was later sought to open the library in the evenings for more general use, which required an increase in the staff, it was forthcoming only on condition that the sign was removed. Thanks to the resourcefulness of the Headmaster, Wilkie Kambule, they managed to keep it none the less. The words 'Sir Robert Birley' were only lightly painted out and remained clearly visible.

In the course of the argument over the naming of the library the blacks had protested to the officials of the Department of Bantu Education that 'Professor Birley is one of our own people'. This tribute rested on much more than the periodic bits of teaching in African schools. The Birleys poured their energies into tackling the whole range of educational and social problems of Soweto. Elinor's contribution was a revelation, more fulfilling for her personally than any of the roles that she had previously played in support of her husband. In Germany she had never shown any interest in queening it as the wife of a high-ranking official of the Control Commission. As a headmaster's wife she had worked assiduously in the background without any pretensions to prestige as a hostess. In South Africa she found a cause which fired her liberalism and to which she committed herself with a fixity of purpose that no obstructive bureaucracy could deflect.

One of the greatest social problems of a vast dormitory like Soweto was the care of small children whose mothers had to travel long distances to work. Elinor became deeply involved in the organising of the system of creches which a group of liberal whites had set up. There were twenty-eight creches and they had to open by 6.30 a.m. to enable the mothers to catch their buses to Johannesburg. The whole scheme would not have been possible without the support of the whites who were prepared to raise funds and organise the delivery of enough food to provide three meals a day for some 2,000 children. The cost to the black families was around £2 a month. It was Elinor Birley's particular responsibility to take the money to the bank, something which it was safe to do only by car. But the scheme itself, known as the African Self Help Association, was run by blacks, and one of its other purposes was to train African women for this kind of work.

The significance of the link between nutrition and education had been apparent ever since Dr Malan's government, formed after the electoral defeat of General Smuts in 1948, had stopped providing school meals. The headmistress of an upper primary school told Elinor of having had children who used to faint for lack of food. This kind of distress had prompted Trevor Huddleston, who was at that time priest-in-charge of the Sophiatown and Orlando Anglican Missions, to begin the African Children's Feeding Scheme which was soon catering for 200,000 children a day and which was the model for similar arrangements all over South Africa. When the Birleys arrived in Johannesburg in 1963, therefore, the scheme had been running for fifteen years or so and it was apparent that it had made an enormous contribution to the standard of work of the children. To support both this and the more recent creche scheme the Birleys were active in maintaining the level of voluntary subscriptions from private enterprise. Even if some of the funds raised were conscience money, it did not matter. What was important above all else was that the children in the creches and in the schools should be physically and mentally in a fit state to take advantage of such educational opportunities as were open to them.

In their work in Soweto the Birleys were identifying themselves with those in the liberal white community most actively opposed to the apartheid policy. They were shocked and incensed at the injustices. A letter which Elinor wrote to a friend in England gave a vivid first-hand account of a particularly Petty Session at one court:

Johannesburg, 29th May 1964

I have just had my first taste of South African justice as meted out to the 'Bantu'. A friend of mine asked me if I would care to go with her to a Magistrate's Court at Kliptown, where her cook was coming up for non-payment of rent. The summons was sent to the cook's house in the township and served on a *relative* in her absence; in England this would have invalidated the whole thing and I believe that it does here too. However, the summons gave her rather less than a week's notice, as she did not hear of it at once; and as she was due to leave with the family for a fortnight's holiday in the Eastern Transvaal specially in order to do the cooking, she said nothing about it to her mistress. When they got back she did nothing, expecting, I think quite genuinely, that she would get another summons. In the ensuing three months the arrears of rent, about £4.10.0. was paid off and she probably thought that the matter was closed. On Wednesday, May 27th, she went along to pay the rent herself (usually she sends one of the children) and was immediately shot straight into prison for 'contempt' of court. Fortunately someone telephoned her mistress, who after about two hours hard work discovered that she was to come before the Magistrate at Kliptown court to-day. Kliptown is a township for Coloureds (people of mixed African and European blood) technically 'open' which means that it is on, or rather just off, a public road and has no notice saying that no one without a permit may enter, and no police post at the entrance, as is the case on the roads leading to the African townships. But cases from the African townships are tried there too. It is a group of rather mean, though clean, buildings, shoved down anyhow inside a compound without any kind of layout, surrounded by an 8 ft barbed wire and chain-link fence.

We were told to be there at 9 a.m. and when we got there we found an official whom we took to be the caretaker, speaking a very Afrikaans English. He was quite polite and helpful, and we explained the case to him, pointing out that the acceptance of the summons had been signed by someone called Kate, whereas the cook's name was Jane, to which he replied that African women often had a Bantu name as well as an European one! We afterwards discovered that this half-wit was the State Prosecutor. We were told that the Magistrate would arrive about 9.10 (presumably for 9 o'clock): he actually arrived about 9.35 and about 9.45 the court heaved into action. While we were waiting, two prison vans arrived, landrovers with grilles and a barred door at the back. There must have been at least thirty inside each, packed like sardines; anything from murderers and men accused of assault to rent defaulters or technical pass offenders, all pushed in together like cattle. They were handled by African police-men who behaved all right so far as we were able to see, and were not, I suppose, responsible for the squashing which would have been ordained by a higher-up European. But it put us into a cold rage to see them shoved around, when obviously quite a lot of them, especially the women, hadn't the faintest idea really why they were there.

The court room was not very large, about the size of Lower School [at Eton], with a lower ceiling and just about as dark. The prisoners sat in rows on benches facing the Magistrate, stretching from the back of the room practically up to the little dais on which his desk was placed. In between was a small space with the dock on the right and on the left, at right angles to the Magistrate, a small table where the prosecutor sat. We weren't sure what our rights were, so we waited outside till Jane's case came up. It seemed to be a mild one, principally due to misunderstanding, for which she had already served two days in jail. I never thought that in this day and age I should hear a court case conducted in this fashion. Dickens himself would have considered it grossly exaggerated in the 1850s. Right from the start the Magistrate addressed her continuously in a loud voice for which the word 'hectoring' is an inadequate description. I do not think it would have been tolerated in England in a prosecuting counsel who had had the leave of the court to treat the witness as hostile. The proceedings were conducted in English (if you can call it that), though Jane speaks mostly Afrikaans and understands little English. They went something like this. 'Wy dint yew come 'ere to answer this summons?' (No pause to give her a chance to take in the question and answer it.) 'Wot do yew think a summons is for?' (No system of phonetics can convey the vowel clipping and the tinny kind of intonation.) 'Yew natuvs awr all the same, yew think yew can laugh and mike fun of the court, and I'm 'ere to show yew yew cawnt. Yew my think yew awr workin' fer rich people 'oo can py your fines' (this, I take it, was for our benefit) 'but I tell yew I'm sick an' tired of all these rent cyses' (her rent had been paid up weeks before) 'and yew natuvs 'ave got tew be tort a lessin' and so on. . . . There was an interpreter who interpreted pari passu with the magistrate, in exactly the same bullying tone; by the time one had finished the other had started again, so that it was literally impossible for her to have got a word in edgeways. The only, literally the *only*, pause in which she was given time to be heard was to answer a question that might incriminate herself; i.e. did she actually know about the summons before she left with her mistress's family for their holiday. At no other moment during the proceedings did she have what could by any stretch of imagination be called a hearing. After about four or five minutes the magistrate gave up all pretence of interrogation and launched into a harangue on 1) the ingratitude of Yew Natuvs towards a paternal government; 2) that paying rent was more important than their wives, their children or their jobs, and that if they couldn't afford those rents they should move into smaller houses (where?). And anyway they shouldn't be so improvident and have such large families. If they paid more attention to genetics (one supposes he meant birth control) these problems would not arise etc. etc. for another four minutes. Jane stood like a statue looking remarkably dignified (she is an elderly woman) and he looked what he was: a peevish, partial and unsuccessful attorney. I am nearly sure I have seen more than one sentence of his set aside on appeal recently with some pretty scathing comments from the judges. At the end of it all she was fined 1 Rand (10s.) or five days, so we paid it and took her home. But by all accounts if we had not been there it would have been *R*10 or a fortnight, that is two weeks' wages.

You can imagine our state of mind while all this was going on; I think at least that it was fairly clear to the Africans, and I very much hope that it was. We discovered afterwards that each of us had been impressed by the iron self-control of the other, and had hoped that we ourselves would be able to hold out. If we had not realised that any sign of disapproval would inevitably react on Jane, I doubt if we should have lasted out.

It really is most unpleasantly like the Nazi era. One says to oneself again and again, 'It can't be true, civilised people don't behave as badly as that, at least not the ones in really responsible positions', and then you find that exactly those people do even worse.

I was told later by my friend, after she had had a chance to talk to Jane, that Jane never even saw the summons. When her daughter, Kate (aged thirty) had signed it, the policeman realised that he had got hold of the wrong person and *took both copies of the summons away with him*. Jane said that the conditions in the gaol were filthy. She could smell the blankets before she was even in the same room with them; the food consisted of raw mealie meal and raw butter beans; the prisoners were packed together solid with only a thin mat on a stone floor to sleep on.

This was the kind of experience which stiffened Elinor's resolve to put her energy into pitting her wits against the authorities.

There was unlimited work to be done helping to relieve the suffering caused by restrictive regulations. At the heart of the problem was the rapid pace of industrialisation which was continuing to attract black labour into the towns. But though blacks were needed there as workers, they were not wanted as residents. The pass and influx control laws designed to restrict the numbers entering the urban areas gave rise to a very large number of arrests and prosecutions. In one suburb of Pretoria talk of bringing back a curfew on blacks which had been in force during the war led to the coining of the phrase 'white by night'. However unrealistic, there was, during the Birleys' time there, beginning to be some talk of keeping Johannesburg white by night. Elinor became a member of the Black Sash, the women's organisation which had taken to standing in silent protest against the Government's actions, and which devoted itself to helping victims of the apartheid policy. This policy could for example lead to black workers being charged with the absurd offence of 'harbouring their wives' near their place of work, rather than leaving them confined in the bleak women's hostels or the distant homelands to which they had been ordered. The most important thing that the Black Sash did was to set up 'advice offices'. This work was at an early stage in the 1960s, when the women concerned were regarded in the white community as harmless eccentrics, but it has since grown and become well established as a white liberal organisation deeply trusted by the blacks. Birley addressed a number of meetings of the Black Sash and made the greatest impact on the occasion when he quoted the German Jesuit priest, Father Delp, who just before he was executed by the Nazis wrote in a letter: 'This is a time of sowing, not of harvest. God sows, some day he will also reap again. I want to strive for one thing – to fall into the earth at least as a fruitful and healthy seed.' It was made clear to Elinor how heartening a message this was to the Black Sash groups throughout South Africa.

Apart from the work of groups like the Black Sash, the most fortifying feature of the political situation which the Birleys encountered was the strength of the white liberal tradition. Among those of British descent there was a substantial community which did not draw its vitality from the narrow aim of preserving the privilege gained through a very recent acquisition of power and status, but which retained attitudes which went with membership of the wider community of the Commonwealth. In Jewish circles, too, there were many who were vigorously opposed to oppressive legislation. This outlook found expression through organisations such as the South African Institute of Race Relations. Birley had a good deal to do with this and with the Christian Institute of Southern Africa which could count among its leaders prominent Afrikaners.

Elinor Birley (*second from left*) at a Black Sash protest meeting

Members of the African Special Branch taking photographs and names at the meeting, as recorded by a visiting Old Etonian

Birleys at a party given for Senator Robert Kennedy in 1966 during his visit to South Africa

Sir Edward Boyle visiting one of the Soweto crèches

Robert and Elinor with children in Swaziland in 1966, shortly before their return to England

Both bodies were constantly quarrying uncomfortable statistics about, for example, the measures taken to remove blacks from areas designated by law as white and confine them to the Bantustans.

The foremost problem was to find ways of giving practical help to those who had suffered for their opposition to apartheid, without straying into the paths of incitement to violence which were inevitably becoming more appealing to the politically active members of the black community. One way was to help the families of political prisoners. Elinor helped to organise correspondence courses for prisoners held on Robben Island and made determined efforts to ensure that the material did actually find its way through the obstructive bureaucracy. Among the many people they were able to help and support outside the prisons was Nelson Mandela's wife Winnie. Elinor was 'Auntie' or 'Mama' to their two daughters whom she helped to send to school in Swaziland. By the time the Birleys returned to England Winnie Mandela and Elinor were the closest of friends.

The white liberal tradition was at its strongest in the universities and it was here that Birley was in a position to make his most telling contribution. It might well have been that the great majority of the English-speaking South Africans had simply accepted apartheid in the hope that their own comfortable lives would not be disturbed, but the younger generation was exposed to more actively liberal debate at places like Wits. Birley was able to put some heart into those who were striving to win them over to the idea of a more just society. He could take the keynote of his work from a plaque in the great hall of the University:

DEDICATION AND AFFIRMATION

We affirm in the name of the University of the Witwatersrand that it is our duty:

> To uphold the principle that a University is a place where men and women, without regard to race and colour are welcome to join in the acquisition and advancement of knowledge; and to continue faithfully to defend the ideal against all those who have sought by

> legislative enactment to curtail the autonomy of the
> University.
> Now, therefore, we dedicate ourselves to the maintenance of
> this ideal and to the restoration of the autonomy of our
> University.

Behind this statement lay a long story of defiant resistance to
government policy by the more progressive academics at Wits.
Birley arrived at a time when their energies were flagging and
what he did above all was to boost their morale. In addition, on
the margin of university life he became a patron of the South
African Committee for Higher Education, the independent
body organised by Anne Welsh, now Anne Yates, which became
a focus for resistance to university apartheid in a practical way
through its pioneering educational work in downtown Johannesburg. Birley saw the potential of this organisation in its early,
struggling, stages and there was a natural ease about the way in
which he won the confidence of those associated with it.

This was particularly so in the case of the student leaders who
supported SACHED. Birley's natural sympathy with young
people of independent mind was a huge advantage. Jonty
Driver, now Headmaster of Berkhamsted and at that time
President of the National Union of South African Students,
had been suspicious of the idea of an ex-English public school
headmaster, turned Professor of Education, and had had to be
bullied into going to see him. But when they did meet, 'Robert
Birley disarmed me from the start by calling me Jonty, as if we
were contemporaries . . . and did he not give us sherry, which
was something professors did in novels but not in South Africa
in those days? And he had big comfortable armchairs, and we
sat and talked. . . .' For young men like Driver, Birley brought
a breath of relaxation into the highly charged atmosphere of
South African student politics.

Perhaps more fundamental than his support for the progres-
sives was the way in which he brought fresh thinking to the
academic work of the university. Naturally attuned to the high
standards of Oxford and Cambridge, he raised the sights of
South African undergraduates accordingly. They responded to
the intellectual challenge he offered more readily than to similar
challenges from their own teachers.

When the discussion came round to the immediate political problems, though, it was not by any means easy to win over the majority of his students, however impressionable, to his point of view. On the other side of the coin of repressive legislation was the rapid economic growth of South Africa and an expanding labour market that was proving a magnet to workers from neighbouring black African states. Stability and an economy, the growing vigour of which was particularly apparent in the boom town of Johannesburg, could be argued to offer a better prospect for the long-term improvement of the lot of the African worker than political upheaval. Such juxtaposition of arguments was reminiscent of a distinction that A. D. Lindsay was wont to draw in his teaching, and in writings such as *The Two Moralities*. On the one hand there was what he called the morality of 'my station and my duties' which had to be recognised if society was to function in an orderly way. On the other hand he pointed out that 'if we live in a country which is influenced at all by Christianity or indeed by any of the higher religions, we are most of us aware of another morality and its challenge, and are at least occasionally stirred by that challenge. When we are so stirred we often find the morality of my station and its duties enjoining one thing and the morality of perfection enjoining another, and we are troubled as to which we should obey.' What Birley did was to face his students with just this age-old problem. At the end of one of the discussions at Wits a young man cried out: 'I don't know what to do; I often think it would be easier if I were black.'

Birley's own position was quite clear, even if at times he found difficulty in conveying it in a way that would be sensitive to the dilemma of his white students, at the same time as doing justice to the blacks. As with all difficult issues he found a partial way out in wrestling with its history. It was a stroke of luck to find that at Wits he occupied an office opposite that of G. H. L. Le May, Professor of Politics and a former Balliol tutor. Copper Le May was at this time working on his book *British Supremacy in South Africa 1899–1907* and Birley was able to read it in draft. From it he gained some knowledge of the Milner papers and the background to the South Africa Bill of 1909 which Balfour declared to be 'the most wonderful issue out of all these divisions, controversies, battles, bloodshed, devastation and horrors of war and of the difficulties of peace'. He gained some understanding of the delusion that the democratic constitution granted to the Union, and the grandiloquent and optimistic pronouncements that accompanied it, could somehow dissipate the anti-British resentment in the Boer community. He was able to trace the earliest signs of the realisation by Milner and Smuts that the Anglo-Dutch friction was, in Milner's words, 'child's play, compared with the antagonism of White and Black'. The lesson was the now obvious one that such reconciliation as took place had to be at the expense of the non-white peoples and that the pressure of their political aspirations was bound in the end to expose the lack of a genuine uniting force.

Understanding the origins of a mentality which looked back in resentment and looked forward in fear did not, on the face of it, make it much easier to deal with the Afrikaners. It was the time of some of the more absurd manifestations of their attitude to the mixing of the races. Basil d'Oliveira, for example, the England test cricketer of Cape Coloured origin, had returned to South Africa on a coaching engagement and his hosts held a special dinner for him. They wanted to invite Tom Reddick, a former Middlesex player who had emigrated to South Africa and coached d'Oliveira when he was young. It was necessary to ask for special leave to do so. From Pretoria the officials replied that, yes, Reddick could attend the dinner – provided that he did not eat. The Birleys experienced similar absurdities at first hand. When the Association of Jewish Women, one of the groups whose work they admired, arranged a party for handicapped children, permission was granted for it to be multi-racial provided that, firstly, the whites and non-whites came in by separate entrances, secondly that they occupied separate parts of the hall, and thirdly that refreshments were served to the white children only.

This intensification of 'petty' or 'social' apartheid which was very evident during the Birleys' time in South Africa was a symptom of a more sinister underlying mentality, reflected in the steady growth of Security Police activity. One instance of this activity which Birley liked to quote concerned a young Anglican priest who was being thoroughly outspoken in his opposition to apartheid. The Police deputed someone to infiltrate one of his confirmation classes. The agent was so impressed by the priest's attitude that he revealed the purpose for which he was there and asked if he could continue his instruction for confirmation.

Birley found little time or opportunity to try to make an impact on Afrikaner thinking, though he did sometimes visit Afrikaans-medium secondary schools, especially to help them with the English for their matriculation papers. On one occasion he found them wrestling with Matthew Arnold's 'Sonnet on Shakespeare'. 'They found that very difficult. I don't blame them. One tends to take it for granted. It *is* very difficult,' he wrote to his sister. There was, too, a little contact with Stellenbosch, the least reactionary of the Afrikaner universities, where there were murmurings of discontent over the ban on multi-racial sport. But the freest discussion that he was able to engage in was among the Afrikaner journalists and the best of these were among the most enlightened people he met anywhere in South Africa.

Birley's main achievements had to remain however in the communities of the English-speaking whites and the blacks. Among the latter the task was predominantly one of practical help – in helping to alleviate the personal distress arising out of the break-up of families caused by the pass laws, to promote the welfare of children and to improve their education. Particularly towards the end of his time in South Africa, when he was a figure well known to the press, he had the opportunity to give national publicity to the shortcomings of the school system on the basis of both his work with the 1961 Education Panel and his many visits to individual schools.

The Education Panel spent about two years preparing its second report, *Education and the South African Economy*, which was written by its Secretary Michael O'Dowd, an executive of the Anglo-American Corporation of South Africa, and published in 1966. Throughout this period a working group of four had met at Birley's flat in Wits. They set out to trace the connections between education and economic and social development, and, using projections of trends, to build up a dynamic picture of the present and future needs of the country. The comparative education methods, deployed by O'Dowd and the two other members of the group, Nigel

Tucker and Raymond Tunmer, were advanced for their time
and initially took Birley by surprise. But he adapted to the new
ideas very quickly and soon joined in the discussions of social
development and economic growth with enthusiasm.

At the heart of these discussions lay the nature of the
industrialisation which South Africa was experiencing and the
demand that this would create for skilled labour. The issue was
exemplified in the question of automation. In Afrikaner eyes this
offered the attractive prospect of reducing the need for labour to
the point where industrial and commercial concerns could be
operated by whites alone. If the need for black labour declined
and disappeared, so too would the townships of Soweto. There
was particularly vigorous argument over the passage in the
report which dealt with this:

> The most recent form of mechanization is the use of com-
> puters. By far the most important use of computers is in the
> performance of calculations which would otherwise not have
> been attempted at all, so opening up completely new
> economic and scientific possibilities. Computers, however,
> can also be used to mechanize completely certain repetitive
> clerical functions, and in some fields they can actually direct
> the operation of certain machines. This latter function is
> sometimes called automation, and when used in this way,
> computers do replace workers.
>
> Although the computer is a most important technical
> advance, it does not, for the purposes which interest us, differ
> in any fundamental way from other mechanical devices which
> have been introduced into industry over the years. It is simply
> a machine which is capable of doing work which was previ-
> ously done by direct human labour. It is true that a computer
> can sometimes do the work of a great many clerks but then a
> steel rolling mill can do the work of a great many blacksmiths.
> Nor does a computer differ from other forms of machinery in
> requiring skilled management, operation and maintenance.
>
> For all these reasons it is unlikely that computers will alter
> the basic patterns of change in the labour force which have
> developed since mechanization began.

Birley, to whom it was most important to be persuaded on this
point, finally said, 'Yes, I see now that if the Industrial Revolu-

tion had not taken place, there really would have been a lot of people who would have had to emigrate to America.'

The report, which was accorded no official recognition whatsoever, proved quite soon to be seminal for the development of South African education policy. Echoes of it and unacknowledged quotations began to find their way into the speeches of Ministers. Fifteen years later an official committee of enquiry, known as the De Lange Commission, reported in a way that demonstrated the farsightedness of the 1961 Education Panel and in particular the small group of which Birley was an important member. They had accurately predicted the rate of economic growth over the period in question, though they had underestimated population growth. They had been right about the need for more and better qualified teachers, a problem which was not tackled until too late. There was a similar failure to follow their advice – advice which in the event proved correct – on the expansion of technical education of blacks. Finally, the De Lange Commission reiterated the warnings of the 1961 Panel about the deteriorating pupil/teacher ratio in black schools; for the 1980s and 1990s it recommended exactly what the panel had advocated for the 1960s and 1970s.

Apart from his contribution to the discussions within the panel Birley was a vigorous publicist for their arguments. In interviews with the national and international press he constantly drew attention to the need for more money to be spent on black schools. He used the panel's analysis to demonstrate that improving black education in this way was not merely altruistic but was an essential investment to meet the growing need for skilled labour. The alternative would amount to a deliberate decision to reject economic expansion for the whites and this, he pointed out, was something that had never been done before in history.

For the English-speaking whites in particular it mattered greatly to maintain contact with an outside world that was becoming increasingly hostile. Birley's contribution was to give heart to the minority who were not prepared to sacrifice the principles of Western democracy and to help to preserve at Wits an island of liberalism where unfettered thinking could continue to flourish. Perhaps not many of his students would continue to question for long the assumptions on which their country was being run, but not all could forget completely the challenge of an alternative morality that had been put to them.

Birley was so obviously respected in the university world in South Africa that when in March 1966 disciplinary problems caused violent disturbances in the University College of Rhodesia and Nyasaland, he was the man chosen to conduct the official enquiry.

It was just the kind of problem that he relished tackling. The College, which had opened in 1957, was the most genuinely multi-racial university institution in Africa. Black and white students were accommodated in the same halls of residence, a degree of racial integration that was scarcely known elsewhere in the Central African Federation. When the Federation was dissolved and the College became a purely Rhodesian institution, the strain on its policy of integration inevitably increased. The poor employment prospects of black students as compared with the whites caused a frustration within the College which all too easily identified itself with the wider political frustration in Rhodesia after the Unilateral Declaration of Independence.

As well as analysing this general situation in his report, Birley, with his taste for illuminating anecdote, included an account of a specific incident which took place a year before the disturbances:

It is the practice when the students organize their annual Rag for them to elect by vote three young ladies, one of whom is the Rag Queen and two are 'princesses'. The three parade through the streets of Salisbury on a float. In March, 1965, three European girls received the most votes, the fourth place going to an African girl. One of the European girls withdrew, so that, in accordance with the voting, one of the 'princesses' should have been the African girl. I understand that the Committee felt themselves to be in a very difficult position. They believed that to have an African girl as one of the 'princesses' would considerably reduce the amount of money collected and, furthermore – I believe that this was the main reason for their decision – that she would certainly be insulted as the float passed through the streets of Salisbury. The girl herself said that she was willing to be a 'princess' in the procession. In the end, the Committee decided to replace her by a European girl. It has been put to me by an African student that the decision was a wrong one, but he appreciated the motives of the Committee. He himself had twice sold copies of the Rag Journal in Salisbury and he said that it had been an unpleasant experience. An Asian student, who is closely in touch with the African students, told me that the decision had created great resentment among them, and that they did not understand the reasons for it. (The Committee could hardly have been expected to make them public.)

As he pointed out, this apparently trivial episode was as telling an instance as could be found of the difficulties facing a multiracial institution in a society which very largely rejected racial equality.

From Birley's investigation of the complicated circumstances of the disturbances which took place a year later the picture emerged of a university administration that could not evade the charge of being remote and pettifogging. It had failed to gain the confidence of the black students who had as a result fabricated a stereotype of authority which appeared to be denying them their rights. Birley's report made no bones about this.

When politically conscious people are denied – or feel that they are denied – their proper rights to express and gain their rights by means of normal political action, they fall back on what seems the only alternative. That is the language of protest. If those protests can be made stronger by means of demonstrations or such actions as boycotts, so much the better. Rightly or wrongly the African students felt that the attitude of the European students in the University was such, and the attitude of the College authorities in failing to appreciate their case was such, that they had no alternative but to make a protest, and as emphatic a protest as they could. And it would be absurd to suppose that they were not influenced by their general views of the Rhodesian situation. The College seemed to them to be becoming a microcosm of the country.

The specific cause of friction lay in an order issued by the Rhodesian government, prohibiting students from taking part in political activities. In fact the College had secured the withdrawal of the order, but the black students were convinced that the price of this withdrawal was the introduction of internal disciplinary measures which amounted to the same thing. Their resentment was therefore in no way dissipated. In their eyes the College was conniving with the government.

The action which they took amounted to a familiar catalogue of noisy demonstrations outside rooms in which College committees were in session, with accompanying allegations of intimidation and assault. An assistant technician was hit on the head by a stone thrown in the vicinity of the Department of Agriculture. (Birley noted in parentheses that he had been informed by the Professor of Agriculture that the stone weighed 205 grammes.) A number of witnesses believed that the underlying aim of the demonstration was to force the closure of the College as a means of embarrassing the Smith government. This Birley did not accept. He considered that the purpose was to remedy what the demonstrators felt to be their just grievances.

Underlying these grievances were questions of political and academic freedom which drew the teaching staff into the controversy. Just as the administrators had alienated the black students so too they had failed to gain the confidence of the staff as far as the efficient conduct of university business was concerned. Against this uneasy background it was natural that the situation should give rise to unrest among those lecturers who were particularly committed to the multi-racial dimension of the institution – and perhaps in some cases almost exclusively to the rights of the black students. When the police were called to the campus, they first refused to give their lectures, and then organised a 'teach-in' on academic freedom.

Birley was well disposed towards their idealism:

Anyone coming to a University institution which is an experiment, and a constructive one, *ought* to be an idealist. He or she will be of very little use to the University if they are not. But their idealism will not be confined to the University. They will be hoping for the creation of societies in which different races learn to live together. For this reason it is only to be expected that many of the staff at the University College, especially among its younger members, will be distressed at recent developments in Rhodesia. To put it quite bluntly – and it would be unrealistic to avoid this issue – to ask that the staff of this College should simply accept the social and political trends of Rhodesian society in the recent past and the present is to ask that they should not be the kind of persons who ought to be on the staff of a multi-racial University institution.

It was significant that this general statement in the report preceded the reasoning whereby he arrived at the conclusion that the actual action taken by the lecturers was ill-judged.

The report recommended that no disciplinary action should be taken against students or staff, that the administration should be overhauled and that the College should appoint an adviser to students and wardens of halls 'whose teaching or research duties will be very light'. There were, too, to be guarantees that legal advice would be provided for any student who was arrested. In sum the report was a sensitive exercise in conciliation of a constructive kind. It bore the fundamentally optimistic mark of an author who was unusually disposed to see the good in people and to turn a blind eye to their frailties. At the same time it was a skilful study of the limits that difficult circumstances can place on the principle of academic freedom.

One way or another it was concern for freedom that characterised all Birley's activities in South Africa. When he was invited back in 1970, it was to deliver the Richard Feetham Academic Freedom Lecture at Wits and the Malherbe Academic Freedom Lecture at the University of Natal. In 1974 he was once again in South Africa and returned to the same theme in an apologia which deserves quotation at length:

Is it possible to find in this country the appropriate term which sums up a distrust, in fact a dislike, of free discussion because, it is thought, it may well become dangerous? Not, I should say myself, in some simple word or phrase. But not long ago I came across something which seemed to me to show very clearly what was involved. It was in an account of a discussion which took place in 1956 between the Prime

Minister of the time and Dr Verwoerd, the Minister of Native Affairs, on the one side and representatives of the Christian Council of South Africa on the other. The subject was migrant labour. Dr Verwoerd, as one might expect, dealt with the issue very skilfully. The Prime Minister does not appear to have spoken until the end of the discussion and then he said a few words and he ended with these, 'The Government shares with the churches a concern for a stable life, but it must always be remembered that it is the first duty of South African government to preserve white civilization.'

There surely we reach the heart of the matter. The policy not only of the South African government, but of the majority of the whites which supports it, seems to us from the outside world to be a completely defensive one. And it is when a society is on the defensive that criticism and, therefore, inevitably academic freedom also, seem to be so dangerous.

There are, however, certain aspects of the principle of academic freedom which we ought to consider before we allow ourselves to get into the very dangerous position of taking its value for granted. First, academic freedom can very easily become something very isolated. This is the doctrine of the ivory tower, that within the well constructed defences of a university, freedom to criticise and freedom to discuss may be allowed and that in return for this privilege the university itself will take care never to move outside these defences. This was precisely the mistake made by the German universities before the days of Hitler. In fact, it was held that by moving outside its defences a university inevitably compromised itself. This point of view was brilliantly expressed by a very great German writer on education, Friedrich Paulsen. 'Scholars cannot and should not engage in politics. They cannot do so if they have developed their capacities in acordance with the demands of their calling. Their business is scientific research, and scientific research calls for constant examination of thoughts and theories in order to harmonise them with the facts. Hence they are bound to develop a habit of theoretical indifference towards opposing sides, a readiness to take any path in case it promises to lead to a theory more in accordance with the facts. Now, every form of political activity, and practical politics particularly, demands above everything else a determination to follow *one* path that one has chosen. Political activity . . . produces a habit of mind that would prove fatal to the theorist, the habit of opportunism.'

And the result of this doctrine? It was clear enough in Germany. It led to an attitude which can only be styled one of complete irresponsibility. It meant that the universities felt no obligation whatever to criticise political views which they knew to be false, and, which was even more disastrous, which they knew to be morally wrong. In the end it meant that academic freedom itself seemed to make it appear to be wrong to oppose a political party which was openly bent on destroying it.

But should a university spend its whole time – or much of its time – arguing about political issues? Certainly not. A university – and this is surely a commonplace – has two main functions. One is to increase Man's knowledge of his universe and, which is just as important, his understanding of it. But this is not quite as straightforward a task as one might think. If I had to choose one moment for the beginning of our Western European civilisation, of which South Africa is a part, it would be the publication in 1637 of Descartes' *Discourse on Method* because of this statement in it, 'I perceived it to be possible to arrive at a knowledge highly useful in life; and in place of the speculative philosophy usually taught in the schools [he meant, of course, what we would call the universities], to discover a practice, by means of which, knowing the force and action of fire, water, air, the stars, the heavens, and all the other bodies that surround us, as distinctly as we know the various crafts of our artisans, we might also apply them in the same way to all the uses to which they are adapted, and thus render ourselves the lords and possessors of nature.' I need hardly expatiate at the University of the Witwatersrand on this union of pure science and technology.

And surely we are becoming more and more aware that Descartes' splendid claim has a way of standing on its head as it were, and the problems of pollution and the environment show us that nature may end up by becoming the lord and possessor of us. It is surely the duty of a university to deal with such a problem as this.

The second function is this. We must remember that most of the members of a university are not professors and lecturers but students. A few of them will continue in universities, but almost all will go into life outside them. The university, then, is inevitably a preparation for life, and this means that it must teach its students to think clearly, to understand what a problem really is – and surely something more as well. There is much to be said, I feel (especially, perhaps, I feel it when I have been reading some recent work of sociology), for the opinion once expressed to me that analysis is usually much the same thing as paralysis. It is especially the task of a university to teach men and women to think constructively and I believe that all the time they should be encouraged to apply such constructive thought to the problems of the society in which they live.

I remember once having a conversation at this university with a journalist from one of the best known Afrikaner Nationalist newspapers. He asked me what I thought of his own people, by which he meant the Afrikaner Nationalists. I said that I divided most of them, thought not quite all, into two classes. The first, a rather small one, I called 'the thousand years Reich' men. It is true that Hitler's Reich (he invented the phrase of course), only lasted for twelve years, but that was neither here nor there. They felt they had a lasting solution to the problems of their society, as long as they stuck to it. But the main body, I said, I called the *'après nous le déluge'* men. 'I see,' he said. 'You mean that we are being very selfish towards our own grandchildren.' 'Well,' I said, 'you have put it much better than I did, but I suppose that is what it comes to.' 'In our hearts of hearts,' he said, 'we all know that.'

The task of the university – and at the moment I am thinking especially of its students – must seem, then, peculiarly difficult at this moment, to foster constructive and positive thinking in a society which has come to take up so negative an attitude.

The constructive and positive thinking which Robert Birley himself had contributed to the problems of South Africa was significant not only for its substance but for its timing. He had arrived in Johannesburg at a stage when the liberal community was feeling increasingly isolated and demoralised. The interest of the outside world, which in the aftermath of Sharpeville had been intense, had largely waned. Some radicals had given up and emigrated. Of those who had stayed, some were banned and others were giving up their opposition to apartheid to avoid being banned also. It was a moment when they badly needed fresh inspiration.

Birley provided this inspiration. Colour-blind in his lack of concern for the social conventions, he was here, there and everywhere. He met lawyers involved in political trials. He met relatives of some of those who were on trial or imprisoned. He relished telling of how he would go from visiting some young man in a police cell to an educational meeting in Pretoria Cathedral hall. He attended the trials of prominent black militants and made a point of talking about them in white circles. He was best placed to concentrate above all on drawing attention to the shortcomings of black education and campaigning for improvement, especially in the numbers and qualifications of the teachers. It was a constructive contribution to the problems of a country which fascinated him for the rest of his life. In England, becoming a Professor of Education at Wits was scarcely what anyone would have expected Robert Birley to do on leaving Eton. For his friends in South Africa it came to appear the most natural climax to his career.

CHAPTER THIRTEEN

The City and the Country

When Birley returned to England from South Africa at the beginning of 1967 he was 63, an age at which most men consider themselves to have earned a quiet retirement, and at which those who wish to go on working find the opportunities to do so dwindling rapidly. For him there was no question of retiring, but just how he was to occupy himself was not at all clear. The most obvious culmination of a varied career would have been a mastership at Oxford or Cambridge and this possibility had indeed arisen during his time at Wits. When Lindsay Keir's term came to an end in 1965, Birley had for a second time been a candidate for the Mastership of Balliol.

It was a story that went back to the last year of Birley's time at Eton. Balliol had been looking ahead and had sent one of the Fellows, Richard Cobb, to sound out the historians at the school about the idea of their Head as a possible Master. Cobb's enquiries revealed that Birley had become too conservative for the younger and more lively men. Far from being Red Robert, he was in their book not even 'pink Robert'. This was enough to cause the idea to be dropped. One or two other outside candidates were also contemplated, but eventually the election appeared to be resolving itself into a contest between two internal candidates, scientist Ronald Bell and historian Christopher Hill. Once it began to appear that Hill was in front, Birley once again came into the reckoning. A few days after the election had finally taken place the Fellows were startled to read a blow-by-blow account of the episode in the Atticus column of *The Sunday Times*. C. P. Snow having, in his novel *The Masters*, treated the general public to an inside view of the manoeuvrings in a similar situation in Cambridge, the story rang a loud bell. It was a notable leak.

For the columnist it had clearly been huge fun to penetrate the confidentiality of the proceedings. His piece began:

At dinner at Balliol College in Oxford last Wednesday an undergraduate sent a note to his tutor asking if he could see him after the meal.

The reply was, 'Not before 10.30 (not because that is when the pubs close, but for reasons almost as weighty).'

By 10.30 Mr Christopher Hill had been elected the new Master of Balliol by a gathering of Balliol Fellows meeting in conditions of elaborate secrecy. A weighty session indeed. And an unexpected result.

It appeared that Bell, the 'pleasant, politically orthodox scientist' had not been a match for Hill, the most distinguished seventeenth-century historian in the country and a former Communist who had left the Party at the time of the Hungarian revolt. It was to combat the enthusiastic canvassing of some younger Fellows on behalf of Hill that Birley was brought in at a later stage of the contest. His Eton conservatism was no longer such a drawback, for he was known to have been sympathetic to radicalism in South Africa in the wake of Sharpeville. He had, too, been to stay at the College as Lindsay Keir's guest shortly before the election was due to take place. This was important because he had been out of the swim of English life and the Fellows were more likely to be impressed by meeting him than by reading what he had written. In fact he and Christopher Hill represented the two traditions from which Masters are generally drawn, those of public service and scholarship. What told in favour of Hill in the end was not only the positiveness of his following but the more general feeling that the College needed a different kind of man from Lindsay Keir. If it was a scholar that they wanted, then, for all Birley's gifts in that direction, Hill was the obvious choice. But it was a very close thing, going to a second vote before there was a majority.

To come so close to such a triumphant climax to an academic career was bound to be a severe disappointment, but it was some consolation to be going back to South Africa where in the event Birley stayed for a further two years. What he did get the opportunity to do on his return to England was in a way more imaginative and provided an unusual outlet for his scarcely diminished intellectual energy. He was invited to become a professor, and head of the department of social sciences at the

City University. The City was one of ten colleges of advanced technology which in the wake of the Robbins Report of 1963 had been granted charters and had now to learn how to be universities. It had been founded as the Northampton Institute in 1894 with, as its object, 'the promotion of the industrial skill, general knowledge, health and well-being of young men and women belonging to the poorer classes'. It had been one of the places to pioneer, in the early years of the twentieth century, sandwich courses that alternated between full-time study and industrial experience. It had gone on to play a part in the movement to raise technological education in Britain to a status comparable to that which it had enjoyed for so much longer in France and Germany. But the step of becoming a fully-fledged university was by far the biggest in its history. It had to expand and mature very fast.

In engineering and applied science which had predominated in the work of the Northampton this was less of a problem than in liberal studies which had been, characteristically enough for an institution of this kind, lodgers rather than members of the family. Management was the most firmly established subject in this category and after the creation of the university, those who taught it very quickly hived themselves off to form a Graduate Business Centre. This left a heterogeneous collection of specialists in economics, sociology, psychology and philosophy, none of them enjoying enough of a reputation at the Northampton to warrant the creation of a department in its own right. It was this leaderless group that Birley was given charge of, and out of which he had to create a new department. His job was to give it the confidence to keep its end up alongside the other departments whose value and status were so much more secure. And beyond that was the question of whether he could help to give confidence to the university itself – one which bore the name of the City but of whose existence many of those who worked in the Square Mile were quite unaware.

The City did have a tradition of supporting education largely through the role the Livery Companies had played in maintaining schools, many of which bore their names – Stationers, Coopers, Haberdashers, Merchant Taylors. It was natural that Birley should help in the effort to harness this tradition to the interests of the new university. In his second year there he wrote an article in the *Financial Times* tracing the development out of the old Northampton and pointing out the importance of the new university and others like it for economic recovery. 'What is needed is that both in the City and in industry generally it should be recognised that the days when British industry could be left to amateur technicians are over. There is much leeway to make up; a glance at technological and management education in the United States and the support it receives from American industry should make it clear. The rapid advance of an institution like the City University shows that it can be made up. The time has come for the City, which can regard this University as one of its own institutions, and for British industry generally to realise that on the dynamic work of these new creations of a national educational policy their own good fortune will increasingly depend.'

Another way of making the City University better known was through its relationship to Gresham College. In 1575 Sir Thomas Gresham, a wealthy Mercer who had been Lord Mayor of London, included in his will plans to found a college in London for the gratuitous instruction of all who chose to attend the lectures. The plans included provision for seven professorships, in Divinity, Astronomy, Music, Geometry, Law, Physic and Rhetoric. In due course the Mercers' Company and the Corporation of the City of London as trustees set about putting Gresham's intentions into practice. The Chairs were filled, and it was stipulated that the lectures given by the incumbents should be open to the public. Although the success of these had varied, the important thing was that they had survived, and represented a 400-year-old tradition which could be grafted on to the City University as a new way of realising Thomas Gresham's original ambition. To help to forge the link Birley was appointed Gresham Professor of Rhetoric, with the duty to give six lectures a year. Here was a new lectern from which he could deliver learned papers on whatever subject he liked. His first series was given in 1968, his last in 1981 when he was finding it painfully difficult to get about. In all he gave getting on for a hundred lectures, which together made up a kind of retrospective exhibition demonstrating the range and individuality of his interests. The other Gresham Professors were men of comparable distinction but they were visitors.

Birley was the only one who was, as it were, fully resident at the City and this close association made the lustre which he contributed to his new institution all the brighter and more welcome.

Birley set about the task of building his department with gusto. In recruiting new staff he was less interested in lists of publications than in sparkle of personality. Among the students he found a latent demand confirming his belief that the premature specialisation in the schools went against the grain for many able young people. He found scientists and engineers asking if they could study poetry because they had had no time for it from the age of sixteen onwards. There was a course which imaginatively combined philosophy and physics. The philosophy tutors wanted to concentrate on scholarly study of the minor figures; the students, backed by Birley, wanted to take on the major ones. The flavour was that of general culture rather than earth-shifting research. The tone was being set by someone who was essentially a schoolmaster, filling the gaps that school education should not have allowed to become so large; it was not being set by an academic social scientist. So though the department prospered, defended in the University Senate by the most towering figure on the staff, it was not in a position to make a great contribution towards broadening the scope of the university as a whole. While the star performers among the new technological universities, like Loughborough and Bath, branched out confidently in new directions other than engineering and applied science, City found it more difficult to flower. This, however, had a good deal less to do with Birley's comparative lack of interest in social science research than with the fact that it was simply not so easy to grow in the shadow of the University of London.

Apart from his efforts to broaden the experience of scientists and engineers, the feature of university life for which Birley most deserved to be remembered was relations between staff and students. The two groups were at odds over various matters which crystallised in the demand for student representation on the Senate. This was a common demand at the time, and at the City it was met with greater poise than in a good many other universities. In the course of the negotiations Birley showed himself at his most patient and statesmanlike. From the outset he believed that the students had a good case and he spent endless hours discussing it with them. Although the old Northampton had had a conventionally authoritarian tradition, a number of the staff responded to the lead he gave, particularly David Jenkins, the Deputy Registrar, and Brian Enright, the Librarian. It was a measure of the students' trust that they were prepared to take a cue from Birley and his associates when it was given; they retired from meetings at crucial moments when their mentors judged that it would harm their case to stay. Jenkins, who became Birley's closest friend at the City, later moved over to the teaching staff and in due course became Dean of Gresham College. Enright became Librarian at the University of Sussex and then at the University of Newcastle-upon-Tyne.

When they returned from South Africa the Birleys still had their Canterbury bolthole but it was unsuitable as a base from which to travel regularly to the City, and too small to serve as a permanent home for the longer term. The solution was first to rent something in London and then to look for a larger house in the country for use at week-ends, in vacations, and in due course for retirement. After some anxiety the City part of the arrangement worked out well. There were two squares near the university where flats which belonged to Trinity House could be rented. Applicants were carefully screened and when Birley put his name forward he found himself being interviewed by one of his old monitors from Charterhouse. He enjoyed describing it afterwards as probably the first time in history that a prefect had had such an opportunity to get his own back on his old Headmaster – and not taken it. The flat in Trinity Church Square proved an ideal pied-à-terre. For the move from the Canterbury house the Birleys returned to their first love in Somerset, where they had spent many happy holidays in the years before the war. They bought Lomans, a former farm-house on the outskirts of Somerton which was large enough to accommodate the stream of friends who came to visit them.

More often than not these friends found themselves being conducted around the beautiful village churches of the neighbourhood, just as the Charterhouse boys had been thirty years earlier. Birley never lost his enjoyment in pointing out the curiosities that abounded in them, foremost among which were invariably the topless angels on the ceiling at Muchelney. The most important feature of Lomans itself was that its layout lent itself to housing Birley's vast collection of books. There were bookcases all over the place, not only downstairs but on the landing and in the bedrooms. The antiquarian treasures were reserved for the study, the sanctum of his bibliophilia. In retirement he was able to take more and more pleasure in this, not least through his membership of the Roxburghe Club, the aristocratically flavoured group of book lovers which met regularly to savour privately the delights of distinguished libraries. It was a convention of the club that each member should have a book bound, and should present copies to all his fellow members. Birley's contribution was 'Love In It's Extasie: Or The Large Prerogative, A Kind Of Royall Pastorall Written Long Since, By A Gentleman, Student At Æton and Now Publisher – with an Introduction by Robert Birley'. It was a great sadness that he was too ill to attend the 1982 meeting of the Club which was held in his beloved Eton College library.

While Lomans supplied the peaceful atmosphere of the country at week-ends, the City was an ideal base for the hyperactive life which Birley was given to leading during the week. He seemed to be lecturing here, there and everywhere. There were the Chichele Lectures at All Souls in 1967 on 'The British Empire in prospect and retrospect' and a host of other less formal occasions. The mark of these was how he continued to let his enthusiasm run away with him, often alas oblivious to the circumstances of his audience. At those lunches to which a speaker was invited in order to liven things up with a short paper, Carthusians and Etonians would find themselves being addressed by their old Headmaster. The minutes would tick away and there would be increasingly anxious and frequent surreptitious glances at watches. But Birley would be blithely unaware of their predicament. He would talk on and on, impervious to all hints, until at long last they were released to scurry back to their offices, flustered and appallingly late.

Mostly the addresses would arise out of the various causes that remained close to Birley's heart and into which he poured his energies for the rest of his life. The German connections remained strong, above all through the friendship with Hans

and Lilo Milchsack. He never missed a Königswinter conference if he could help it, and he went to Berlin whenever
possible, sometimes with groups of the Königswinter par-
ticipants. Going to see the Wall always added a flavour of
realism to their debates on international politics. On one of
these visits the East German official at Checkpoint Charlie had
been scrutinising the passport of one of the group. 'Herr
Stansgaaate,' he called out. There was no response. 'Herr
Stansgaaate.' The call was repeated several times more before
the penny dropped and Birley told the sheepish holder of the
passport to own up. It was Tony Benn, whose renounced title,
Lord Stansgate, had returned to haunt him. Birley also became
more and more interested in the Anglo-German Youth Exchange Scheme run from Berlin by Doris Krug. For many
years he gave the opening lecture at the 'Young Königswinter'
conference, arranged by this organisation to bring together
promising young men and women in their twenties from Britain
and Germany as a way of promoting mutual understanding.

Another enduring interest of Birley's was the public schools.
He was a governor not only of Charterhouse, but of Rugby,
Malvern and King's School, Bruton. While he had been Head
Master of Eton he had managed to monopolise one of the two
Headmasters' Conference nominations to the Committee of the
Governing Bodies Association and soon after his return from
South Africa he became one of its two Vice-Chairmen. He
represented the fully independent schools while Hubert Ashton
and later James Cobban represented the direct grant interest.
Birley's influence had waned by the time it came to the
foundation of the Independent Schools Information Service,
ISIS, in 1972. But it was characteristic that he should not be
excluded entirely from the triumphant initiative which brought
the girls' schools into an organisation which many headmistresses believed was going to operate predominantly for the benefit
of the boys' schools.

One of the greatest obstacles to a rapprochement was the way
in which the boys' schools had taken to admitting girls to their
sixth forms. Despite the assurances that were given, the tension
continued and Birley became convener of a small group formed
to look at the problem. The first meeting was potentially
explosive because it was to be attended by Miss Chalice, the

Headmistress of Queen Anne's, Caversham. This redoubtable, opinionated lady could be expected to give the headmasters a rough ride. Birley accordingly had the idea of holding a dinner at his Club beforehand, with a rule that there was to be no talk of politics until the meal was over. The meeting ended in an amicable agreement on the ground rules for consultation between any schools involved in a transfer of pupils. Afterwards Joyce Cadbury, a leading representative of the governing bodies of the girls' schools, remarked that there was only one point on which she remained uncertain – whether it was the food or the wine that had done the trick.

Birley's interest went well beyond the mainstream public schools. He was quick to become involved in any educational enterprise which had an international purpose. He was patron of the network of language schools built up by Frank Bell in the 1960s. He was, too, successively chairman and president of the Educational Interchange Council. When, in 1979, it had to go into liquidation, Birley wrote to Bell who had succeeded him as chairman some thirty years earlier: 'You have been very much in my mind. There is no doubt that during thirty *most* critical years EIC has done most valuable work. I know it is impossible to assess it mathematically, but I have no doubt of it at all. The new Cambridge Modern History speaks of this as "The Age of Violence". True enough, but there have been some constructive efforts which have saved us from disaster since the end of the war. I rate EIC very high in my list of these. And I shall never forget what a help it was when I was working in Germany after the war.'

It was natural that Birley should also take a keen interest in international boarding education. He had got to know Kurt Hahn in the inter-war period and was closely acquainted with the circumstances that led him to leave Germany and found Gordonstoun. A remark that Hahn once made to him stayed with Birley for the rest of his life. 'Whenever you have to deal with a boy who is a rebel, remember that you must not fail at some time or other to get him to face the question, "Are you going to be a fighter, or a quarreller?"' During Birley's time as Educational Adviser after the war, the forceful and earnest Hahn was constantly getting in touch with him, putting forward ideas for new boarding schools – which were utterly impractical in the prevailing conditions. It was in due course necessary actively to dissuade him from turning up on the doorstep in Germany. And then on one occasion when Birley went to a meeting in Paris, there was Hahn, waiting for him as he stepped off the plane. When, much later, Hahn's inspiration found expression in the creation of the United World Colleges of the Atlantic, Birley was among the most enthusiastic supporters of the venture. Eventually, at the suggestion of Sir George Schuster, he was made a governor of Atlantic College in South Wales.

Characteristically Birley found time not merely to attend governors' meetings at Atlantic College but to do some teaching. And learning. He had not expected to find, in the course of a lesson on nineteenth century liberalism, that there was fierce argument over Bismarck, not between the French and the Germans in the class, but between the North Germans and the Bavarians. His favourite story about the College concerned a black South African girl who was sufficiently energetic and determined to be able to raise the money needed for another African to follow her there. This was a boy from Lesotho. Coming though he did from a country with no coastline, he turned out to be more skilled in the maintenance of boats than anyone they had ever had at the College before. He too raised the money for someone to follow him but insisted that it should not be solely for the benefit of Africans. His successor was from South America. Perhaps the most positive contribution that Birley himself made to Atlantic College lay in helping to establish the acceptability of the International Baccalaureate as an entrance qualification for British universities. He was chairman of the meeting of university registrars at which this was achieved.

Birley's educational interests widened out still further through his connection with the Selly Oak Colleges. On the death of Charles Gillett, the previous chairman of the Central Council, the feeling had been that it would be appropriate to look outside the Birmingham Cadbury community for a successor. The Colleges were no longer predominantly Quaker, but an international ecumenical institution which called for a figure distinguished in the educational field and with international interests. It was Sir Kenneth Grubb, an influential

Anglican in the World Council of Churches, who suggested Birley, with the characteristic observation that 'he can read and write'. The only worry was whether, with all his other commitments, he would be sufficiently prepared to give his mind to it. When Paul Rowntree Clifford put it to him on a visit to Lomans, all doubts were dispelled at once. It was quite clear that it would be no sideline. And so it proved. If there was ever a problem during his chairmanship, he would drop everything and go to Birmingham. Though not as decisive as some chairmen, he was admirably patient in defusing explosive situations. He was quick to see to the heart of an issue and very skilled at discovering who needed to be persuaded to help if the outcome was to be successful. He had long since become a master of the art of manipulating the old boy network in the furtherance of worthy causes.

Selly Oak was a way of fulfilling his religious convictions. Though to all appearances an orthodox Anglican, Birley had little interest in theology. At Eton he had gone to great lengths to ensure that religious instructions was not dogmatic, and to encourage the small group of Roman Catholic boys to attend mass at their own church which was some way from the school, at the far end of Eton High Street. This used to make them late for Sunday tutorials, and when Birley discovered that an anti-Catholic master was making life difficult for some of them on this score, he dealt with the problem urgently and effectively. At Selly Oak he identified himself most strongly with the ecumenical commitment of the Colleges. This was consistent with his enthusiastic membership of the All Souls Club, a group of Anglicans and Free Churchmen formed in response to the Lambeth Appeal to all Christians in 1920, and which, by the time Birley became a member, had been opened out to include Roman Catholics. They met three times a year for dinner, after which the host read a paper. On the last occasion when Birley was host, at the Travellers' Club, he spoke about great religious art, having come armed with a library of books which were passed round in the course of his address. It was this intuitive response to religious inspiration, rather than any analytical turn of mind, that was the key to his own beliefs. When he saw a point he was less anxious to discuss it in any fundamental sense than to be planning how to do something about it. He remained formally an Anglican, but he gave the impression that in later life he had come round to the idea that a practical morality was its own best pleader.

Nothing however fulfilled Birley's humanitarian urge so fully as his continuing interest in South Africa. Dotted about the various tables at Lomans were issues of the Black Sash journal, pamphlets about the work of the Christian Institute and various other organisations sympathetic to African nationalism. There was a signed copy of *Cry Rage!* by James Matthews and Gladys Thomas, circulated in a limited edition in 1972, poems which with varying degrees of ferocity conveyed the smouldering resentment of the blacks. At the milder end of the spectrum were the lines:

> we have been offered
> pie in the sky
> but never smelled it
> neither will it appease
> our hunger for rights
> that are rightfully ours
> we watch through the window
> as they sit feasting
> at a table loaded with equality
> and grow frantic at its flavour
> how long can we contain the rumble
> of hunger in our belly?

And more fiercely:

> rage sharp as a blade
> to cut and slash
> and spill blood
> for only blood can appease
> the blood spilled
> over three hundred years
>
> our limbs have been torn
> our bodies crushed
> the soil streaked with gore
> drained from our broken bodies

bring out your guns
make ready your jails
the land has not graves
enough to contain us
your prisons not cells
enough to hold us

you have taught us
that you have no reason
so reason not with us
when our rage will find you

rage sharp as a blade
to cut and slash
and spill blood
for only blood can appease
the blood spilled
over three hundred years

Birley's interest lay above all in giving practical help to meet the cost of education. In 1970, in association with his great friend, the liberal lawyer Ruth Hayman, he formed the Lomans Trust 'to raise money to provide bursaries and assist in the secondary education of African and coloured children in South Africa'.

Birley was also keen to help young Africans to come and study at British universities. There was the poignant case of Wellington Tshazibane, an able boy from a poor home who had gone to Orlando High School. Birley had then been instrumental in getting him to the University College of Fort Hare to read Physics. In 1969 he came to Wadham College, Oxford as a beneficiary of funds raised by the students at the College to help fellow students from underprivileged societies. Three years later he graduated with a degree in engineering and went on to take a postgraduate course in Design at the University of Salford. He was determined to return to South Africa, but his Tutor at Wadham, Colin Wood, prevailed upon him not to do so until he had had time to help him to find a job. An interview was arranged with a representative of Anglo-American who was visiting Britain, and who took him on as a trainee engineer on the spot. In December 1976, on suspicion of involvement in a bombing incident in Johannesburg,

Wellington was arrested at Jan Smuts Airport as he flew in from Lesotho after his regular ten-day shift at one of the mines there. The next day he was found hanged in his cell in a Johannesburg prison. Following his death Birley was one of the signatories of a letter inviting old members of Wadham to make donations to a Memorial Fund for the purpose of supporting African education. The money was readily raised, and was used eventually to help another African to finance his studies at the University of the Witwatersrand.

Many of those who knew Birley in England were unaware of the range of his activities on behalf of underprivileged communities: as Chairman of the Christian Institute Fund; as a member of the Council of the Minority Rights Group; and as a member of the Rhodesia group of the British Council of Churches. Much of the thrust of his work was to build up opportunities for young people in developing countries to study abroad. He was on the Executive Committee of International Students House in London and President of the World University Service. These were the more visible signs of his activity. Behind the scenes he was constantly using his ingenuity to help Africans. On one occasion at the Passport Office in Petty France he was trying to get visas for two of his many protégés. An old pupil who worked there and whom he had swiftly buttonholed protested: 'Surely, Sir Robert, you are not asking me to break regulations.' 'I am not asking you to break them, but to *bend* them', was the reply.

The picture of Birley the crusader against apartheid remained to the end somehow at odds with that of Birley the successful headmaster. At the memorial service in Eton College Chapel which commemorated primarily his stewardship of two great schools, two Africans in the congregation were deeply upset. Their impression of the service was that Birley's South African activities had been subordinated to the earlier part of his career, and they could not understand it. 'He got me out of prison,' said one of them afterwards, to whom it appeared that the Establishment had reclaimed him.

As the retirement years went by, it was inevitable that the frustrations of being able to get about less and less easily should take their toll. Birley grew old as he had lived, frenetically scribbling notes for lectures, and increasingly loquacious once he had mounted one of his hobbyhorses. The perfect recipe for old age, a sonnet by Christophe Plantin, a sixteenth-century figure more famous for his printing than his poetry, hung framed in his dressing room:

LE BONHEUR DE CE MONDE

Avoir une maiſon commode, propre et belle,
Un jardin tapiſſé d'espaliers odorans,
Des fruits, d'excellent vin, peu de train, peu d'enfans,
Poſſéder ſeul, sans bruit, une femme fidèle.

N'avoir dettes, amour, ni procès, ni querelle,
Ni de partage à faire avecque ſes parens,
Se contenter de peu, n'eſpérer rien des Grands,
Régler tous ses deſſns sur un juste modèle.

Vivre avecque franchiſe & ſans ambition
S'adonner ſans ſcrupule à la dévotion,
Domter ſes paſſions, les rendre obéiſſantes.

Conſerver l'eſprit libre, & le jugement fort,
Dire ſon Chapelet en cultivant ſes entes,
C'eſt attendre chez ſoi bien doucement la mort.

Though true in most details, in sum it suggests a serene tranquillity that Birley's restless temperament never really allowed him to experience.

The greatest pleasure for the Birleys in their later years was seeing their grandchildren grow up. Julia, the elder daughter, had married Brian Rees, a House Master at Eton and afterwards Headmaster of Merchant Taylors', Charterhouse and Rugby. Their five children stayed frequently at Lomans in the school holidays, as did the three children of the younger daughter Rachael who had married art historian Paul Hetherington. There was profound sadness, too, for at the cruelly young age of 47, Julia died of cancer. The Birleys followed the children's fortunes at their various schools with consuming interest. One of the very last memories of R. B. at Eton was the sight of him being helped up the steps to attend a performance of *Ralph Roister Doister*, in which one of the Rees boys was taking part.

Elinor attended her husband with devotion to the end,

driving him to speaking engagements when he was scarcely able to walk, looking after the stream of friends who came to see him, and making light of the demands on her as he became less and less able to order his own life. In the last months many a visitor learnt something from her fortitude. The end was peaceful. In the last day or two he was awake for brief periods only. He died on 22 July 1982.

CHAPTER FOURTEEN

Robert Birley

Quiet poise of manner; sober elegance of dress; athletic frame recalling sporting prowess in youth; easy conversation, wary of intellectual earnestness – none of these were attributes of Robert Birley. Few men in his position could have failed more completely to live up to the conventional idea of the modern public school headmaster. But however skilfully he acted up to his individualism, he was anything but a poseur. If, as Bernard Berenson once said, genius is the capacity for productive reaction against one's training, then Birley set out early on the road to genius. One of the men he met in South Africa remembered him from schooldays at Rugby half a century earlier. 'We all know that it was you who organised the strike of fags,' he said, 'no wonder you're a devil of a nuisance.' The memory of a tyrannical fagmaster has prompted many a retrospective denunciation of public school education. The nerve to stand up and do something at the time is more productive than the harboured grudge, but less common. Birley's strike succeeded and life became tolerable at the bottom of the Rugbeian heap.

In that same year at Rugby, Birley was taught history by C. P. Evers, the kind of highly respected master who stood no nonsense – imperturbable, sound and conventional in everything he did. One morning the boys were reading a chapter in their textbook about Ireland in the eighteenth century, the standard account of the land tenancy arrangements, when all of a sudden, to his pupils' alarm, it seemed as though this pillar of conformism had been caught up in a private earth tremor. 'This book is intolerable,' he shouted, throwing it on the table and striding up and down, cursing it roundly. It was self-satisfied, he fumed. It was not only self-satisfied, it was plain wrong. 'Now,' he said, 'this is what really happened . . .' and he launched into his own account of the matter. For Robert Birley, stupefaction made way for exhilaration. When the earthquake had subsided, he resolved that he would never again take a school textbook seriously.

Such were some of the seeds of disputatiousness that were sown in Robert Birley's schooldays. Perhaps it was just as well that he had no great bent for languages and was not, like nearly all those considered 'good at work', placed on the Classical side. There is limited scope for argument in the early stages of the study of Greek or Latin. In history on the other hand, disinclination to take at face value what one is told by one's elders can begin to thrive much sooner. It was in the soil of Rugby that Birley's determination to find out the facts for himself struck root, a soil more fertile than might have been expected amid the cluster of Butterfield buildings exuding the forbidding conformism of the Victorian middle class. By the time he went to Balliol the habit was firmly established. It was entirely in character that in his second year he should plunge so wholeheartedly into the research on the English Jacobins which made him Gladstone Prizeman in 1924. Ever afterwards, in a lifetime as a teacher, he saw the encouragement of the inquiring mind as being precisely what school was for and what teaching was about.

When it became obvious that he was cut out for an academic life, the only question was whether this should be as a schoolmaster or a don. Either was very much on the cards and it was a fortunate chance that propelled him out of a dismally unpromising fourth year at Oxford into a temporary teaching post at Eton. He would not have been the natural choice of many headmasters offering a first job, obliged as they are to think not only of what a young man can do in the classroom but also of how active he will be in the less formal world of extra-curricular activities. Birley lacked the physical co-ordination that most of these activities called for. He could not have coached games or given instruction in practical hobbies or taken an OTC parade to save his life. It was a clumsiness that made him a slightly improbable figure as a new young master. The first party he went to at Eton was a jolly affair involving a treasure hunt. With mischievous ingenuity the host had planted one of the clues at the top of a rope in the gym. It was the much older lady partnering Birley in the game who had to shin up and get it. But whereas at smaller schools there would have been a premium on versatility, Eton's size made it comfortably able to afford some full-time intellectuals. Eton was the school which offered, more than any other, the opportunity to lead something approaching a don's life.

Christ Church which soon emerged as an alternative might not have been so very different. If he had gone there first, the chances are that he would have fitted in as happily as he did at Eton. He would have learnt too that there was no substance to his subsequent doubts about his ability to teach undergraduates. What mattered, however, was that Eton was where he did go, and that it very quickly became evident that his great gift was for school teaching. The professional scholarship of a university department was not his true métier. His research was as unsystematic as it was enthusiastic. On the one hand he delighted in unearthing the most obscure and unrepresentative details, like the fact that 'for a short period, February 4th 1194 to April 6th 1199, England was part of the Holy Roman Empire – a fact, I may say, always omitted from English history textbooks'. On the other he had a penchant for oversimplification that would have been the despair of any supervisor of a doctoral thesis. But these two deviations from the main stream of academic research were formidable assets when it came to teaching boys. Even those most indifferent to the measured flow of the main stream could be swept up in the torrent of ideas, characterisations and idiosyncratic information that poured forth in Birley's history lessons.

The inexhaustible antiquarian enthusiasm, from which all this derived, never waned throughout his life. It was at its most powerful when the Eton College library was close at hand during his time as Head Master. His own personal collection of old books enabled it to continue into his retirement. A letter to a friend who was to visit him at Lomans three years before he died included a characteristic arrangement:

Wednesday 30 May–Friday 1 June will be perfectly all right for us. There is, however, one slight complication. On the 31st May I shall be talking to the local branch of the Council for the Preservation of Rural England. I am talking about William Turner, Dean of Wells for a short time in the middle of the sixteenth century. I think he must have been in some

ways about the oddest Dean in the History of the Church of
England. But he was the first English Ornithologist and
wrote a wonderful book on Plants. He combined being a
vigorous supporter of the extreme Puritans with advocating
toleration. He constantly urged that the money gained by the
Dissolution of the Monasteries should be used to improve
Education. I think he is a somewhat neglected figure in
English history.

BUT there will be no need at all for you to attend. I hope
you will not mind being left alone in the house for about two
hours.

Crippled with arthritis as he was, the same impatient enthusiasm drove him to fulfil every possible speaking engagement, until he became totally bedridden. The day before he
died his few waking minutes mostly involved calling Elinor to
pick up the books which had slithered off the bed when he had
fallen asleep.

The antiquarian interest went back to the early days at Eton
where he was introduced to the College library by Monty
James. It was then that he learnt the ferocity of endeavour that
scholarship demands. It may well have appeared to his pupils
that the flow of his teaching had a naturally inexhaustible
source, but he worked enormously hard for the stamp of
authenticity that it bore. The result was that the boys could feel
that they actually knew the great figures of history whom he
described with such verve. For he managed somehow to speak
of them in contemporary terms, and without hedging his view
of their achievements about with the cautious reservations of
those who are frightened of being contradicted. He was far from
being totally self-confident in these years, but in the classroom
his nervous shyness evaporated. Where discipline was concerned, boys would of course try to discover how far they could
push him, but it was never very far. Even as a green young
master feeling his way he had the natural authority of a born
teacher.

From the beginning Birley was absorbed by Eton and yet at
the same time he was above its parochialism, as his work for the
unemployed demonstrated. Many years later the Slough authorities acknowledged his long and sympathetic association with

their town by naming a road after him. Very appropriately Birley Road runs close by the site of the old Slough Social Centre.

His stature among his colleagues grew steadily, especially when it became an open secret that he had been seriously considered as a successor to Cyril Alington. When the appointment had been made it soon became evident that the new Head Master was not nearly so congenial to him as Alington had been. So there was a certain irony about the fact that it was actually Elliott who set things in train for the fulfilment of his young colleague's ambition to be a headmaster himself. At Charterhouse Frank Fletcher was most anxious that he should not be succeeded by J. F. Roxburgh, an Old Carthusian who, having made a name at Stowe, had a natural desire to move on to his old school. The trouble was that Fletcher could not think of any other strong candidate that he could recommend to the Governors. It was Elliott who, in the course of a visit on HMC business, learnt of the dilemma and asked if he had heard of a young man called Birley. He had not (despite the fact that they were both members of the UU), a meeting was arranged, and the first great turning point in Birley's career was in prospect. His ambition had developed early, and his hard work had brought an early reward.

Among those who did not know Birley there was astonishment at the appointment of this precocious young man whom *The Times* described as '6 foot 6 inches tall, looking like a Holbein drawing of one of the early Tudors, and with a curious interest in medieval crucifixes in which the figure of Christ is clothed'. Among those who did know him it was no great surprise. Letters of congratulation poured in from far and wide. A former pupil, Peter Fleming – brother of Ian and a very successful author of travel books – wrote from Khotan in Sinkiang en route for a crossing of the Himalayas: 'thanks to the kindness of an 85-year-old Armenian suffering from elephantiasis – the nearest thing to a White Man seen for some time, I have just read in the *Weekly Daily Mail* (of which the title, now that I have written it down, somehow reminds me of pedants' disputes about the Double Time Sequence in *Othello*) of your appointment to Charterhouse; and I much want to congratulate you, though I fear that, by the time you receive them, my congratulations will be not only out of date but inapposite, since you will have been raised to still greater glories long before I have reined my sweating yak back on to its haunches before the nearest Post Office.' Birley was immediately and greatly missed at Eton. Cyrus Kerry wrote to acknowledge how much he had done for the boys in his House. And a week or two after the beginning of the new half George Lyttelton ended an affectionate and characteristically sparkling letter thus: 'I miss you very much. I have few passions. Eton is one of them and I can hardly forgive you for not still carrying a great deal of the old lady's weight.'

The transition to headmaster was abrupt and in banishing bowler hats and putting the woods within bounds, Birley was giving early rein to his more liberal instincts. In the event however it was not this kind of forthright decision that was to characterise the style of the new headmaster. If he was a beacon of liberal light, its beam shone obliquely upon the very conservative world of Charterhouse. He manœuvred cautiously, taking people with him when he could, but eschewing flamboyant decisiveness if he could not. It was singlemindedness of a discreet kind. The freshness that he brought to the school was of course most immediately apparent to its intellectual aristocracy, for whom his teaching was an inspiration on their path to the colleges of Oxford and Cambridge. The liberal light shone rather less brightly for the remainder, the lumpenproletariat destined for the Army sixth, who were not so readily excited by hearing about 'one of the most important, if not *the* most important, events of the century'.

Yet even among boys of no particular position in the school there were favourable first impressions. One of them wrote to his mother: 'The new Headmaster is very capable and, I think, very likeable. He preached his first sermon to-day which was a great success. He is very easy to listen to and can talk for a long time without making one feel bored.' As his father, who quoted this confidence in a letter to Birley, remarked, 'This is great praise from a boy like Tony who is very quiet normally and is protected by a thick armour of British reserve behind which it is difficult to penetrate.' It was not necessary to be one of the favoured minority, for whom the best teaching was reserved, to experience the unobtrusively civilising affect of Birley's headmastership. Opportunities to enjoy the arts grew steadily. Robert Neild, later Professor of Economics at Cambridge, for whom Charterhouse was monumentally dull and oppressive in comparison with Abinger Hill, his progressive prep school, remembered discovering the haven of a lushly furnished room which had been set aside for musical appreciation. The radiogram installed in it was the height of sophistication at the time. The master in charge was George Snow – whom Birley had encouraged to follow him from Eton, where his talents had not been fully appreciated. Snow went on to become Headmaster of Ardingly and Bishop of Whitby.

At Charterhouse Birley's reputation grew apace. An early uncertainty and a shy, even gauche manner were no serious handicap in someone who was so patently sincere and so infectiously enthusiastic. At the Founders' Day Dinner in December 1982, the first after Birley's death, the proposer of one of the toasts remarked that he had changed the life of every boy with whom he came into direct contact. He could never have been accused of confining his attention to the star performers, as immature headmasters are prone to do. He was every bit as assiduous in furthering the interests of the frail, the odd and the weak. He might have appeared a terrifying figure, but he was never unkind, never guilty of boosting his own confidence by undermining that of others. He followed the lead of the headmaster who is reputed to have declared: 'Let the manifestations of your wit be like the coruscations of summer lightning, lambent but innocuous.'

In these years Birley was very much the man for his time, acutely aware of the threat of war and then growing steadily in stature as he guided the school through it. He would have cut no figure in the Army, Navy or Air Force. But as a headmaster he found it in him to establish an easy relationship with the high-ranking officers with whom he came into contact. Throughout the war Old Carthusians bothered to write to him with accounts of the active service on which they were engaged. For those who were conscientious objectors he had an equally ready ear, even though he was himself anything but a pacifist. He had always followed A. D. Lindsay's line that doctrinaire pacifism was actually a danger to peace, because peace abroad could only be assured on the same principles as at home, by the insistence on respect for law.

Birley's sermon on Victory Sunday was one of the best he had ever preached. Presenting the war as a spiritual crisis, he explained that the Nazis' way of life had been inspired by a principle which they had called the principle of leadership:

> This has sanctified power itself, and has allowed it to exist as an end in itself, untrammelled by considerations of morality or of the interests of others. This error is so monstrous, so immensely wicked, that it has brought with it inevitably almost unimaginably horrible things, which we had forgotten were possible among men. In international politics it has led to the insane ambition of one people to dominate the world, because they were persuaded that they were better fitted to wield power than any other. It has led to unbelievable cruelties, to the most savage persecution of other races and those of any nation, including their own, who thought otherwise, to the removal from their homes and families of millions of men and women and children, to vast destruction and misery. The immense scale of it all is something we can yet hardly realise. It has meant the harnessing of the creative powers of man to the service of evil and the very skill and industry of man has been turned to his own destruction. All this, we can now see was inevitable; it followed relentlessly from that great original error, the belief that power carried with it no responsibilities for others, but was its own justification.
>
> Now, against the background of this great spiritual evil, let us turn back once more to consider from what we have been delivered. I do not think that I need elaborate this. We now know what conquest by Germany would have meant to us, because we have seen what it has meant to other nations. From this island, looking at Europe, we can see it all too clearly.
>
> If then, for a moment, we consider what it is that we have faced in this war, it will make our thankfulness something far deeper than mere rejoicing at a realisation of our escape. For rejoicing by itself, thankfulness alone, can be something very shallow. We can only give it meaning if we do not think only

of what we have been spared, but also of the opportunities now presented to us. And I wish this evening to suggest one way in which you can look forward to the opportunity which has been given you.

First, we should realise that the evil, against which we have been fighting, is something bigger than Germany. For various reasons, arising from their national history and temperament, it found its home most completely among the German people. But evil may arise anywhere and the temptation to misuse power may come to any man. And the way to fight it among men is to give them some other aim which means more to them. The Nazis rose to power because the Germans were a nation which despaired of the future and had lost its faith. Too many thousands of them felt that they were no longer needed, that their lives had no real purpose. Granted that Hitler and the Nazis were devils, but they came into a house which had nothing but empty rooms.

Modern civilisation makes it all too easy for the rooms in the house of any nation to be empty. Material comforts do not fill those rooms. They do not themselves give men vital interests in their lives, the feeling that their lives have a purpose, that they matter in the one way that means anything, that they matter to other people. But you here are very fortunate. You are given many interests in your lives; you learn fellowship with others, the sense of being responsible for the well-being of others. I believe that the best way in which you can show your gratitude for the deliverance which you have had is to dedicate yourselves to the task of helping others who have not been as fortunate as you in securing these things. Never let this country become a house with empty rooms. If difficult times are ahead of us, if for instance we suffer again the desolation of wide-spread unemployment, give yourselves up to the task of ensuring that the men of this nation never lose faith in themselves. Hold yourselves responsible for that. Remember the lives of thousands and thousands of your own age, living in great cities in times of peace, who have little to live for beyond the dull round of repetitive work in factories, when they are in employment, and those amusements in their hours of leisure which can never satisfy their real needs, and then think of your own lives, how you have so much which is really satisfying, in your relationships with others, in your intellectual interests or literary or artistic, or in games or in the love of the countryside. There is an immense duty before you, in the years after the Japanese war is also won, to make an England fit, not 'for heroes to live in' (the old phrase betrays itself in its exaggeration), but for ordinary men and women to live in with full and satisfying lives, as you yourselves are given so great a chance to live. The Nazis filled an empty house with the spirit of evil. There were days before this war when England was becoming spiritually empty. We can repay that debt that is ours, if we never allow that to happen again.

It was not long before Birley's thoughts about reconstruction turned to the Germans. He wrote a letter to *The Times* about re-education. He wrote his much praised report on his visit to the British Zone in the autumn of 1946. He was a natural choice to become, as one of his friends put it, headmaster of Germany.

Birley's liberal conscience was finding expression in a major cause for the second time in his life. At Eton it had been the relief of the unemployed in Slough, now it was the reconstruction that was to bring relief to the suffering victims of war. He was coming to be known nationally, especially in view of his membership of the Fleming Committee. After twelve successful years the time was ripe for him to leave Charterhouse and the opportunity to go to Germany as Educational Adviser was a golden one., It was none the less a wrench and a risk, and there was the temptation to hedge his career bets by asking for secondment, but both the governors and he himself realised that it had to be one thing or the other. As at the time of his appointment as Headmaster, letters of congratulation poured in. Chuter Ede, the Home Secretary, wrote to say that 'no one could command greater confidence in the country than yourself in this post, on the proper filling of which so much of the future happiness of mankind depends'. To his letter of welcome to the Control Commission General Robertson added: 'I hear . . . that there is great sadness at Charterhouse about your departure. This is inevitable but I believe that the work which lies before you out here is worth a great sacrifice.'

Robertson was far from alone in expecting and finding Charterhouse's loss to be Germany's gain. That may sound grandiloquent, but whatever the confidence some members of the Cabinet had in Birley, no one could possibly have expected that a headmaster of limited experience and no military background would fit in so well at the Control Commission and make such a profound impression on the Germans. He never claimed to understand the intricacies of the German educational system and he was not, as legend is inclined to have it, the architect of its reconstruction. What he did supremely well was to give heart and hope to those to whom it did fall to rebuild the schools, the youth organisations and the universities.

It was a crusade of reconciliation. At the celebrated week-end gatherings at Birley's house, Germans of embittered and diametrically opposed political views, who would not have spoken to one another elsewhere, met to discuss questions of the day and of the future in an atmosphere of cordiality that took them by surprise. He brought the Education Ministers together for a week-end once a month and out of these informal gatherings grew the powerful *Kultusministerkonferenz*. Still more important than the encouragement of German educationists and politicians to come together and solve their problems was the task of finding practical ways of carrying through the high-sounding mission of bringing Germany back out of isolation into a respected place in the comity of nations. Though he did his share of preaching about this, Birley's great contribution was the practical one of adding his weight to the various initiatives to bring Germans to Britain and Britons to Germany. His period as Educational Adviser may have been comparatively short, but he continued to be involved long afterwards: through the German Academic Exchange Service; which he did so much to re-establish; as Chairman of Wilton Park, the re-education centre for German prisoners of war which went on to be first an Anglo-German, then a more fully international discussion centre; and as the oracle of Königswinter.

Whether or not he was aware of the fact, it was never likely that Birley would be in Germany for long. Eton was already looking round for a successor to Claude Elliott, and the Provost, Henry Marten, had long since made up his mind that his protégé of the twenties was the man. After a little over two proconsular years in Germany Birley was back in England to fulfil his highest ambition, to be Head Master of Eton.

The crusading reputation which Birley had acquired was hardly calculated to commend itself to his new constituency of Old Etonians and parents of boys at the school. Four years of Labour government had put the political left in a position of unprecedented influence. The appointment of 'Red Robert' as Head Master of Eton seemed a provocative breach in the innermost defences of the Establishment. On this score Birley's reception in the autumn of 1949 was far from uniformly cordial. The boys had come to be very fond of Claude Elliott who had become more gentle and charming with the years. Now they were faced with a terrifying figure whom their parents for the most part regarded as a dangerous socialist. Within Eton, among the staff who remembered his earlier days there or who had known him during his years at Charterhouse, the feeling was quite different. A fair number were personal friends and there was a small caucus which had pushed hard for his appointment. Quite apart from this support, there was no reason for the housemasters to feel threatened. Within living memory they had still been freeholders who actually owned the bricks and mortar of their houses. The independence that this tradition had produced needed more than a Robert Birley to constitute a threat in those days. It was more from the outside than from within that his reputation for radicalism was feared.

In fact such fears were groundless. For the first generation of boys who went through the school under Birley little appeared to change. Indeed a good many of them never exchanged a word with him, apart from the moment when they received the book which it was his duty to present to each of them when they left. While he had been at Charterhouse he had made no particular secret of his disapproval of the Eton Society, the small and self-perpetuatingly exclusive club of boys commonly known as Pop. To friends he even confided his view that it ought to be abolished. If the thought ever did cross his mind when he returned to Eton as Head Master, he was too realistic to entertain it for long. Pop was far too formidable – and valuable – a *corps d'élite* to be tampered with, let alone abolished. For its part it shared the view, comforting to traditionally minded parents, that the real power lay with the Provost and Fellows, and that Red Robert was therefore a figure of limited relevance to the style in which they ordered the life of the school. When this figure of limited relevance had the effrontery to 'sack' one of their number from the Society, it was seen as an unparalleled outrage. And was avenged. Towards the end of Birley's headmastership, when he was recommended for a knighthood by the Ministry of Education, the proposal was – as Peterborough in *The Daily Telegraph* subsequently reported – blocked by the Old Etonian mafia in Harold Macmillan's government. It was not until his return from South Africa that he became KCMG, when, as the *Telegraph* columnist went on to say, 'admirers may well feel that a life peerage would have been a more adequate reward'.

The Red Robert myth was a telling expression of the conundrum of Birley's personality. For an Old Etonian or a parent of a boy at the school it was all too easy to interpret his openmindedness as seditiousness. Some saw it as scarcely short of treasonable to be hobnobbing with the likes of Fenner Brockway. Yet whatever threat did exist was never to Eton. There could have been few more articulate defenders of the independence of the public schools, few more passionate believers in the unique contribution to national life that Eton itself had to offer. If Birley's restless temperament threatened anything, it was the conformism within Eton, something which he refused to regard as the true genius of the place. For as life outside the school became more competitive, so within it more and more store was coming to be set on the conventional techniques of 'getting on'. There was a keener and keener edge to the contests to be elected to positions of prominence in house and school. And at the top of the pyramid, getting into Pop was something of a purpose-designed training for political intrigue. Birley did not disapprove of the system, indeed he regarded its capacity to teach the practical skills of politics as the most important feature of an Eton education. But what he did strive to do was to imbue it with an idealism that rested on old-fashioned Whiggish values of principle and service. To be sure, he was prepared to let the place become more meritocratic, but he had a sharp eye for the point at which a meritocracy becomes a mediocracy. He liked to believe that unorthodox flair of the kind that he himself had in abundance could not only be accommodated but could continue to flourish along the narrower paths of advancement that modern life permitted.

Nothing characterised so clearly what he stood for as his view of the academic work of the school. He wanted the mark of an Etonian to be simply that he was educated rather than drilled; that he had an inquiring, flexible, spontaneous mind rather than a dull organisation-based mentality. It was in this sense that he resisted the onset of A levels, a sense that removes any real meaning from the superficial labels of conservative or progressive. In an address to the British Association in 1953 entitled *Greek or Chemistry or Both?* he developed C. P. Snow's two-culture theme, explaining the difficulty in historical terms and drawing prophetic inferences for the present day:

I believe that we must face the existence of this dichotomy in our culture, even though we realise that we cannot possibly close it as completely as in Dr Johnson's time, or in Galileo's. We might express it in this way. There are to-day in our society two classes who have perhaps the greatest influence. On the one side there are the executive civil servants. Many of them will have received a classical education, nearly all an education based on the humanities. On the other side there are the scientists. Their educational background will have been quite different. From the age of fifteen or sixteen, in this country, they will have concentrated on scientific studies. Probably for some time before they will have studied more science that the boy or girl who has another specialist subject in view. Both will have undergone a severe, in fact a splendid, intellectual discipline. But the education of the civil servant will have been intended, fundamentally, to enable him to understand Men, while that of the scientist will have been intended to enable him to understand Nature. It is hardly necessary to exaggerate the seriousness of the effects of this difference, but perhaps it is worth saying this. The civil servant will have to deal with a world largely dominated by the effects of scientific discovery: his education will have done nothing to help him to understand – not the technique of the scientist, for that we must agree is not to be expected – but his attitude and his approach to his subject.

The scientist will find himself faced by immense social responsibilities as a result of the power which science provides: his education will have done nothing to prepare him to shoulder these responsibilities.

In the analysis that followed nothing was oversimplified, no panacea was suggested, but Birley did make very clear his belief that the pressure to take examinations earlier and earlier was a pernicious obstacle to true education, and one that he was not prepared to accommodate at Eton:

if I may be personal for a moment, I am glad that I am head master of a school where traditionally the School Certificate was taken late. When the minimum age limit, was imposed, I found that my friends who were headmasters were faced with appalling problems in rearranging the curriculum. As far as I remember it cost me one evening's work. Which only shows, perhaps you may say, that, if one remains quite stationary for long enough, one finds oneself eventually in the van of progress.

At the heart of Birley's view of Eton was an almost mystic conviction that the best inspiration for enlightenment for the future lay in the educational values which the school had stood for in the past. He turned a blind eye to the philistinism, the bullying and beating that had marked its history. For him Eton was the school which more than any other had had the opportunity and the obligation to civilise those who in the future would occupy leading positions in national life. For him it was the school best placed to keep alive the peculiarly English, quaintly traditional, duty to educate a governing class. Those who had been to Eton would be of a special stamp, as much at home encouraging the arts or advancing the cause of science as wheeling and dealing in the lobbies of the Houses of Parliament. Beyond that it was not merely the prospect of power that should inspire them, but the vision of statesmanship.

In keeping with this lofty idealism Birley was himself a supremely inspirational figure, especially for those who worked under him. New masters would find themselves summoned to the Head Master's study for a kind of informal induction at the start of their first half. Roger Thompson who was appointed in 1957 when Birley's powers were at their peak recalled the scene:

> He sat in a big chair beside the fire surrounded by opened books, page-marked books on every available flat surface, puffing with nervous energy on his Churchmans cigarettes (never inhaling), flicking ash and stubs with great accuracy into the grate. He told us that teaching was like champagne – we had to fizz and bubble if we were to capture the minds of our divisions. He himself, as I later learnt from Colleger pupils, broke all the rules of the book. He talked all the time, often neglecting questions and not obviously encouraging the discovery method. Yet his almost boyish enthusiasm for the subject inspired the most sullen and uncooperative of his listeners; they all said he was the best teacher they had ever encountered. I once saw an essay book which he had marked. He would footnote his comments throughout the essay and then make his points at the end in his bold fluent hand. The comments were considerably longer than the original forty-minuter, and he had exhausted the letters of the alphabet for his footnoting and started entering a^1 b^1. It made my meagre three or four line criticisms and marginal corrections look very thin.

The tirelessness was an object lesson to them all. Once during what was the busiest week-end of the half he put on an exhibition of all the different Bibles from the College library. Every exhibit had a long note written in his own hand, and he himself was there for most of the day pointing things out to lower boys or masters who dropped in, with equal enthusiasm.

Birley's extraordinary scholarship, evidenced in the unending stream of arcane facts and startling analogies, always took precedence over the day to day demands of administration. His unpredictability in this sphere could be exasperating, his sense of priorities skimble-skamble. The classic story is told of a housemaster who wrote two letters to Birley. The first, which he laboured over, was a detailed proposal for Eton boys to teach English to immigrant children in Slough; the second was a routine note about a boy missing Chapel on the last day to attend a wedding in Ireland. To this the housemaster got a reply of two pages with minute instructions about Green Line buses, main line train times, ferries, and so on, which would make it possible for the wretched boy to attend Chapel *and* wedding. To the first – the kind of scheme, ironically enough, that a young Robert Birley might have thought up – he never received any answer.

That Birley coped with administration at all was remarkable, given that he was fundamentally unsystematic and conducted most of his correspondence in longhand. He was fortunate in having a succession of devoted secretaries who were capable of getting by without copies of his letters. He was not entirely without the ability to delegate. Indeed he was rather proud of the staff officer approach which he had learnt in Germany. But he was so unsystematic and unpredictable about it that it was always on the cards that he would create more problems than he solved. His remark to Tom Creighton in Berlin to the effect that there was something to be said for bad administration was particularly revealing. He could never have associated himself with the sterility of what can pass for good administration. Knowledge and interpretation were for him the really important things in life. It was precisely his personification of humanistic values that made him not merely a greatly respected figure within Eton but a charismatic one at the many public engagements which he fulfilled outside it. He had begun as a controversial and frightening figure with a reputation for socialist sympathies and an unhealthy enthusiasm for Abroad. By the end it was more natural to think of him as a fount of conservative wisdom, a reassuringly benign presence personifying traditional educational ideals within Eton and outside it.

To those who were in day to day contact with Birley in those peak years he was unforgettable, a supremely theatrical figure in a supremely theatrical school. Scholarly stoop, ungainly gait (probably some of the flattest, if not *the* flattest, feet in the profession), clownish boots, voluminous cassock and billowing gown, craggy long face with great bags under Searle-cartoon eyes – had he been an actor, he would have been overworked as every director's choice to play opposite Margaret Rutherford. He was no self-advertising showman but he loved the ceremonial of tradition, loved being in a position that brought invitations to attend the great occasions of state. All this made him far more of a conservative than he liked to let on, but the values that he believed in conserving were essentially patrician, far above the bourgeois snobberies of the Lanchester tradition. He wanted the public schools to change with the times, as he believed all the great institutions of British life had done. Yet for all the talk of places being kept for state scholars, he did not greatly change Eton. Though he never quite lived down his early radical reputation, the fears in the Old Etonian backwoods found no justification. Indeed Birley was the last great figure of the public schools before they chose to shed that designation and call themselves independent schools.

In that he was perhaps fortunate. He never experienced the tremors that ran through the schools in the later 1960s when 'permissiveness' in social behaviour was obscurely perceived as some kind of liberating virtue, and protest against restrictions became a teenage way of life. It is a churlish thought, but in those years it was in many ways easier to react constructively to youthful protest in a South African university than in an English public school. For the two situations were so very far from comparable. In England there was no justification for the rebelliousness of young people that came anywhere near the injustices of South African society. By that token it was quite consistent that Birley, a fundamentally conservative figure in England, should have identified himself in so thoroughgoing a way with the radical struggle against apartheid. Again it is churlish but it needs to be said that it is easier as a bird of passage with no preferment at risk to articulate the more liberal thoughts of those for whom a very comfortable way of life is being threatened. In South Africa the main concern of most whites was quite understandably to get into harbour and stay there. It was much easier for someone in Birley's position to leave harbour and sail close to the wind. None the less it was a substantial achievement to do so with such skill and judgment, going as close as it was possible to do without capsizing. It was a balance between courage and sensitiveness that could be widely admired, for above all he never sounded self-righteous in his defence of liberal principles.

His defence of liberalism was no purely theoretical one conducted in the seminar rooms of Wits. In his address at the memorial service for Birley in St Mary's Cathedral in Johannesburg John Kane-Berman recalled what it was like to accompany the Birleys on one of their return visits to South Africa:

> I drove them half-way round the country and was astonished at how many people they knew in remote parts of Zululand or the Transkei. Frequently along the way we called in at mission hospitals or other places where they would be welcomed with open arms. And somehow they never seemed to tire. On one occasion during this trip, Sir Robert had delivered a formal lecture at the University of Natal in Durban, and then he and Elinor slipped away late at night, not to bed as everyone else was doing, but to the university's black medical students' residence, where a group of about fifteen was waiting. This was in August of 1970, and one of the students in the group was Steve Biko. He and his colleagues and the Birleys talked long into the night. But it was typical of Sir Robert that the conversation would turn as much on his own joy at teaching Shakespeare to children in Soweto as on the heavy political questions that are of course uppermost in many of our minds.

Ideas, values, principles were important to Birley but they meant little if they did not find their expression in real people. It was an outlook traceable to his own education in the Balliol precept, 'First lesson, men are greater than theories.' In less elevated vein it simply reflects the true schoolmaster's inability to forget the individuals he has taught, long after what he has taught them has been forgotten.

Robert Birley's greatness is to be found in the least splendiferous strand of his distinguished career, the unquenchable vitality and intelligence of his teaching, whether it was as the Head Man in the division rooms of Eton, or as 'the Old Man' in the classrooms of Orlando High School in Soweto. It was in this element, quintessentially his, that he encouraged and inspired so many, a private example that far outshines any public honours that were heaped on him – and this is the memory that most deserves to endure.

INDEX